YOUTH URBAN WORLDS

IJURR-SUSC Published Titles

YOUTH URBAN WORLDS

Aesthetic Political Action in Montreal

JULIE-ANNE BOUDREAU
AND
JOËLLE RONDEAU

ILLUSTRATIONS BY
LUKAS BEECKMAN

This edition first published 2021

The right of Julie-Anne Boudreau and Joëlle Rondeau to be identified as the authors of this work has been asserted in accordance with law.

Registered Offices
John Wiley & Sons, Inc., 111 River Street, Hoboken, NJ 07030, USA
John Wiley & Sons Ltd, The Atrium, Southern Gate, Chichester, West Sussex, PO19 8SQ, UK

Editorial Office
The Atrium, Southern Gate, Chichester, West Sussex, PO19 8SQ, UK

For details of our global editorial offices, customer services, and more information about Wiley products visit us at www.wiley.com.

Wiley also publishes its books in a variety of electronic formats and by print-on-demand. Some content that appears in standard print versions of this book may not be available in other formats.

Library of Congress Cataloging-in-Publication data is applied for

Paperback: 9781119582212
Cloth: 9781119582229

Cover Design: Wiley
Cover Images: Photographs by Joëlle Rondeau, Mélissa Moriceau

Set in 11/13pt Adobe Garamond Pro by SPi Global, Pondicherry, India
Printed and bound by CPI Group (UK) Ltd, Croydon CR0 4YY

C097112_230221

Contents

List of Figures

Series Editors' Preface

IJURR Studies in Urban and Social Change
Book Series

The IJURR Studies in Urban and Social Change Book Series shares IJURR's commitments to critical, global, and politically relevant analyses of our urban worlds. Books in this series bring forward innovative theoretical approaches and present rigorous empirical work, deepening understandings of urbanization processes, but also advancing critical insights in support of political action and change. The Book Series Editors appreciate the theoretically eclectic nature of the field of urban studies. It is a strength that we embrace and encourage. The Editors are particularly interested in the following issues:

- Comparative urbanism
- Diversity, difference and neighborhood change
- Environmental sustainability
- Financialization and gentrification
- Governance and politics
- International migration
- Inequalities
- Urban and environmental movements

The series is explicitly interdisciplinary; the Editors judge books by their contribution to the field of critical urban studies rather than according to disciplinary origin. We are committed to publishing studies with themes and formats that reflect the many different voices and practices in the field of urban studies. Proposals may be submitted to Editor in Chief, Walter Nicholls (wnicholl@uci.edu), and further information about the series can be found at www.ijurr.org.

Walter Nicholls
Manuel Aalbers
Talja Blokland
Dorothee Brantz
Patrick Le Galès
Jenny Robinson

Preface

As we are putting the final touch on this manuscript, the world is going through a major health crisis. The outbreak of the COVID-19 pandemic has meant that billions of people are now confined to their houses, with varying degrees of social and state control. The scale at which we live our everyday lives has shrunk to the micro-local at the same time as it remains globally networked through digital media. What will become of urban life in a context where going out on the street is severely restricted?

When we began writing this book, I (Julie-Anne) had just published *Global Urban Politics: Informalization of the State* (2017), where I argued that in a world of cities, the political process works differently than in a world of nation-states. Institutionally, the architecture of the state has rescaled giving more weight to cities. At the interpersonal level, urban life propels a political logic of action based on spontaneity, affectivity, and mobility. And ontologically, in a world where urbanity is a hegemonic force, people's conceptions of space, time, and rationality are changing. Consequently, I argued that urbanization is a force of state informalization whereby the distinctions between the state, the market, and civil society are becoming more blurred. The state, I argued, no longer had the monopoly over the distribution of justice and authority.

As we are finishing this book, the state has become very present in our daily lives: closing down international borders, daily messages by elected leaders on the progress of the virus, imposing strong police or military presence on the street to ensure people respect the quarantine. This situation illustrates very well that state formalization processes are elastic: formalization is never complete. In certain periods it recedes and informalization (unwritten rules) seem to take over. At others, the state returns in force to assert its power. However, with its scientific hyperrationality in the management of the current health crisis, the state has some difficulty in imposing its reason on city life. Urban life is composed of multiple protection systems. In the case of the pandemic, the more obvious is the public health system. But urbanites also resort to other protective and coping mechanisms, such as faith, hope, or community. In these isolating times, it has been deeply moving for many to see videos taken by people on their high-rise balconies in Milan, Rome and Madrid, coming out cheering and clapping at a rallying hour every evening, to give one another courage and salute "front line" workers. Only a few days later, it was people in similarly-shaped urban environments all across the world that started to act in such way, spontaneously responding to calls echoed through social media and reverberating enticingly against the materiality of the contemporary urban world. Being together apart, in such dense urban environments, fully present in a here and now that is suspended in space, at a time when it has become very difficult to plan anything in the future, and yet enables the creation of a situation where everyone can recognize themselves as an actor and be energized by what is going on: we would say that this a deeply urban way of acting politically.

These "other" forms of protection are intensely aesthetic and affective. They emerge out of and through the lived conditions of urbanity. They cannot be reproduced by a state leader standing outside of a government building, clapping in front of journalists and recording cameras at the same hour. It does not have the same effect, even if a similar intent might motivate the act. Something is escaping, or perhaps more accurately exceeding, the hyperrational crisis management of the state. And yet, not everyone has the privilege of such balcony, or lives in a dense city environment, or has the means to stay in, checked out of the workplace during a global pandemic. Indeed, this contemporary urban world is uneven and variously affects the conditions of our entangled everyday lives. How can we grasp what is going on, simultaneously and differently, at the street level?

Such a question is why this book is an epistemological intervention in the study of politics. We argue that in an urban world, ethnography is essential to make sense of the political. Even in moments of intense state presence like the one we are currently experiencing, an urban epistemology is very fruitful for understanding the level of integration between state rationality and everyday life; that is, to evaluate the effectiveness of state policies (to put it in public policy language), and analyze the infrastructures that people and other agentic forces make together and out of each other, differently, spontaneously and sometimes autonomously from the state too.

This book is also an empirical contribution to the study of urban youth cultures, mobilizing various voices from Montreal. We see it as a contribution to the transition between two decades. The ethnographic material presented here dates from the 2010s, a period of very rapid urbanization and globalization, excessive mobility, consumerism, and interconnected political mobilizations around the world (Arab Spring and Arab Winter, student strikes, urban revolts, Indigenous Idle No More movements, anticapitalist and anti-austerity protests, climate strikes led by youths walking out of school…). With 2020, the world has slowed down: the coronavirus has brought air travel to a standstill and there is a strong push for climate change action (slow academia, relocalized, sustainable food systems, energy transitions, carbon taxes). Urban life after the COVID-19 will not be the same.

Yet, with the interdisciplinary theoretical contribution using cultural and urban studies to understand political processes, we see this book as a reflection on our collective and immediate future. Being sensitive to aesthetic political forms reveals the creative possibilities of urban everyday life. It can inspire collective and concerted action from the local to the global scale. It has become urgently clear that the continued acceleration of an hypermobile, hyperconsumerist lifestyle, fuelled by racial capitalist-extractivist modes of global urbanization, will bring the world directly to its end. Around the world as we write these lines, states are implementing state-centred measures based on their imagined "monopoly" of violence, scientific rationality, and disciplining. There are many other possibilities for action that are not state-centred. As the teenage son of a colleague once said: "Mom, another end of the world is possible." Such statement seems illogical; yet, it illustrates our argument in this book. Urban life is replete with unexplored potentialities based on different rationalities, rhythms, ways of being, forms of action. In youth urban worlds we can find inspiration for collectively building this immediate future.

This is why we wish to dedicate this book, first and foremost, to youth. They are the ones who will be living through the next six, seven, eight decades of deeply uneven global changes, set to unfold at an unprecedented speed and scale, while having to contend with the consequences of today's record levels of public debts, in uncertain times. We all have the power and responsibility to influence what these futures may hold. This new decade, we are told, is going to be a crucial one for collectively orienting the conditions for the survival and well-being of all life-forms on this planet. Youthfulness is power and agility. The youth urban worlds we have been privileged to partake in, from Montreal, have taught us that beyond the ballot box, beyond political leaders, or the kind of political education that might be received in schools, a youthful collective has its own agentic power to experiment with, to transform what exists, what has come to be known and named, and might come next. More than age or a stage of psychological development, youthfulness can be a way to act politically in the world.

This is what we wanted to represent with our choice of photos for the book cover. Youthfulness of course requires young people, like Arthur Guirand who is posing from the roof of a building squatted for a clandestine Queer humour show in the rapidly-gentrifying white working class Hochelaga neighbourhood, with Montreal industrial landscape in the background. Youthfulness is also palpable in certain street moments, like this break dance circle in downtown Montreal; a challenge to the all-white artistic representation of Montreal promoted by the City administration during its 375th anniversary celebrations (the flags on the street lights advertise the city's 375th anniversary). Finally, with the biosphere, iconic monument of Montreal built for the 1967 International Exhibition, we wanted to visually represent how youth urban worlds are globally-connected. Its architecture evokes a bubble rising in the air, or what Sloterdijk (2011) would call a sphere, involving human and more-than-human agency.

The ethnographies presented here result from collective work that spanned a decade. It is the fruit of collective research projects, seminars, and interactions with the many students who came through the Laboratoire de recherche Ville et ESPAces politique (VESPA): Nathalie Boucher, Frédérick Nadeau, Ajouna Bao-Lavoie, Julien Rebotier, Godefroy Desrosiers-Lauzon, Stephanie Geertman, Martin Lamotte, Laurence Janni, Dounia Salamé, Antoine Noubouwo, Muriel Sacco, Alice Miquet, Olivier Jacques, and many others.

Let us say a special word for the students who conducted research with us for this book: Leslie Touré-Kapo and Désirée Rochat were active researchers and local coordinators in the mapcollab project discussed in chapter 2, Alain Philoctète participated in our ethnographic research conducted in Saint-Michel in 2008 (also chapter 2), Denis Carlier, Mathieu Labrie, and Alexia Bhéreur-Lagounaris participated actively in the research project on the 2012 student strikes (chapter 3), Maude Séguin-Manègre and Marilena Liguori collected data for chapter 5.

It goes without saying that such material was collected thanks to the generous funding of the Canada Research Chair program (2005–2015), the Social Sciences and Research Council of Canada for the mapcollab project (chapter 2), the Fonds de recherche Québécois Société et Culture for Jo-elle's Master's scholarship (chapter 4), and the Programa Interinstitucional de Estudios sobre la region de America del Norte for the project on "voluntary risk-takers" (chapter 5). We wish to acknowledge our coresearchers in these projects, especially David Austin, Steven High, Coline Cardi, and Marie-Hélène Bacqué.

Although the material has been expanded here, fragments of this book were previously published in different forms: Ateliers mapCollab, 2018. *Mon quartier, notre vie. Regards transatlantiques.* Montréal: Del Busso Éditeur; Boudreau, J.A. 2017. *Global Urban Politics: Informalization of the State.* Cambridge: Polity Press; Boudreau, J.A., M. Liguori, and M. Séguin-Manègre. 2015. "Fear and youth citizenship practices: Insights from Montreal" in *Citizenship Studies.* Vol. 19(3–4): 335–352; Boudreau, J.A. and M. Labrie. 2016. "Time, space, and rationality: Rethinking political action through the example of Montreal's Student Spring" in *Human Geography.* Vol. 9(1): 16–29; Rondeau, J. 2017. 'Une autre relève agricole: Analyse des rôles des acteurs d'une formation en agriculture urbaine dans la production d'espaces et de pratiques agricoles alternatives au système alimentaire agro-industriel en milieu urbain', Master's Thesis, Institut national de la recherche scientifique, Montreal; Boudreau, J.A. 2018. "Contextualizing institutional meaning through aesthetic relations. A pragmatist understanding of local action" in W. Salet (ed.). *The Routledge Handbook of Planning and Institutions in Action.* New York: Routledge; Boudreau, J.A. 2019. "Informalization of the State: Reflections from an Urban World of Translations" in *International Journal of Urban and Regional Research.* DOI:10.1111/1468-2427.12701.

We wish to highlight the incredible work of the Studies in Urban and Social Change Editorial Board in providing feedback on this manuscript, and especially the two anonymous reviewers. Never had we received such detailed and thoughtful comments. Some of their insightful formulations have made their way to the following pages.

Working in Montreal involves constant switches between French and English. Because we wished with this book to locate Montreal in global debates about urban politics, we decided to first write this book in English. But because we also wanted to converse with Montreal youths, we also wrote the book in French. The contemporary urban world is a polyvocal and multilingual world of translations. This is something young Montrealers taught us. And our warmest acknowledgement goes to them, to all those who speak in the following pages.

As we finish writing this book, youths already bring us on another adventure. TRYSPACES: Transformative youth spaces is the collaborative research project emerging from these ethnographies (funded by a Social Sciences and Humanities Research Council of Canada's Partnership Grant, 2017-2023). This is why we briefly discuss in the conclusion the theme of transgression, which will be the focus of our next adventure.

References

Boudreau, J.A. (2017). *Global Urban Politics: Informalization of the State.* Cambridge: Polity Press.

Sloterdijk, P. (2011). *Bubbles. Spheres Volume I: Microspherology.* Los Angeles: MIT Press.

FIGURE I.0 Map sketch by Joëlle Rondeau, based on 'Map of Montreal sociological neighbourhoods in 2014', published by Service de la diversité et de l'inclusion sociale, Ville de Montréal (5 October 2014), under the Creative Commons Attribution 4.0 International License.

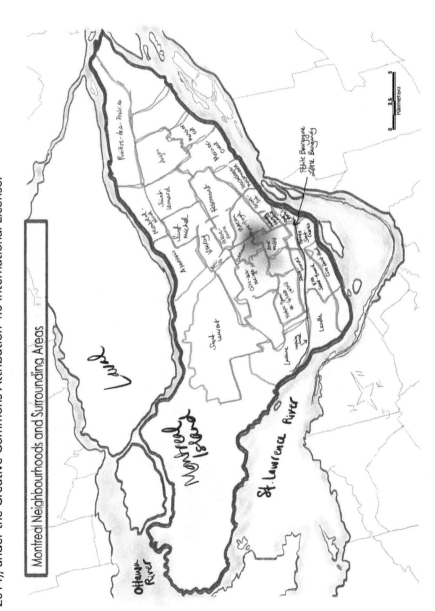

Introduction
Voices From Montreal

Montreal, what makes it beautiful is simply its diversity, but also the place it opens for alternative expression, be it from an ecological, artistic, or ... political ... point of view.[1]

(Ivan, student who participated in the 2012 strikes)

MAKE-UP

They put make up on her.

Who you may ask.

Ils ont mis du maquillage sur elle.

Qui, demandes-tu?

I'm talking about the planners, the renovators.

They put make up on her. My home is what I mean by her. The building where I have spent 95% of what I now refer to as my conscious life.

I feel it's a ploy to attract investors, to attract the rich, to attract money and prestige.

...

We live there, have lived there, and will continue to live there. That is, if permitted. We are the ones who carry stories. We are the ones who inflict pain and have had pain inflicted upon us.

We are the fighters, the protecters, the by-standers.

We are the listeners, the see-ers, and the gossipers. We have fought the battles and continue to fight ...

The new windows, new balconies, new backyard, new everything presents a new beginning. The open wounds covered up, never mended. A new beginning that doesn't include us. A new beginning that neglects the historic warriors.

(Kabisha, 14 June 2014, mapcollab.org)

Youth Urban Worlds: Aesthetic Political Action in Montreal, First Edition.
Julie-Anne Boudreau and Joëlle Rondeau.
© 2021 John Wiley & Sons Ltd. Published 2021 by John Wiley & Sons Ltd.

Ivan is one of the students who opened his urban world to us, one year after the 2012 student strikes that came to be known as the Maple Spring (*Printemps érable*; see Chapter 3). He describes political action in Montreal with reference to its history and culture of social mobilization – '*the space for alternative … ecology, … art, … politics*'. Such description is consistent with the way most youths who will speak in this book describe Montreal. In the second excerpt from Kabisha, produced during our MapCollab workshops,[2] Montreal's diverse cultures are described in more sour terms. Her words are highly political, screaming against gentrification and exclusion. Like Ivan, she highlights aesthetics. Allow us to let another young Montrealer speak before coming back to Kabisha:

> *It's also a city where we witness and we easily see just by being there … You know, there are big contrasts of human realities that coexist in this city. And this, I think, creates tensions that are palpable, that favor people's involvement when they have the occasion maybe.*[3] (Hubert, student who participated in the 2012 strikes)

Like Kabisha, Hubert speaks of spatial contrasts and socioeconomic inequalities. And like her, he emphasizes their embodiments: '*Just by being there*' we can '*witness and see … contrasts in human realities*'. '*We are the ones who carry stories. We are the ones who inflict pain and have had pain inflicted upon us*', writes Kabisha, '*We are the listeners, the see-ers, and the gossipers*'. Politics is something we feel and live, just by wandering in the city. Montreal, as these youths whom we will meet express, is the globally connected urban milieu where their lives unfold. More than just the backdrop for their actions in the world, this place affects and is affected by their experiences and various engagements. It gives shape and malleability to their reality, a canvas and a medium to speak their truths, to experience and understand their lives in relation with the worlds they inhabit, with which they engage and communicate. What can we learn from these voices from Montreal, interconnected in an increasingly urbanized sociopolitical global order that both transcends and exceeds the international order of sovereign nation-states?

David Harvey (1985a, p. 266) was concerned with the need to better understand how 'the urban milieu, considered as a physical and social artefact, mediates the production of consciousness in important ways, thus giving urban life and consciousness many of their distinctive qualities'. He published *Consciousness and the Urban Experience* as a companion volume to the perhaps more well-known *The Urbanization of Capital* (1985b). His starting point was the recognition that the 'particular kind of urban experience' resulting from the production of an increasingly urbanized space necessary to the survival of capitalism in the twentieth century is 'radically different quantitatively and qualitatively from anything that preceded it in world history' (Harvey 1985a, p. 265). While his studies on the urbanization of capital focused on the production of a 'second nature' of built environment with particular kinds of configurations under capitalist processes (Harvey 1985a, p. xvii), his concern with the publication of a companion volume was to examine the implications of the urbanization of social relations on political and intellectual consciousness, a parallel process to the urbanization of capital which produces the physical and material space of the city. His contention was that capitalism 'has also produced a new kind of human nature through the urbanization of consciousness and the production of social spaces and a particular structure of interrelations between the different loci of consciousness formation' (Harvey 1985a, p. xviii). Harvey shed light on the importance of taking the 'urbanization of consciousness' as a real social, cultural, and political phenomenon in its own right.

In doing so, and although he was criticized for its superstructural model of consciousness, Harvey was bringing the insights of thinkers of urbanity, or urban ways of life, such as Louis Wirth and Henri Lefebvre, to bear on a Marxian interpretation of the urban process under capitalism. Indeed, living in a world of cities requires a profound rethinking of how we act politically, how we engage with our world and create meaning through urban research.

This book explores how urban cultures affect political action from theoretical and empirical perspectives. Based on four ethnographies of youth political action in Montreal, it shows that urban cultures are challenging the very meaning and contours of the political process. Using the perspectives of racialized youth, 'voluntary risk-takers' such as dumpster divers, Greenpeace building climbers, students taking to the streets during the 2012 'Maple Spring', and urban farmers, it develops the theoretical idea of aesthetics as a an increasingly important dimension of life and mode of political action in the contemporary urban world. The embodied forces of attraction and desire that animate youth political action are too often ignored in studies of urban politics. This is especially true in cities of the so-called Global North. This is why in this book we wanted to engage with theoretical frameworks developed in the Global South and from Black studies in order to understand Montreal. This scholarship helps to shed light on the diverse forms of aesthetic political action perceived in the different yet interconnected youth urban worlds in which we have been immersed. These diverse ways of acting politically, through aesthetic relations, are not all consistent with one another and tell us much about the transformation of the political process in a world where the state can no longer pretend to have sole monopoly over the channelling, organization, and mediation of conducts and resources.

In order to understand these urban political forms, we are moved to 'look' for and be affected by politics in places that political scientists would not generally identify for political analysis. Understanding the urban culture behind action cannot come from observing political campaigns, ideologies, political organizations, or interviews with the leaders of social movements. Instead, the ethnographic work presented in the following pages delves into the common symbols, sensations, and perceptions that structure the individual and collective imaginary, youth political gestures, and the implicit 'grammar' that gives meaning to these multiple gestures and feelings in different youth urban worlds situated in Montreal. We argue that living in an urban world transforms conceptions of time, space, and rationality, and that these emerging notions based on nonlinearity, mobility, and affectivity have a significant effect on political actions (Boudreau 2017).

Space–Time–Affect: The Urban Logic of Political Action[4]

Much has been said in recent decades about the fact that we are living in an urban world. The United Nations and generously funded research and art projects of all sorts are repeating that more than half the world population now lives in cities (Burdett and Sudjic 2010). Such statements are debatable given well-documented difficulties in measuring urban populations (Brenner and Schmidt 2014). However, whether more and more people actually live in cities that are covering more and more territory is not important here. The fact that people are adhering to this globalized discursive trope is.

Our conception of the global world – the images we disseminate and reproduce of this urban world – is indeed dominant. Living in a world of cities is very different from living in a world of nation-states. We argue that doing urban research in a world of cities is also very different from doing research in a world of nation-states, because urbanization shapes objects of analysis and constitutes the medium through which we do research. We begin this book with the following: in a world of cities, political action unfolds very differently than in a world of nation-states because urbanity affects our conceptions of space, time, and rationality. This argument is fully developed elsewhere (Boudreau 2017), but it is important to expand on key points to situate how these transformations in our frames of perception and cognition affect the political process and how we can read and make sense of it.

As urban social movements, flashmobs, and occupations have shown over the last few decades, where, when, and how politics unfolds is no longer exclusively in the voting booth or the union meeting, during elections or strikes, and through strategic thinking about how to win the competition between opposing interests (Merrifield 2013). As state institutions lose their monopoly over governance – that is, over the distribution of justice and authority – urban ways of life are bringing new political forms to the fore. This, of course, does not mean nation-states have disappeared or that their power has diminished. Our argument here is simply that other spatiotemporal conceptions and rationalities have been made visible. This is an argument that was already emerging in the 1980s and 1990s with postmodern critiques of positivism and developmentalism. The state-centred worldview, a 'particular but contestable way of understanding the world that began to take shape in the 19th century and crystallised in the 20th century' (Magnusson 2010, p. 41), was never fully rational, but our scientific methods sought to highlight its rationalism. With the rising hegemony of urban worldviews, postmodern epistemological critiques resonate more easily with everyday practices. Furthermore, the retrenchment of the state through urban neoliberal processes over the last few decades has contributed to an increased visibilization of urban political forms, whether because they sought to fill the gaps of eroded social safety nets or because they tried to develop delegated power arrangements for service delivery. Neoliberal urbanization has thus affected the way institutions and people interact, understand their roles, sustain a now global urban order, and make political claims. Rather than solely focusing on such structural processes to examine the texture and unfolding of urban politics, we contend that a fruitful approach is to consider the effect of urbanity on the ways we act, interact, and think about the world. Such an approach brings to the fore the conceptual density of aesthetics as a critical mode of political action in a world of cities formed through unequal global urbanization processes.

'Urbanity', or 'urban ways of life', refers to a set of historically situated conditions that affect the way we act, interact, and think about the world. As cities become more prominent in our conceptions of the world, the way we sense and conceive of space, time, and rationality of politics changes. It exemplifies, as David Harvey wrote in 1985, how '[w]e always approach the world with some well-honed conceptual apparatus, the capital equipment of our intellect, and interpret the world broadly in those terms' (Harvey 1985a, p. xv). In the modern world of nation-states, which dominated the past century and rested on a Westphalian international order, we learned to think of the political process in terms of containers. Politics, understood in this context as conflicts generated by the confrontation of opposing interests, took place within the confines of national boundaries. The modern democratic and sovereign state was there to mediate conflicts by guaranteeing the stability of the rules of the game (elections, protection of civil rights, monopoly over legitimate violence, etc.). The state was thought to have full control over its territory and was there to protect us. It was the main interlocutor of all political claims. If we were unhappy with a specific situation, we turned to the state to claim for change. In this bounded world, conflict and contention were tolerated as long as they sustained the state.

In the contemporary world of cities, where nation-state sovereignty and boundaries are profoundly challenged by global flows, the state still plays a central role. But cultural and economic flows, and the mobility of people and merchandise across borders, have significantly affected the bounded spatial conception of the world. In a world of cities, politics is no longer seen as the exclusive domain of the state. Action unfolds in networked, fluid, and mobile spaces that are not fixed by clear borders. Global social movements, social media campaigns, and political tourism are evidence that in order to understand politics, we need to think in terms of networked and not only bounded spaces.

In the modern world of nation-states, time was seen as directional and with constant velocity. We thought of politics in strategic terms: a political act was enacted with a clear goal and was thought out carefully in order to evaluate its chances of success. We thought of the world in linear terms. For instance, there were developed and underdeveloped countries. The assumption was that with time, underdeveloped countries, often 'young' nation-states having won decolonial struggles, would modernize and catch up. Time, particularly the temporality of political change, was conceived as a historical march towards progress.

In the contemporary world of cities, we still act strategically and hope for a better future. But other forms of political action are increasingly visible. Acting spontaneously, without strategy, developing tactics as we respond to immediate situations, without thinking too much of the consequences of action, acting out of passion or rage more than ideology... this brings our attention to a different conception of time and political change. The temporality of action is fragmented, composed of multiple situations and dominated by the 'here and now' more than the future, by tactic more than strategic thought. Multiple synchronous paces and circular (cyclical or sequential) temporalities clash with directional trajectories and stable duration.

In the modern world of nation-states, the stability of the space of action and of linear time facilitated pretension to scientific rationality as the motor of legitimate action. We calculated, planned, and acted because we thought we could master the parameters of the issue at stake. Of course, we still act this way, but we also increasingly assert other rationalities of action based on creativity, unpredictability, sensorial stimulation, intuition, emotion, and loss of control.

This leads to a more diffuse form of political action, where leadership is absent (or at the very least, invisible or negated). Action unfolds in a specific time and place through a network of relations. We often recognize political action only if we decentre the gaze from leaders and analyse specific situations instead (how actions unfold in time and space). How and where are we, then, to look for urban politics?

Living in a world of cities compels us to feel and look for politics in different places. To take such politics seriously, we need to be sensitive to unusual political forms. The state-centred model of political action that permeates conceptual frameworks for analysing urban politics can constitute an epistemological obstacle in this regard. Through these lenses, urban politics is predominantly known and thought through what Warren Magnusson (2010) calls 'statist thinking'. While very useful for understanding state action, such a lens cannot encompass the totality of the political process.

Let us flesh out this argument more fully to locate another understanding of urban politics and its locales. As Magnusson (2010, p. 41) explains, statist thinking is an epistemological limit historically related to the development of political sciences in the context of the formation of the state throughout the Modern period and the development of social sciences in the nineteenth century, 'when the world was divided up in a new way for purposes of academic study'. Bourdieu has also closely examined the development of such increasingly specialized fields related to the sociohistorical and situated conditions of modernity (Hage 2012). Through this sociohistorical process, the division of academic disciplines, following the sectoral divisions of state departments, held the promise of facilitating the production of scientific knowledge and the development of an efficient state administration. While sociology was given the mandate to study society, economics focused on the economy; 'anthropology, the origins of man; geography, the environment in which men lived; and political science "the state"' (Magnusson 2010, p. 41). Ghassan Hage (2012) and Ben Highmore (2010) have also pointed out that the domain of aesthetics was not left out of this process, as it became an increasingly specialized field concerned with the arts, 'increasingly limiting itself to only certain kinds of experience and feeling, and becoming more and more dedicated to finely wrought objects' (Highmore 2010, p. x; see also Saito 2017).

It is easy to observe that a state-centred bias has been carried over in urban political studies. It is exemplified in conceptualizations of urban politics as being 'about authoritative decision-making at a smaller scale than national units – the politics of the sub-national level ... with particular reference to the political actors and institutions operating there' (John 2009, p. 17). From there follows that urban politics is studied with a focus on municipal jurisdictions: land use, housing, public infrastructure, waste, water, and so on.

These accounts are, in this sense, municipalist (focused on formal state institutions). Nevertheless, political scientists have recognized that municipal politics is perhaps more permeable to informal actors than politics at other government levels. Urban regime theory is the most elaborate example of the intertwinement of the formal and the informal at the local level in the North American context (Stone 1989).

As the anthropologist Ghassan Hage (2012, p. 3) argues, '[t]he existence of a specialised political field, for example, has not meant that the political no longer exists except in specialised institutions'. Indeed, the 'political is still diffused throughout the social, that is, a dimension of life remains political through and through regardless of which social domain one is examining, and despite the existence of specialised political institutions and practices' (Hage 2012, p. 3). Of course, this is a claim made forcefully by voices formerly excluded from these specialized institutions, including academia: Black feminists, disability scholars, Queer activists...

Warren Magnusson (2010, p. 43) challenges political scientists and urban studies to embrace politics from what he calls an 'analytic of urbanism' that presents an 'opportunity to challenge the whole edifice of contemporary political science', from the perspective that 'the form of political order that arises from urbanism [what results from distinctively urban practices] is different from the one implicit in the project of state building'. He stresses that this state-building project and the rise of nation-states did not extinguish the urban political orders nested within, and simultaneously exceeding, the scales of state power, further adding that in some cases, such urban political orders even predate state political orders (Magnusson 2010, p. 45).[5]

Characteristically, cities are produced by multiple authorities; they function through distributive agency involving the active and reactive materiality of buildings, non-human living beings such as plants, animals, birds. We will see in the following chapters how these proto-agents affect the unfolding of political action in dense, interconnected urban environments. Theoretically, we are inspired by various moves to relational epistemologies, including topological thought in urban geography and assemblage theories that consider more-than-human sources of agency and relational production of urban space (Amin and Thrift 2002; Amin 2004; Farias and Bender 2010). However, these theorizations are not always ethnographic or participatory. For these reasons, they do not always accommodate very well the messiness, ambiguity, and sensuality of being and living in the city. They are also less apt to account for and articulate the variety of urban knowledges produced by actors situated in or engaged at different scales of urban political life (Johnson-Schlee 2019).

Our focus here is on the transformation of political subjectivities and modes of political action at a relational, street level, and this requires ethnographic immersion. Immersion enables us to emphasize networked relations as being spatially and temporally continuous, producing youth urban worlds which connect and have connected Montreal as a node in various global urban world orders. Within these situated and interconnected contexts, we see urbanity as a logic of political action permeated by distinct features of an urban consciousness (distinct ways of perceiving space, time, and rationality).

In Chapter 2, we will meet Tivon, a young man living in the Little Burgundy neighbourhood. He slams, he writes, he dances, he acts through an urban logic of political action. Although many social scientists would not see political action in Tivon's life because he doesn't participate in street demonstrations or political organizations, we argue here that by paying attention to how politics unfolds in an urban world, we can see in Tivon's life many political gestures. Describing one of his video projects, he writes: '*It's crazy how things change. Condos are going up at a faster rate than ever and the word gentrification doesn't even explain how the riches of the community are being replaced with the riches of the word*' (mapcollab.org). He expresses concern about the pace of change in his neighbourhood, and points to the inability of words to keep up. Words become useless to express his political outrage. He further alludes to how his neighbourhood is linked to the '*riches of the wor[l]d*', thereby expressing a networked spatial conception linking the local with the global.

As he describes another photo, he pursues: '*This is my daily eye level street view. This may be your first time seeing this view. I have seen this view almost everyday for the past twenty years!*' (mapcollab.org). Tivon grounds his political analysis in everyday life. You may not think this is particularly interesting, he seems to say when describing an ordinary 'eye-level street view', but this is my standpoint, my entry point into the world. He is inviting us to enter this everyday world in order to understand his politics. The inadequate intensity of the word 'gentrification' and everydayness impelling political gestures, these are two examples of what we want to call the aesthetics of political action in an urban world. They call attention to the importance of conceiving a political relation aesthetically.

Acting Aesthetically: Political Gestures, Political Acts, and Political Action

Transformations in our conceptions of space, time, and rationality bring to the fore and reinforce aesthetic forms of sociopolitical relations. In her seminal treaty on justice and differences, Iris Marion Young (1990) foresaw the importance of the 'normative ideal of city life'. Against the idealization of community (anti-urban) life, Young advances 'city life' as what we should valorize. 'City life', she writes, 'instantiates difference as the erotic, in the wide sense of an attraction to the other, the pleasure and excitement of being drawn out of one's secure routine to encounter the novel, strange, and surprising' (Young 1990, p. 266). She normatively prioritizes eroticism against community recognition or the protective feeling of membership. Eroticism comes close to what we call acting aesthetically. 'The erotic meaning of the city', she pursues, 'arises from its social and spatial inexhaustibility [what we have called a networked conception of space]. A place of many places, the city folds over on itself in so many layers and relationships that it is incomprehensible' (Young 1990, p. 267). Young is identifying here the need to act aesthetically, to trust our senses and not only our rational and cognitive capacities to name and categorize the world.

Our engagement with the notion of aesthetics builds on various traditions of thought which foreground a pre-Kantian conception of aesthetics: aesthetics not as a theory of the arts or of taste, but as the realm of sensory experience and perception. 'Aesthetics is born as a discourse of the body', writes Terry Eagleton (1990, p. 13) in his study on the birth and importance of the category of the aesthetics in Modern thought. He reminds us that '[i]n its original formulation by the German philosopher Alexander Baumgarten, the term refers not in the first place to art, but, as the Greek *aisthesis* would suggest, to the whole region of human perception and sensation, in contrast to the more rarefied domain of conceptual thought' (Eagleton 1990, p. 13). If, by the nineteenth century, Western philosophical engagements with aesthetics had become increasingly focused on the fine arts, particularly within the Anglo-American tradition (Saito 2019), philosophers interested in investigating the aesthetic experience of the world beyond the artworld began to challenge these trajectories and their limited scope. This led to the development of the fields of environmental aesthetics and everyday aesthetics in the second half of the century (Carlson 2019; Saito 2019). However, the rise of modern European metropolises also attracted the attention of philosophers and sociologists who sought to understand an aesthetics of urban modernity, as experienced particularly in Berlin and Paris (Thibaud 2010).

We need to engage with these various traditions of thought to explore how contemporary urban cultures are transforming the political process. Analyses of the sensible experience of urbanites and the transformation of the structure of this experience have influenced urban thought for over a century. Georg Simmel, Walter Benjamin, and Siegfried Kracauer are well known for their analyses of the sensible culture of the modern city and the significance they put on microscopic scenes, gestures, or experiences of everyday life in order to capture the aesthetic differences and effects of the urban experience in modern European cities (Thibaud 2010).

Because of global urbanization processes, the urban experience is no longer spatially and temporally bounded to the city. In *The Politics of the Encounter*, Andy Merrifield (2013, p. xvii) provocatively suggests foregoing the concept of the 'city'; in his own words, 'to give up the ghost of thinking in terms of absolutes – of entities with borders and clear demarcations between what's inside and what's outside' and instead embrace 'the urban process as a form that is formlessly open-ended' (Merrifield 2013, p. xviii). Yet, as we explore it here, the urban process remains in important ways shaped by situated aesthetic experiences and political acts that accumulate in given urban environments (see also Boudreau 2017).

To explore the significance of the ontological shifts from a world of nations-states to a world of cities, as described earlier, epistemological perspectives from the field of environmental aesthetics are useful. Rather than focusing on the aesthetic appreciation of mute and passive objects, this tradition of thought has been centred on the aesthetic experience and appreciation of any kind of everyday life situation (routinized or breaking from the perceptions associated with the routine) and any kind of environment, including urban environments.

Arnold Berleant is a New York-born philosopher who became a prominent figure in this field, laying the groundwork of the theory of aesthetic engagement (Carlson 2019). Foundational to this theory, by contrast to the posture of a detached and contemplative observer, is a continuity of perceptual engagement in the environment; the sensuous and sensate body's full immersion 'in a single intraconnected realm' inhabited by 'humans and all other things' affecting and affected by everyone and everything (Berleant 1992, p. 9). It rejects the notion of environment as a container or an object that exists independently or externally to the perceiving subject. 'There is no outward view, no distant scene. There are no surroundings separate from my presence in that place. There is rather a full awareness focused on the immediacy of the present situation, an engaged condition that encompasses richly inclusive perceptions and meanings', writes Berleant (1992, p. 34). It foregrounds an ontology of the relation and the milieu rather than an ontology of the object (Thibaud 2010, p. 11).

The development of environmental aesthetics has been closely related to the environmental movement as it emerged in the United States in the 1960s and 1970s. Two rather distinct orientations have crystallised within the field over the years: cognitive and noncognitive. The former is centred on the importance of having 'knowledge of what something is, what it is like, and why it is as it is' (Carlson 2019) in order to appreciate its aesthetic dimensions and qualities (e.g. the earwigs in Chapter 4). The latter is focused on the realm of precognitive sensations and inclinations, including the imagination, which arguably participate in shaping aesthetic experience and informing aesthetic appreciation. The aesthetic of engagement is most closely associated with this noncognitive orientation (Thibaud 2010; Carlson 2019).

While the field has led to the development of a significant body of research on the aesthetic experience and appreciation of urban environments, the intellectual and academic projects sustained through this scholarship have in many cases remained attached to the normative political goal of distinguishing how environments lead to or could increase human well-being and quality of life (Thibaud 2010). An implicit normativity orients this engagement with aesthetics. This is not our primary focus here.

Nonetheless, as part of a broader turn to affect in geography and urban studies, this field has opened theoretical perspectives by which to interrogate, beyond representational models of signification, the role of sensations, perceptions, feelings, and meanings as they are shaped by and give shape to routines of our everyday lives and urban experiences.

In this book, we explore more specifically the significance of diverse aesthetic relations and political forms influenced by the contemporary conditions of urbanity, by various urban political orders (pertaining to substantially different youth urban worlds), and by the aesthetic feel of certain places in an interconnected yet specific urban environment: Montreal. In this endeavour, we closely examine the workings and political effects of two precognitive modalities of aesthetics engagement and political action that have not received enough attention in academic scholarship: seduction and attraction.

Let us for a moment return to Young's account of eroticism. Young (1990) emphasizes people's relation to the spaces, times, and peoples of the city. In short, although she does not use these terms, she acknowledges that agency is distributed among human and other-than-human actors. The problem with the ideal of community life, she insists, is that it rests on the need for recognition. City life, in contrast, thrives on attraction to differences, not the search for recognition. Speaking of other-than-human forces, Stengers (2005, cited in de la Cadena 2010, p. 352) notes that 'the political arena is peopled with shadows of that which does not have a political voice'. She is referring here to material forces, such as mountains and forests – and, inspired by Young, we could add specifically appealing buildings, objects, markets, and so on. City life is characterized by attraction to such material and human forces. Connolly (2011) speaks of the 'proto-agency' of non-human actors which disrupts our sense of perception through unexpected vibrations. When we allow proto-agents to disturb our sense of perception (when, to use de la Cadena's words, we let earth-beings have a political voice), we distribute agency outside the sovereign, rational individual. In other words, in a world of cities, we need to zoom in on precognitive encounters between bodies, material artefacts, and spaces *as elements of the political process*. These encounters involve finesse, attuning, fascination, attraction, magnetism, seduction.

Conceiving of political action through a distributive sense of agency can challenge the democratic notion of personal responsibility. If agency is distributed, how can we attribute the effects of action to someone? In order to untie this conundrum, we follow Krause (2011, p. 301) in defining agency as 'the affirmation of one's subjective existence through concrete action in the world'. Whatever we do, intentionally or not, it has an effect in the world. For example, we might unintentionally look at a group of Black youths gathered at a subway station in the Saint-Michel neighbourhood with disgust or fear, and it would have an effect on the individuals receiving this gaze. Such political gesture may not be rationally and strategically planned as a racist act, but it has an effect. We are responsible for our gesture, even if it was not cognitively planned. The embodied political gesture of looking with disgust or fear at other bodies in this specific moment and place produces effects on those bodies and on the signification of that place. In short, distributive agency, in the sense of analytically incorporating all forces at play in political action, from proto-agents and earth-beings to reflexive individuals, does not mean stripping away political obligations and responsibility for one's involvement in the situation, intentional or not.

A critical attention to the political effects of precognitive and distributive aesthetic modalities of political action therefore also requires that we understand aesthetics not only as a domain of sensations, but also as a socially, culturally constructed domain of judgement. Perceptions (skin colours, body shapes, greens coming out of concrete) and the values ascribed to them (what is considered beautiful, disgusting, fearful, etc.) are influenced by ideologies and social education, and in turn effectively 'partition the sensible', as Jacques Rancière (2000) would say. Rancière's understanding of the distribution of the sensible (*le partage du sensible*) has 'in recent years become de rigueur in Anglophone political theoretical mobilizations of the relationships between aesthetics and politics' (Jazeel and Mookherjee 2015, p. 354; see also Shapiro 2010; Dikeç 2015).

In English, we must read 'distribution' with the double meaning that the French word *partage* implies; that is, as distribution and/or partaking. For Rancière, the political consists of aesthetic practice insofar as 'it sets up scenes of dissensus' whereby the excluded, unseen, or those who don't have a recognized (legitimized) political voice make a sensible appearance which disrupts the democratic sensorium by exposing the polemical distribution of its constituents and the modalities of their perception and partaking in what is to be held in common (Rancière 2000; Vihalem 2018, p. 6). In Rancière's words (2000, p. 24; our translation), the relationship between aesthetics and politics is situated at the level of this 'sensory cutting of parts of the common of a community, the forms of its visibility and its arrangement'.[6] As the philosophy scholar Margus Vihalem (2018, p. 7) remarks, 'Rancièrian aesthetics, especially due to its political implications, partly moves away from Kantian aesthetics, although it preserves and further develops the fundamental intuition of Kantian aesthetics, namely that the aesthetic is what pertains to "a priori forms of sensibility"'. This approach fruitfully suggests that the distribution of the sensible operates out of and through a certain regime of perceptibility which assigns meanings, value, place, parts, temporalities to sensations in a social democratic order. Yet, by focusing on moments of political dissensus or interventions that disrupt the polemical order of the distribution of the sensible, Rancière does not consider the empirical difficulty in identifying what Jazeel and Mookherjee (2015, p. 355) want to call 'genuinely political interventions from what we might otherwise regard as anodyne postpolitical re-orchestrations of the social order' (see also Papastergiadis 2014).

We turn to Panagia (2009) to broaden our understanding of aesthetic political action that does not necessarily involve instant disruptions in the distribution of the sensible, but that nonetheless creates sensory lifeworlds affecting what is available to be sensed (in terms of both sensations and meanings) in urban youth worlds. Panagia's reflection on the politics of sensation is useful here because it enables us to pause in the 'experience of sensation that arises from the impact of an appearance' (Panagia 2009, p. 187), which, in his words, disfigures or disarticulates the conditions of perceptibility that would make recognition possible. 'Rather than recognition', writes Panagia, 'I suggest that the emergence of a political appearance requires an act of admission: an appearance advenes upon us, and we admit to it. An act of recognition *might follow from the durational intensity of advenience but it does not follow causally* in that there is no necessary condition that makes it so that it must (or even can) recognize any or all appearance' (Panagia 2009, p. 151; our emphasis).

In order to understand this conception of aesthetic politics, we need to look at both how action unfolds and its effects. We find it useful to distinguish between political action and political gestures. *Political gestures* involve the body in aesthetic ways (marching in a demonstration, screaming to a police officer, going to a punk concert) but may not necessarily register attention in their unfolding, or be performed with an intent to register attention. As Black studies and Black feminist theorists show, some forms of aesthetic gestures do not necessarily unfold as interventions into the sensorium of a dominant order, seeking to disrupt structures that determine regimes of perceptibility. For instance, Black feminist scholar Patricia Hill Collins (1998, p. 48) calls attentions to speech acts of Black women 'breaking silence' by 'giving testimonials that often disrupt public truths about them' from the authority of their own lived experiences. But, as she remarks, '[a] second type of knowledge exists, the collective secret knowledge generated by groups on either side of power that are shared in private when the other side's surveillance seems absent' (Collins 1998, p. 48). Political gestures in this context, conversations shared around the kitchen table or in student union offices for example, are not performed to register attention. 'For oppressed groups, such knowledge typically remains "hidden" because revealing it weakens its purpose of assisting those groups in dealing with oppression', writes Collins (1998, p. 49).

Political acts are creative moments that break from the routine and, through their unfolding, intrinsically legitimate the actor. An 'act' is not a reaction to a situation, but the creation of an actor who can legitimately be present in a situation they participate in creating. In turn, a *situation* is a moment and space where actors share a common sense of what is happening; they can sufficiently read what is happening to be able to engage in the interactions unfolding. Millions of banal situations unfold in our urban lives. A situation can become a political act when we make political gestures and give special meaning to what is happening. Take the following situation at the Saint-Michel subway station. A police officer approaches a group of youngsters hanging out near the entrance gate. He asks them to move and disperse. The group poses a political gesture by asserting the presence of their bodies there. They negotiate with the police officer. This creates a situation they can identify, unlike routine or banal instances of urban interactions, and thus they constitute themselves as actors. This is a political act. The police officer smiles, stays a little while with them, and then continues his route. The group stays a little more time and then leaves. Had they not asserted their embodied presence to the police officer, this would not have been a situation that broke from routine. It would not have been a political act. The accumulation of such political acts in our everyday lives and their transformation into a politicized narrative is what we call political action.[7]

In other words, what matters in the exercise of power is our experience of its effects. In order to capture these effects, Allen (2003) distinguishes between different modalities of power, each with their own relational peculiarities. *Domination* is an instrumental form of power relation exercised at someone else's expense; it restricts choice and closes down possibilities. *Authority* is also an instrumental power relation, but it does not involve the imposition of a form of conduct leading to submission. *Coercion* directly involves the threat of force to exact compliance, whereas *manipulation* implies the concealment of intent. *Seduction*, for Allen, is a modality of power relation that arouses specific desires by taking advantage of existing attitudes and expectations. Thus, it is the modality most relevant to aesthetic political relations. Because its effects are unpredictable, it is the opposite of domination. Seduction can be refused. It works through suggestion and enticement rather than prescription. If someone is not attracted to seducing acts, they will have no effects.

In his insightful empirical study of why criminals act when they do, Katz (1988) argues that a crime can occur only when a criminal senses a distinctive sensual dynamic at play in a specific moment and place. He explores how the criminal is attracted to the sensual possibilities opened by the situation and seduced by its 'symbolic creativity'. He is attentive to the 'mode of executing action, [the] symbolic creativity in defining the situation, and [the] esthetic finesse in recognizing and elaborating on the sensual possibilities' (Katz 1988, p. 9). He argues that 'to one degree or another, we are always being seduced and repelled by the world', that we 'are always moving away from and toward different objects of consciousness, taking account of this and ignoring that, and moving in one direction or the other between the extremes of involvement and boredom'. He pursues: 'In this constant movement of consciousness, we do not perceive that we are controlling the movement' (Katz 1988, p. 4). In other words, for Katz, seduction and attraction are almost synonymous. He does not ascribe to seduction an intentional strategy. Instead, he focuses on the effects of seduction and the 'esthetic finesse' required to respond to it. As an emitting modality of power, seduction needs a receptive effect. This is what we will call *attraction*.

In order to explain what we mean by 'attraction', allow us to describe a situation experienced by Julie-Anne in the Prado Museum in Madrid. The Prado has a very large collection of Goya's paintings depicting royal characters and religious scenes. When Julie-Anne visited the museum, she focused on the story these paintings were telling, on how Goya depicted power. When, at the end of the day, she went down to the museum's lower level, she encountered his *Pinturas Negras*, painted on the walls of his house toward the end of his life (during the 1820s). These murals depict barbaric scenes from everyday life in quasi-phantasmagorical forms: embodied human interactions, eating, blood, fear, crowds, sickness, music, ageing bodies, raging gods, expressively reading a book, sexual desire, fire... (see Figure I.1). As she encountered this 'aesthetic appearance' (Panagia 2009), Julie-Anne could no longer move her body. She could not read what she was seeing anymore; she could almost feel the warmth of the blood on her fingers, the fear of the crowd. She stayed for nearly an hour, without moving, until her husband came for her.

Exiting the museum, they sat on a bench under the fresh shade of a canopy tree for another hour, where Julie-Anne couldn't stop speaking, spitting out her

FIGURE I.1 'Saturno', Francisco de Goya, 1823.

emotions, trying to make sense of what she had sensed and the difference bet-ween her rational relation to Goya's 'power' paintings and this political work. The *Pinturas Negras* have been analysed as Goya's radically political position generated by the sourness he felt at the end of the Napoleonic Wars (Junquera 2003). They were painted in his country house just outside of Madrid, where he retired disgusted by urban power plays and barbaric humanity. They play with bodily functions such as blood, vomiting, and modified body parts in order to express a profound rejection of urban political life. It is this rejection that makes these paintings so urbanely intense, as opposed to the clean depic-tion of state and imperial power that transpires from his previous works.

The *Pinturas Negras* tell a story of aesthetic political action in the sense that they represent everyday scenes of power relations that are intensely emotional and embodied. They depict political gestures of fights, bodies resisting, and shocking inequalities. But beyond the story they tell (what they cognitively represent), Julie-Anne's encounter with them was a 'pregnant moment' of aesthetic politics. These moments occur when action-oriented perception is temporarily suspended, when we sense that something different is happening without being able to articulate it with words. During these 'fugitive glimmers of becoming' (Connolly 2011, p. 7), what we sense 'breaks our confidence in the correspondence between perception and signification' (Panagia 2009, p. 5). In other words, in these pregnant moments, we can no longer rely on our cognitive capacities to understand what is going on. Julie-Anne could only, as Panagia would put it, admit this 'aesthetic appearance' was affecting her.

Philosophically, Panagia emphasizes the immediacy, the here-and-now, the shock of an aesthetic appearance. When we are faced with something that speaks to our senses (such as the *Pinturas Negras*), we cannot name it (recognize it as something we know). We can simply 'admit' that it is touching us. Panagia suggests that aesthetic appearances are political because they provide us with opportunities for responsiveness. The intensity of this experience is generally neglected from political analysis because it cannot be described with words and thus articulated as ideology or interests. 'Under the pressures of immediacy', Panagia writes, 'we lose access to the kinds of conditions that make it possible to determine things like motivation, use, or belief – all forces that constitute the nature of interest' (Panagia 2009, p. 27). Pregnant moments are regulated by attraction.

It was only after this moment of 'immediacy' that Julie-Anne tried to represent, rationalize, and explain what she experienced. To this day, the *Pinturas Negras* still exercise a strong force of attraction on her. They have modified what she can see, sense, utter, and think about politics. Some artefacts (proto-agents, earth-beings) are so powerful that our cognitive abilities no longer function to relate with them. When we stop looking at a painting for the story it tells (relating to what is represented on the canvas) but instead feel we can enter and touch the colours and forms it offers without identifying what it is that is touching us, we find ourselves in an intense pregnant moment that will affect our sensing.

The *Pinturas Negras* qualify as bearing what the German philosopher Wolfgang Welsch (2002) would call 'transcultural effectiveness'. With regards to Japanese art, he describes a situation comparable to Julie-Anne's experience at the Prado. His words are insightful in defining attraction:

> As distant as those works or conceptions may be in time and space, we yet feel, strangely enough, that it is we who are at stake here. Irresistible fascination is the outset. We sense a radiation emanating from these objects: though not made for us, they seem to approach us, to address

us, we are strongly attracted and even fascinated by them. They appear to bear a promise – one, perhaps, of unexpected insight or of future enrichment. In any case a promise we should respond to. They seem to bear potentials able to improve and enlarge our sensitivity, our comprehension and perhaps even our way of being. (Welsch 2002)

Beyond works of art, everyday urban life is filled with pregnant moments. Living in a world of cities compels us to be sensitive to unusual political forms and immerse ourselves in everyday lifeworlds. We are inspired by Bence Nanay (2016), who stresses the multiplicity of aesthetic experiences and 'resist[s] the urge to find some kind of essential feature of aesthetics: it comprises a diverse set of topics'. Because we are concerned with aesthetics as it relates to different dimensions of urban life and the politics embedded in and produced through urban experiences, our analyses mobilize conceptual resources from the main fields of aesthetic studies briefly discussed so far: everyday and environmental aesthetics (Berleant 1992, 2012; Blanc 2013) and aesthetic politics (Panagia 2009).

In the following chapters, we more specifically emphasize aesthetic political relations that operate through seduction and attraction, involving the strange feeling of being sucked into them, as within a magnetic field. This defines a pleasurable sensation, a hopeful horizon, 'a promise we should respond to' (Welsch 2002), because attraction involves responsiveness. Aesthetic political relations thus open up the imagination, prefiguring or charting new or other ways of being in the world (Murphy and Omar 2013; Carlson 2019). *Seduction* and *attraction* are twin modalities of power at play in aesthetic political relations. Examining their functioning entails looking at the execution of power (agency) and its *effects* in the world. In order to do so, agency is understood as *embodied* and *distributed* among human and other-than-human actors. Political action, therefore, results from embodied *political gestures* and the sensual, intuitive response to situational opportunities producing *political acts which can become transformed into a politicized narrative through their accumulation in everyday life*.

In short, aesthetic political gestures and acts are expressive of what Black feminist scholar Christa Davis Acampora (2007, p. 5) calls 'aesthetic agency' and potentially 'transformative aesthetics'. She writes that 'the core idea of aesthetic agency is that integral to our understanding of the world is our capacity for making and remaking the symbolic forms that supply the frameworks for the acquisition and transmission of knowledge' (Acampora 2007, p. 5) and our sensory dispositions. In this book, we explore this by immersing ourselves in various youth urban worlds.

Youth Urban Worlds

In *La révolution urbaine*, written in the midst of the 1968 movement in Nanterre (Paris), Lefebvre (1970) specifically locates the potential for a Marxist revolution in the urban historical period. Indeed, urbanity, youthfulness, and political action have long been interrelated. This raises the question: Is the contemporary visibility of urban and youthful political action the simple continuity of the urban revolts of the 1960s across the world?

In the 1960s, as in the 2010s, young people were facing rapid processes of urbanization and globalization. They were constructing a clear generational rupture, what has been called a 'cultural revolution'. There are, however, two major differences between the two historical contexts. The 1960s was a flourishing period of nation-state construction, with the development in the Global North of the welfare state and the rise of social populism and national economic protectionism in the Global South. The 2010s was rather a period of nation-state austerity measures and economic deregulation, in the North as in the South. The 1960s urban political mobilizations occurred in a period of economic boom, just before the economic crises of the 1970s and the rise of neoliberalism. The 2010s mobilizations represent instead the culmination of the struggle against neoliberalism in a context of global economic urban crisis generated by a mortgage debacle. One could argue that the global urban youth movements of the 1960s and 2010s represent the beginning and the end of what Tarrow (1998) would call a 'protest cycle', characterized by the visibility of youth and an urban logic of political action that fosters specific repertoires of action: spatial occupations, arts and cultural creativity, alternative lifestyles and rhythms, sexual liberation, embodied and spiritual explorations, global connections and interactions, closeness to 'nature', and more-than-human agency.

The development of global urban youth movements since the 1960s has been studied in France and Italy as the New Social Movement approach. In this literature, the objective is to uncover the structural socioeconomic and cultural transformations that led to the emergence of newly politicized issues (such as sexual orientation, feminism, and ecology) outside of the labour–capital nexus (see e.g. Melucci 1989; Touraine 1992). Inspired by Marx's idea of labour as the motor of history, these authors define a social movement as a force that has transformative social power. The fact that social movement theory is interested in newly politicized issues that are particularly visible in young urban dwellers' lifestyles might have initiated a reflection on the impact of youthfulness and urbanity on social mobilization. Yet, Lefebvre (1970), although not a social movement theorist per se, but widely perceived as writing within this context, is the only author who has explicitly raised this question. For this, he was criticized by Castells (1972) and Harvey (1973). In *The Urban Question*, Castells emphasizes that there is nothing specifically urban about the way history progresses. According to the young Castells, the prevailing motor of action is still class struggle. He rejects the idea that an urban mode of production is displacing the industrial capital–labour nexus and sees youthfulness as an irrelevant variable. He interprets political claims arising in cities as the contemporary manifestation of the capital–labour conflict, shifted from the workplace to the collective consumption spaces of the city. In *Social Justice and the City*, Harvey makes a similar argument, suggesting that the urban is still heavily dependent on industrial capital and thus cannot be analysed as a new mode of production. His evidence is that in the 1960s and 1970s, industrial capital was still far stronger than land capital.[8] Until the 1990s, social movement theory did not theorize the urbanity of these new movements. Youthfulness was always implied given the demographics of activists in these movements, but never directly theorized.

In the field of youth studies, beginning with the Chicago School, youngsters were associated with deviance: hoodlums, aggressors, wasters, and so on (Thrasher 1927; Cohen 1955; Becker 1973). The focus of this work was on explaining why social problems emerge and their consequences for the ecological equilibrium of cities. At its beginnings in Chicago, youth subcultural studies tended to explain transgressive youth behaviour by emphasizing that marginalization produces specific sets of needs and behaviours and that deviance is more prominent in cities because urbanity challenges traditional community ties (Simmel 1903; Whyte 1943). In order to face marginalization, it explained, youth with similar problems of social adjustment will get together and invent their own frames of reference as a sort of support system. Subcultures generally refer to relatively distinct (urban) social subsystems within a larger culture (Williams 2007). By the 1970s, however, youth subcultural studies in the United States was moving from sociology to criminology, emphasizing youth as potential criminals and leaving behind the earlier focus on youth cultural production.

Meanwhile, in the United Kingdom, Richard Hoggart was creating the Centre for Contemporary Cultural Studies, moving the centre of subcultural studies across the Atlantic Ocean. Hoggart was less concerned with how marginalized youth get together and more with explaining subcultural formations in terms of power relations. From Chicago's explanation in terms of deviance, Hoggart and his team positioned youthfulness as class resistance (Clarke 1976). Henceforth, subcultures were understood as spaces of resistance to cultural hegemony, the most visible sign of which is youth styles. From Chicago's ethnographic methodologies, youth subcultural studies turned towards semiology and phenomenology (Dillabough and Kennelly 2010)[9]. With this turn away from ethnography, the initial theoretical and empirical articulation between youthfulness and urbanity disappeared as subcultural studies moved from Chicago to Birmingham.

Straw (2002) suggests speaking in terms of urban scenes instead of subcultures. The idea of an urban scene emphasizes practices instead of stable identities. Because the city consists of 'experiential fluxes and excesses', individuals rely on urban scenes to find their bearings (Straw 2014). They offer places to see and be seen, but also to experience various identities and share common values. For Straw, a scene is a cultural phenomenon which participates in the effervescence of the city and its sociability. This is interesting because it focuses the analysis on the relationship between specific cultural activities and the space, time, and affectivity of the city (Born, Lewis, and Straw 2017). Yet, by moving away from subcultures, the concept of the urban scene has abandoned the initial concern with deviance and transgression. Political action is absent from this analysis.

During the1970s, in the francophone world, the *sociologie de la jeunesse* developed around very different sets of concerns centred in education and psychology. Researchers attempted to understand biological transformations and educational models. The 1980s marked an important shift towards a nonbiological conception of age in France, as in Quebec. The question became: How do young people enter adulthood? (Galland 2011). French sociologists identified various rituals constitutive of this transition to adulthood, such as moving out of the family home or having a child. Instead of studying marginalization or style (subcultures), the French-speaking debate asked whether age was an efficient angle for social categorization (Gauthier and Guillaume 1999). If the British debate moved away from the urban, the French debate has never spatialized the youth question. It proposes a linear temporal model for understanding how youth grow up, how they grow out of youthfulness. It is not concerned with the specificities of being young and urban. For instance, when hip-hop emerged in the French *banlieues* in the 1980s, the urbanity and spatiality of this cultural phenomenon was not considered relevant either by Bourdieu's (1993) structuralist explanation or by Dubet's (1987) more agency-oriented analysis. In both cases, it was seen not as a youth subculture but as a poor copy of the North American original (Warne 2014, p. 59). The fact that French hip-hop was born in and of the *banlieue* as a specific space and culture was not theorized.

In this book, our approach explicitly articulates urbanity and youthfulness to political action. Like the early Chicago School, we work with ethnography. Like the Birmingham Centre for Contemporary Cultural Studies, we adopt a critical perspective linking youthfulness and political action (although we do not necessarily frame this action in terms of resistance). Like the French *sociologie de la jeunesse*, we are concerned with understanding what it means, socially, to be young, as opposed to being 'adult'. But we wish to explicitly spatialize this reflection. Doing so alongside racialized youths living in racialized neighbourhoods necessitates (as we will see in Chapter 2) that we pay critical attention to the effects of racial discourses, practices, and state apparatuses on experiences of youthfulness. The question for us is not so much: Why and how do young people transgress the adult norm or grow into socially functioning adults? Instead, articulating youthfulness, urbanity, and political action, we ask: Who can claim to be young? Who can assign youthfulness to a political subject? Under what and whose terms? What is youthfulness as a form of political action?

We find inspiration in the literature emerging from studies of youth and urbanity in the Global South. This literature is particularly insightful in theoretically articulating youthfulness and urbanity, perhaps because both are so much more visible in these Southern cities given the intensity of the urbanization process there and the inverted age pyramid in relation to the ageing population of the Global North. Of course, the urban context that inspired these studies is very different from that of Montreal. Nevertheless, if adapted to the specificities of the latter, the theoretical proposals emerging from these contexts are most useful for decentring the analysis.

Studying young trendsetters in Mexico City, Urteaga (2012) suggests seeing *youthfulness as a position from which to experiment with cultural and social change*. Youthfulness for her consists of a specific 'way of being together'. Being together, for youth, is about opening spaces of fluxes and games in which they can constantly recreate their ways of being through aesthetic, a specific conception of work, ways of organizing themselves to work, new verbal and body languages, and forms of social conduct. In short, Urteaga emphasizes the idea of a youthful social and spatial position.

Simone's (2005) work expands on this idea by emphasizing the mobile and fluid nature of this sociospatial position. Studying youth mobility cultures in Douala, he shows how circulation gives youth the opportunity *to experiment through dispersion rather than confinement*, thereby rejecting the enclosed idea of subcultures with clear boundaries. In the politically and economically unstable context of Douala, becoming somebody means being able to move around, to operate everywhere in the city rather than being known locally as the 'son of Mr. X'. In this context, writes Simone (2005, p. 520), 'disrespect for a confined sense of things, therefore, becomes a key element of self-fashioning'. In Douala, being young means *assembling various discordant temporalities and situations of potential informal work, because the present can no longer be considered a platform for the future*. Youth life, in Douala, is a life of permanent circulation, rather than following the well-known track of marriage and formal employment. Simone thus squarely rejects the French aspatialized perspective on the transition to adulthood.

Being young and mobile provides a very different vantage point from that of being married and employed, in Douala and elsewhere. This networked mode of spatial relations changes worldviews (and it is not exclusive to youth, even if it is perhaps more visible for them). The world becomes less linear, built from networks of significant places and collections of temporalities. A vantage point (Urteaga's sociospatial position) not only provides a framework for reading the world, it also constructs a platform for fashioning oneself as a political subject. Bhabha (1994) explains clearly how *travelling* provokes a rupture in one's identity, because being in a new place provokes feelings of estrangement; it displaces one's identity; it changes one's standpoint (in the proper sense of changing what we see and feel as we change where we stand). The more vantage points we experience, the more political subjectivity we develop. This entails discontinuous political ideas: we change more often what we think is the right political claim to make. We can more easily change 'causes', move across value systems and political influences. Political engagement becomes highly dependent on the various encounters we have along our many displacements. Allegiances are often only temporary.

This is what Bayat (2010) attempts to capture with the notion of a youth non-movement, based on his analysis of young people's resistance to the Iranian regime in the 1980s. Looking at almost invisible gestures such as the underground world of youth dancing parties and the informal market for prohibited music, he qualifies Teheran's youth culture as a youth non-movement. Instead of speaking of youth subcultures, Bayat prefers to speak in terms of youthfulness, to emphasize a political form and a way of life, instead of youth as an essentialized and biological category. What characterizes youths are youthful 'ways of being, feeling, and carrying oneself (e.g. a greater tendency for experimentation, adventurism, idealism, autonomy, mobility, and change) that are associated with the sociological fact of "being young"' (Bayat 2010, p. 118). Youthfulness, pursues Bayat (2010, p. 119), is an urban condition: 'It is in modern cities that "young persons" turn into "youth", by experiencing and developing a particular consciousness about being young, about youthfulness'.

The field of youth studies in the Global South explicitly articulates, theoretically and empirically, youthfulness as a mode of action, as a social position, as a set of mobile spaces and temporalities. Based on this work, we prefer to speak of youth *worlds* instead of subcultures or new social movements. We adopt Becker's (1982) interactionist conception of the various worlds that compose social life. A world is always socially constructed and in constant transformation. Becker's basic idea is that people's worlds are constituted by what people do together. Even if his work was central to subcultural studies emerging out of the Chicago School, the concept of youth world can accommodate a much more porous spatiality.

For us, an urban world is constructed by and shapes youth perceptions of the broader world, as well as their interactions with other-than-human forces that people their everyday lives. Instead of defining their worlds as subsystems, alternative cultures, or recognizable urban scenes, we keep Becker's interactionist focus, because it avoids structural and deterministic explanations of why people do what they do.[10] Youth urban worlds are formed through interactions with the spaces and artefacts of the city as much as with other people. In addition, following Nancy (1993), we suggest that worlds are characterized by specific sensory experience, by a shared space of commonality. What we are able to sense depends on our relations and exposure within and between worlds. Unlike urban scenes, however, many of the youth urban worlds we will describe in the following chapters are not easily identifiable, representable, or nameable. We could speak of the anarchist activist scene, the lifestyle sports scene, or the urban farming scene. But we cannot really speak of the racialized youth scene, and not all activists would identify with the anarchist scene. This is why we will speak more fluidly of youth urban worlds.

Because of their impact on conceptions of time, space, and affect, urban worlds are profoundly affecting the political process. Youthfulness as a form of political action rejects the state centrism of many organized social movements. Acting through youthfulness means being politically engaged through urban youth cultures and their habits of speech, their ways of interacting, their artistic expressions, their political experimentation. Street art, do-it-yourself movements, and other forms of inhabiting the city and making space for alternative lifestyles are fruitful ways of achieving this.

The Global Urban Political Moment of the 2010s: Youthfulness in Action

Much has been written about the wave of urban political mobilizations that has swept cities around the world since 2010. The student strike in Chile, #Yo-Soy132 in Mexico, the 'Maple Spring' in Quebec, the various Arab springs, Occupy in several cities, the 15M Indignados in Spain, the Gezi movement in Turkey, the Umbrella Revolution in Hong Kong, Black Lives Matter in North America, Femen in Eastern Europe and then across the world, les Nuits debout in France following the 2015 terrorist attacks, Anonymous, the list goes on… These movements refer to one another. They are globally connected, but fundamentally anchored locally. They are mostly enacted by young people.

Why do they deploy their action in cities? Political economists would respond that urbanization creates increased inequality and injustice (Harvey 2008). Sociologists would insist that cities provide multiple public spaces that facilitate the expression of political opinions and mobilization. Environmentalists might highlight the fact that urbanization and development have produced globally shared problems that are more acutely felt in cities. While these various explanations are all relevant, they do not see youthfulness as a relevant factor, because their focus is not on the changing political form of these mobilizations.

Global urbanization creates very dense connections, from the Internet to mobile activists, from world forums to shared values and discursive resources (the right to the city, the struggle against neoliberalism). In other words, urbanization brings a more networked relation to space, and this enables political events to resonate with one another translocally. This was very clear in the Occupy and Femen movements. Furthermore, worldwide urbanization favours alternative rationalities and builds on emotional intensity. For example, emotions such as rage and outrage are explicitly positioned as the genesis of the Indignados and Juventud Sin Futuro and the struggle to punish the Mexican state for the disappearance of 43 students in Ayotzinapa in the autumn of 2014.

The urban political moment of the 2010s is characterized by specific political forms emphasizing performance more than debate (aesthetics more than representation), embodied and affective gestures, distributive agency, networked spaces of action, open-ended politics of doing (more than a politics of claiming), and individual transformation and spirituality. In many ways, this is very similar to the urban political moment of the 1960s (see in this regard the work of Julie Stephens (1998) on anti-disciplinary forms of protest emerging in that decade), aside from the availability of very different technologies. As Austin (2013, p. 16) vividly reminds us while analysing the 1960s: 'People did not simply imitate or react to international struggles that they witnessed via the media. For many, events around the world highlighted their own local injustices. Inspired by what they witnessed, they experienced a kind of kinetic connection and a common sense of purpose, or what George Katsiaficas (1987) refers to as the *eros* effect – "the massive awakening of the instinctual human need for justice and for freedom" – which could otherwise be described as an almost spiritual sensation that connected dissidents across the globe.' And these dissidents were and are mostly young and urban.

Indeed, around the world, there has been a rapid increase in the number of educated youths living in cities (UNFPA 2014). This generation of urban youth has developed a collective identity through the sharing of images and ideas in physical and digital spaces. Generational sociologists speak of the 'global generation' (Edmunds and Turner 2005).[11] In Quebec, this is often called a *génération d'enfants-rois* (a generation of kid-kings). A viral Facebook post in April 2015 discusses this appellation:

> While the rest of society is resigned, she wants a better world … they wonder why she doesn't vote. They wonder why she feels the urge to break everything … Somewhere, she has a banner on which it is written: 'Fuck toute!' They don't understand. They find this generation of king-children so stupid. Fuck-everything.[12] (Sebastien Jean, 9 April 2015)

In its apparent destructiveness, the banner 'Fuck toute!' (fuck everything) became very present during the spring 2015 mobilizations against auster-ity measures in Quebec (see Figure I.2). It seems even that these youngsters were marching out of indifference, which is an oxymoron: doing and be-ing indifferent (Collectif Débrayage 2016). To us, the exasperation expressed by the banner, intertwining virtual posts with physical graffiti and marches in the city, represents a generational rupture in the way young people prac-tice and understand politics. This is what this book describes through four ethnographies.

FIGURE I.2 'Fuck toute', Beaubien metro station, February 2016.
Source: photo by Joëlle Rondeau.

Inspired by the work of Mannheim (1952), generational sociologists argue that to be qualified as a generation, a cohort needs to share a distinctive social consciousness. Whether a generation succeeds in developing such consciousness depends, according to Mannheim, on the 'tempo of social change'. In times of accelerated social change, youth are less reliant on the older generation's memories (Pilcher 1994). The 'fuck everything' wired generation operates prefiguratively, developing new political forms, following an urban logic of action. Indeed, 'taking young people seriously', as Skelton (2010, p. 145) argues, 'may well lead to new definitions of the political and demonstrate other ways of conceptualizing geopolitics and political geographies'. In the following chapters, as we immerse ourselves in various urban worlds, we will show how 'millennials' engage in a politics of social transformation based on digital and social media, but also – and mostly – on the sensuousness of the street. Rather than analysing these forms of youth transgressions and politics as mere deviance or countercultural excess, we see in these youth urban worlds the stuff of urban change.

Montreal in a World of Cities

It is from our ethnographies of Montreal that the complexity of aesthetic political action theoretically emerged for us. Montreal is a city where politics, arts, and experimentation are intensely felt every day by its dwellers. This is what Ivan, Kabisha, and Hubert expressed at the onset of this introduction. It is also what David Austin explains in the preface to his extraordinarily profound book on 'Race, Sex, and Security in Sixties Montreal'. Quoting him at length is worthwhile:

> My first sense of Montreal's historical importance within the Black diaspora came in the 1980s when I was a high-school student in Toronto. My older brother, Andrew, introduced me to a book that critically assessed the significance of a Black-led protest at what is today Concordia University. Around the same time, I read Walter Rodney's *The Groundings with My Brothers*, a book that I had discovered at the famous Third World Books and Crafts, which no longer exists. The book included three presentations that Rodney had delivered in Montreal in 1968. Clearly, Montreal had been home to major developments in the Black diaspora, and yet oddly very little had been written about it. (Austin 2013, p. ix)

Through oral histories, Austin depicts a Montreal central to the transnational Black Left and where Black political thought and actions have left significant imprints on ways of reading the world, as we will see in Chapter 1.

He highlights the intertwining of embodied suffering and disciplining with racism and youthful politics. The following pages are inspired by his work, thinking about Montreal as a place with its own role in global urban youthful politics. Without explicitly stating so, Austin's work on the role of Montreal in the transnational Black Left movement follows what Simone (2010) calls an 'epistemology of Blackness'. Such epistemology requires situating the analysis in a specific place where, over time, certain ways of doing have crystallized because of the constant movement and intermingling of Black people. As a heuristic device, this epistemology helps emphasize circulations and connections; it enables, through sensibility to affective interactions, a description of specific worlds.

Our own experience in Montreal and the intellectual stimulation it provided us are at the origins of this book, as are our exchanges with students and colleagues who have moved through or near the Laboratoire Ville et ESPAces politiques (VESPA) research laboratory where we speculated and reflected (to borrow from Harvey's (1985a) terminology) on a research programme aiming to explore urbanity as an object of study and a critical epistemology. We strove to consider the ways in which our urbanity in Montreal transforms our understanding of the world while opening up possibilities for acting and engaging with it.

In Chapter 1, we will describe how the intense sensorial experience of long winters, playful politics and street art performance, sexual nationalism, 'White niggers' and racism, linguistic spatializations, a youthful population, and a vibrant punk scene are some of the elements we bring forward to speak of Montreal's urban feel. We could have chosen others, such as the role of balconies and back streets in public sociability. Despite its relatively small size, Montreal has long been a city within a world of cities, a city embedded in world culture and politics. This is notable in its activism, but also in its cultural production since the 1960s. This is why Montreal makes an interesting place to examine the transformation of the political process and logics of political action in an increasingly urban and connected world.

Marcotte (1997, p. 150; our translation) describes the arrival of a new type of character in Montreal novels in the 1980s, a character that has a 'particular way of living the action'. This novel character enacts what we call in this book the 'urban logic of action', an action that unfolds with a concept of space, time, and affect very different from that which was prevalent in the world of nation-states. Marcotte (1997, pp. 150–151) explains that starting in the 1980s, the unfolding of action in novels took place 'within a dilated space, without boundaries or with very thin boundaries, a space that in itself invites crossing, displacement'. With regard to time, 1980s novels emphasize 'infinity in the sense that time is not counted, sliced in function of an objective to attain, but it is lived through privileged instants. On the one hand, the "spectacular" stops, freezes, glorifies the present time; on the other hand, the importance given to look, fashion, dating, periodization, makes of time a pure succession of moments that evidently has nothing to do with what we call a historical movement.' Finally, Marcotte (1997) notes that in contrast with novels from the 1960s and 1970s, the 1980s novel is not marked by historical confrontation. Instead, 'in this space of mobility, in this time freed from the duty of orientation, action unfolds as a vital activity, game, party sometimes'.

In a nutshell, Marcotte's analysis of Montreal novels evokes to us how urban ways of life transform our conceptual apparatus and filters of perception for understanding the world. He synthesizes what we call the exacerbation of an urban logic of political action, characterized by a conception of space, time, and rationality different from that which dominated the world of nation-states. From the 1960s to today, global urban protest movements have made visible new ways of acting politically based on the confusion and dilemmas provoked by urbanization.

A Methodological Note

In order to understand the provocations of these urban political forms, or even to 'see' them, we must enter youth urban worlds, share their everyday political gestures. In other words, we suggest that political analysis requires ethnography, and not only ethnography of the state (Bernstein and Mertz 2011). It is, of course, a matter of academic discipline. Political philosophy and other fields have a very important role to play. Yet, this book is a plea for a stronger recognition of an ethnographic approach to political analysis. This means describing how action unfolds in concrete situations before explaining or justifying it. It means adopting an inductive rather than a deductive posture. It means engaging in ethnographic work 'as a mode of "epistemic partnership"' (Marcus 2006, cited in Papastergiadis 2014, p. 20).

Ethnography has been a prominent method in urban studies for a very long time. Chicago School ethnographies continue to inspire the field of urban studies, incorporating sophisticated intersectional analyses of power relations (see for instance Duneier 1999; Wacquant 2004; Ralph 2014). In the following chapters, we build on this tradition in order to make the argument that the current urban moment is uniquely in need of ethnography. This book suggests that in order to analyse political forms in the contemporary moment, a good unit of analysis is the *relational* micro, because it is at that scale that everyday and aesthetic politics come to make sense. Inspired by urban ethnographies such as Caldeira's (2012) work on taggers and mo-tobikers in Sao Paulo and Ghertner's (2015) analysis of world-city making in Delhi, immersing ourselves in youth urban worlds is a springboard for theo-rizing the political beyond resistance and organized protest.

This book emerges from various ethnographic projects undertaken at the VESPA Lab in Montreal between 2008 and 2016. Taken together, these projects constitute some of the urban youth worlds that we moved through during that period. We selected the following four ethnographies based on a sense of responsibility towards youth and intuitive attraction to objects of analysis often overlooked or disregarded by political analysts, but which open up different possibilities for learning about the transformation of the political process in a world of cities. The selection was based on our aim of presenting a diversity of urban youth worlds in Montreal, balancing the representation of voices and perspectives from within and across them. This is why, in the following chapters, we meet youths from different neighbourhoods, variously racialized and privileged, and learn from the distributed agency of various human and non-human actors.

We individually, or with students, engaged in various ethnographic observations using diverse methods ranging from the use of mobile, multime-dia tools (video, GPS, biometric) and participatory research to more classical interviews and anthropological immersion. Our ethnographic approach has sought to engage with these actors as 'epistemic partners' (Holmes and Mar-cus 2008), recognizing that, in an age of complex interactions and intercon-nectedness, 'members of a community no longer see themselves as stewards of a specific worldview that is rooted in a fixed territory, but as agents capable of upholding and modifying the residual forms of their cultural identity as it interacts with forces from remote and unknown parts of the world' (Papas-tergiadis 2014, p. 21).

Our ethnographic approach involves, through this process, a posture of aesthetic sensitivity that cultivates open-mindedness and receptivity, meaning, in part, that we observe with all bodily senses and cultivate engagement in the urban youth worlds we experience. This posture involves using reflexive empathic imagination to make sense of others' experience of the world – or, when we are not able to engage physically in their experiences, using emo-tional intelligence to learn from emotional cues and consider what we can sense, what touches us but we cannot immediately name or recognize. In such cases, time is needed to let feelings and sensations 'sink' or 'settle' in, to create dialogues for generating meaning.

As we became more engaged in these worlds through generative webs of relationships and the co-constitution of fields of aesthetic perception (where 'sensations and affect co-mingle'; see Ioanes 2017), a theory of aesthetic relations came to make sense as a way of illuminating in contrastive and complementary ways the political process that we are witnessing being transformed. The ethnographies therein exemplify dimensions and modes of acting politically through aesthetics, rather than *verifying* the argument we make. While we focus particularly on seduction and attraction as modes of aesthetic political relations, we do not favour cognitive or noncognitive approaches to aesthetics of urban environments and everyday life, nor do we gesture towards an overarching unifying notion of aesthetic experience and aesthetic practice. We rather let the ethnographies express the various dimensions and ways of acting politically, aesthetically, that we noticed and came to better understand in interaction and dialogue with research participants and colleagues.

In this regard, we have chosen to write through ethnographic material because we see ethnographic description as an act of translation. In their critical work on 'writing culture', Clifford and Marcus (1986) break from the ethnographical tradition of the Chicago School that aimed to represent lived experience 'as it really is'. Instead, they see ethnography as a writing practice involving polyvocality, dialogue, and intertextuality. The ethnographer, they argue, creates affective fictions of the world they describe. This is what we wanted to achieve by writing these ethnographic chapters collectively. We, Julie-Anne and Joëlle, occupy distinct positionalities in each chapter, depending on the youth world we are entering and on the methods and organization of the research projects. We conceived this book as a sounding board for modalities of political action and expression which do not make the headlines in public debates or academic texts, but which nonetheless transform the global urban worlds in which we live, affecting us by changing our political subjectivities at infra-empirical and precognitive levels.

Introducing each ethnography is a drawing of a situation described therein. We conceive these images as entry points into the youth urban world analysed in the chapters using artistic rather than scientific language. These situations were illustrated by Lukas Beeckman based on his reading of the chapters, providing a different aesthetic sensibility by which for the reader to feel these youth urban worlds. Furthermore, a footnote at the beginning of each chapter briefly explains the type of ethnographic material used. Consistently in all these ethnographies, we presented ourselves as researchers from the VESPA. Julie-Anne is Full Professor and thus occupies a different social position than Joëlle, who was a Master's student at the time of research and writing. It is somewhat awkward to write ethnographic descriptions in the third person, but we did not really see how to do otherwise. If, for instance, Joëlle is the ethnographer in a chapter, she writes speaking of herself in the third person so that the reader can identify who is actually physically with the young people they encounter in the book. As this is a piece of collaborative writing between the two of us, Julie-Anne has intervened in the chapters Joëlle initially wrote, and vice and versa. In other words, we wanted to avoid individually signing chapters and to freely intervene and connect our ethnographic materials. This process was enriched by reading research reports and articles produced with other students and research professionals who have come to work and study at the VESPA.

The Organization of the Book

Chapter 1 offers an overview of the historical urban context in Montreal since the 1960s. We strive to first provide a larger and more detailed rendering of Montreal's urban feel by discussing some of the elements that are reciprocally affecting politics and urban youth worlds lived in this city. We then discuss Montreal's place in the global urban political moment of the 1960s and 1970s and highlight how, at one end of a historical protest cycle, this moment reveals changing relations to time, space, and alternative rationalities that contribute to the affirmation of an urban logic of action alongside a nationalist state-centred logic of action.

In Chapter 2, we enter into the urban political world of racialized youth in the neighbourhoods of Little Burgundy and Saint-Michel. We explore how an individual becomes a political subject through daily encounters and situations of negotiation with the state (represented in this chapter through the figures of police officer, school teacher, and social worker). In the context of public debates around street gangs, racial profiling, and radicalization, we argue that analysing these youth worlds as 'anti-social' or 'at-risk' blinds us to what is being constructed on a daily basis. It shows that racialized youth are politically active beyond debates and representations. The 'universe of operation' that characterizes their neighbourhoods requires that we adopt what Simone calls an epistemology of Blackness. With material such as accounts of their daily movements in the city, collective cartographies of their neighbourhood, song lyrics and poems written by the youths themselves, and video vignettes they co-produced with us, the chapter illustrates how racialized youths act through movement, seduction, and distributed agency.

In Chapter 3, we explore the emotional and spatialized experience of youths who participated in the 2012 student strikes. While this ethnography focuses on a more explicitly political event, we do not analyse it using the traditional sociological tools that focus on power relations, strategies, and organization. Instead, we work with emotional mapping, life narratives, biometric data, and video showing how transforming conceptions of time, space, and rationality in the contemporary urban era produce new forms of political action. Through an analysis of students' urban trajectories and their emotionally charged places, we reflect on the effective reach of different modalities of power. Important figures such as the red square and Anarchopanda allow us to reflect on distributed agency and the negation of leadership. The sound of pots and pans and the vibration of ecstatic screaming under the Berri tunnel are used to show how these aesthetic experiences have changed the students as much as the streets of Montreal.

Chapter 4 draws us into the urban political world of beginning and aspiring urban farmers on the terrain of City Farm School, an urban agriculture training programme operating from within marginal and interstitial spaces at Concordia University. Through this ethnography, we follow urban farmers to explore how embodied experiences of the spatialities and circuits of food give meaning to urban agricultural practices as an aesthetic mode of political action. Although the market gardeners we meet are critical of the industrial, corporate-led global food system and are aiming to spatialize alternative foodways and agrarian resources, their logic of action is based not so much on antagonism and contention as on impulsion and aesthetics in a field of interactions with numerous non-human actors. We further analyse how seduction and attraction are twin modalities of power at play in the urban market garden by focusing on the charismatic appeal of non-human earthly beings and the political ecologies that are sustained or disrupted through aesthetic relations.

In Chapter 5, we encounter 'voluntary risk-takers' and edgeworkers. We begin with the story of Hubert, a skateboarder. We also meet dumpster divers, Greenpeace building climbers, explorers of abandoned industrial buildings, practitioners of extreme sports, and graffiti writers. Here, we move through the world of mostly White, university-educated, middle-class youths who choose alternative lifestyles involving variable levels of legal, physical, and social risk. The chapter argues that fear can have a politically empowering effect. It illustrates how fear circulates among these youths, how it is spatialized, how it participates in transforming both youths and the spaces in which they practice, and how this results in distributed forms of political agency. In this chapter, we work with the concepts of choreographic power and urban diviners in order to reflect on provocative subjectivity and the importance of political gestures visible beyond words.

In the Conclusion, we offer an epistemological reflection about ethnography and aesthetics. Responding to structural and dichotomous approaches to politics, we discuss how a situational and performative approach can contribute to better understand how politics unfolds in the contemporary period. This entails adjusting our understandings of agency and power. We insist that class and racial markers are important elements affecting aesthetic political relations. Indeed, looking back at our four ethnographies, we discuss how aesthetic political relations are differentiated in terms of forms and political effects. But, in all four ethnographies, youthfulness is a springboard for political action.

Notes

1. Most names have been changed, unless the person in question gave us permission to use their real one. Citations in their original language will be presented as footnotes: 'Montréal, qu'est-ce qui fait sa beauté, c'est justement sa diversité, mais aussi la place à l'alternatif qui existe, que ce soit d'un point de vue écologique, que ce soit du point de vue de l'art, que ce soit … politique…'
2. MapCollab is a collaborative multimedia research project exploring how youth speak and live their neighbourhood, in Saint-Michel and Little Burgundy (Montreal). It will be extensively discussed in Chapter 2.
3. 'C'est une ville aussi où on constate et on voit assez facilement même juste en étant là … Tsé il y a des gros contrastes de réalités humaines qui cohabitent dans cette ville-là. Pis ça je pense que ça crée des tensions donc qui sont palpables, qui favorisent l'implication des gens quand ils en ont l'occasion peut-être.'
4. Part of this section was published in Boudreau (2018).
5. Magnusson (2010, p. 45) writes: 'the messy urban order of the occidental city did not simply disappear. In fact, it was extended and replicated in the context of Western colonialism and imperialism. In that context, it connected with other forms of urbanism.' Researching and presenting the extent to which such processes took place in the context of Ville-Marie, the colonial city that later became known as Montreal, is a project that exceeds the scope of our present research and, more specifically, the contextualization of Montreal in the next chapter, but it is of timely relevance. On this topic, see Boileau (1991), but also Dorries et al. (2019), referring to different settler-colonial Canadian urban contexts.
6. 'L'important, c'est que c'est à ce niveau-là, celui du découpage sensible du commun de la communauté, des formes de sa visibilité et de son aménagement, que se pose la question du rapport esthétique/politique' (Rancière 2000, pp. 24–25).
7. Inspired by Arendt, Dikeç (2015, p. 46) would put it in the following terms: 'Political action inaugurates space – a space of encounter that at once relates and separates individuals, where the self in her distinctiveness is disclosed in relation to others present.'
8. As the global political economic context drastically changed in the following decades, both Castells and Harvey nuanced these arguments and offered important reflections on the urbanity of social movements. While Castells (1999a–c) turned more towards the networked organizational form of social and political claims, Harvey (1989, 2008)

revisited Lefebvre's early claims to the right to the city and high-lighted the shifts in the political economic context that had enabled the rise of urban movements around the globe.

9. More recently, in the same vein, scholars have used the term 'urban tribes' to designate youth groups (Bennett 1999) or insisted on class, race, and gender intersectional power dynamics (Wilkins 2008).

10. As opposed to Bourdieu's (1979) concept of a social field, which supposes people act the way they do because they are structurally predisposed to act in specific ways.

11. Most youth we encountered in the following ethnographies are aged between 18 and 35 years old, the millennium generation. But our analysis is not restricted to these essentialized cohort markers.

12. 'Alors que le reste de la société se résigne et la regarde de haut comme si cela ne les touchait pas, elle veut un monde meilleur pour tout le monde ... On se demande pourquoi elle ne vote pas. On se demande pourquoi elle a le goût de tout casser ... En quelque part, elle a une bannière où il est écrit : «Fuck toute!» On ne comprend pas. On la trouve donc conne cette génération d'enfants-rois. Fuck-toute.'

Chapter 1

Montreal and the Urban Moment

As a city located on an island at the confluence of the St Lawrence and Ottawa rivers, Montreal can become very hot and humid come summer. Parks fill up with people, many of them young adults, eager to escape the heat of apartments, meet up with friends, sit on the grass, chill out in the shade, play sports, have drinks, and follow the unfolding of the day wherever the fortuity of interactions may lead: a bike ride to a neighbourhood barbecue get-together, a microbrewery patio, a café, a basketball court, a back alley, an open-air music scene, or train tracks and open fields. With their song 'Un été à Montréal', the hip-hop group Dubmatique captured the electricity of a warm, humid day filled with such urban flânerie. There is sensuality, playfulness, a sense of networked open-ended space to the flow, lyrics, and beats of this song. Let us follow these artists' invitation to spend a Sunday in the Park Jeanne-Mance with them. This park is located on the foothills of the Mount Royal, the iconic mountain at the centre of the city. It is there that, since the 1990s, Montrealers have spontaneously met up for the Tamtams, an open-air gathering where they come to jam with tamtams and various other kinds of musical instruments, dance, and relax. OTMC (Ousmane Traoré), a Senegalese-born Montrealer who lived in Paris before co-founding Dubmatique with his friends, raps over the beats: '*I invite you to spend a Sunday in Parc Jeanne-Mance / Wandering around in this ambiance where people mix / And the Possee sits on the grass, "chilling" tranquil / The atmosphere is festive, dressed in my most beautiful musical phrasing / Let me introduce myself within the magmatic mass / With a trick of "pass me the mic" / Smash the ice and make the different classes melt.*'[1]

We use this example to highlight a kind of public sociability that builds on and constitutes the aesthetic political relations that shape urban politics and consciousness in Montreal. As Laurent Vernet (2017, p. 44; our translation) has argued in a study of the Tamtams and Piknic Électronik, two

Youth Urban Worlds: Aesthetic Political Action in Montreal, First Edition.
Julie-Anne Boudreau and Joëlle Rondeau.
© 2021 John Wiley & Sons Ltd. Published 2021 by John Wiley & Sons Ltd.

open-air gatherings taking place every week as soon as the air warms up, 'to join the tamtams or the Piknic Electronik is not … synonymous with connecting with the strangers who make up the crowd. It is probably a "taste for others" [*goût des autres*], a mutual appreciation of the presence of others in very special circumstances.'[2] In Parc Jeanne-Mance and on the foothills of Parc du Mont-Royal, people of diverse cultural backgrounds and social classes mix and mingle (*les gens se mélangent*), creating an aesthetic appearance where interactions are self-regulatory, negotiated intuitively but also in relation to municipal authorities, with whom a pact regarding the shared use of public spaces was reached in 1994 – a pact which still holds today, without the need for institutional enforcement. The lyrics to 'Un été à Montréal' nonetheless underline the visibility of class-based differences and make it clear that possibilities for taking part in such spontaneous gatherings are not equally distributed. OTMC seems to suggest that the seductive spell of this aesthetic appearance simultaneously creates the possibility for taking the mic (or rather, being handed the mic) and making utterance through the noise of the city, motivated by the desire to make such class-based differences melt. This desire and the youthful platform from which it emerges and is sustained resonate with the urban political consciousness and subjectivity that became increasingly audible and visible through the affirmation of urban movements in 1960s and 1970s Montreal. The playful aesthetic relations that unfold via public sociability sustained by this sensual 'taste for others' (*goût des autres*, in Laurent Vernet's words) sharpen trust in the knowledge that come from such sensorial engagement, and inform political consciousness and aesthetic modes of political action.

We start this chapter with reference to the iconic mountain and two rivers that are distinctive geographical features of this city because they are not only significant to the contemporary urbanization of consciousness and formation of urban political subjectivities, as we have just briefly discussed, but are also inextricably linked to the imperial, settler-colonial networks and the urbanization of capital that have given shape to the urban space we move through today. As Victoria Dickenson (2011, p. 38) has written, 'these two geographical features – mountain and river – have shaped settlement patterns and land use by both Aboriginal and European inhabitants', thereby contributing to defining 'human experience in this place'. The meeting of the St Laurence and Ottawa rivers has long provided access to sacred meeting grounds and gathering, trapping, and hunting territories for multiple and diverse Indigenous nations around the area, including the Anishinaabeg Omàmìwinini (Algonquin), Kanien'kehà:ka (Mohawk), Atikamekw, and Wendat (Huron). Still resonating today, 'Hochelaga', 'Moneyang' (Thumbadoo 2017, p. 124), and 'Tiohtià:ke' are Indigenous toponyms given to the Island of

Montreal, which is known as a 'millennial political, diplomatic, economic and cultural hub' (Ville de Montréal 2017). A gathering and trading place, it was a metropolis long before the first French settlements that led to the establishment of Ville-Marie (Fennario 2017). The Ottawa and St Lawrence rivers provided access to the Great Lakes and western areas of the continent, and later strategically connected Montreal to trade networks with Europe and other places along slave trade routes from the West African continent to the West Indies (Castonguay and Dagenais 2011; Nelson 2016). Over time, it became strategically positioned as 'Canada's leading city', from the mid-eighteenth century to the 1970s.

In a convincing analysis of the corporeal representations of Montreal by middle and merchant classes in the city's period of rapid industrialization, Nicolas Kenny (2011) demonstrates that the urbanization of imperial and settler-colonial capital producing the industrial and modern city was also a deeply embodied experience. More specifically, he argues that '[t]he work done on nature to create the modern city had given rise to novel corporeal experiences that reshaped perceptions of the body itself. And as the environment was transformed to meet the imperatives of modern industrialization, so was the body – through which that environment was lived – re-imagined, seen as a fragile organism whose welfare depended on a degree of closeness to the natural world that spawned it' (Kenny 2011, p. 66). His analysis is insightful for its account of the ways in which the body mediated the industrial city through processes which in turn transformed perceptual fields and representations associated with the experience of a modern, industrial urbanity. In our exploration of the contemporary experience of urbanity from this place shaped by two major riverways and an iconic mountain, we also argue that to think, feel, move, and do research through urban worlds is inextricable from the condition of being affected by this environment.

We should pause here to note that while 'Montreal' has come to qualify a city, an island, an urban agglomeration, and broader metropolitan region surrounding the archipelago of the island, we contend, following Castonguay and Dagenais (2011, p. 2), that it is important to keep 'this plurality of spatial frames' in mind as we explore the urban youth worlds discussed in the ethnographies that follow this chapter. These diverse and not mutually exclusive spatial frames reflect and inform various realities, mobility practices, environments, and spatial imaginaries that are unbound to contained scales, whether those are institutionally defined or shaped by geographical features of the land.

In order to better locate the milieu in which political action unfolds in these ethnographies, we need to provide a larger context to the elements that feed into the urban experience, reciprocally affecting politics and urban youth worlds. Thus, in this chapter on Montreal and the urban moment, we strive to first provide a larger and more detailed rendering of Montreal's urban feel.

We then contextualize the significance of this case study to an examination of the transformation of the political process in a world of cities. Montreal, as we will see, is a useful site for understanding how we act politically in such a world. This, we argue, is partly due to its youthful population and the ways in which youthfulness has historically shaped urban culture by being used as a location from which to experiment sociopolitical change, particularly with the affirmation of urban movements connecting Montreal to networks of youthful countercultural ideologies, contestations, and protests in the urban political moment of the 1960s and 1970s. The history of sociopolitical urban movements help us understand how aesthetic appearances shape and transform subjectivities, as well as the narratives that come to give meaning to political actions.

Thus, in the final section of this chapter, by drawing from scholars who have written on sociopolitical actions and literary expressions of 1960s and 1970s Montreal, we will explore how this urban political moment reveals changing relations to time, space, and alternative rationalities that contribute to the affirmation of ways of acting through aesthetics, and of urbanity and youthfulness to experiment sociopolitical change. It is important to look at this historically situated (yet globally connected) political moment because Montreal's place in the global urban cultures of the 1960s and 1970s has had deep and lasting influences on the shapes and narratives of the Montreal urban youth worlds that we will enter in subsequent chapters. This political moment, and the nationalist, sovereignist, state-centred project that it generated in the decades that followed (in spite of the urbanity characterizing it), also sheds light on politics in excess of the conceptual and administrative apparatus of the nation-state or the municipal government. But, to be able to sense and conceptualize these political processes, we must first adjust our perceptual and ontological filters at the level of the street. Let us explore a selection of key elements that feed into the urban experience here. What's the sense and feel of things shaping Montreal's politics?

Montreal's Politico-Sensuous Feel

As banal as it may seem, Montreal's politics is shaped by its long winters, but also by its tensed and spatialized linguistic and racialized differences, by its history of nationalism framed as a Third World decolonizing struggle, by its youthfulness, and by its persistently visible punk culture. What do these elements have in common? The body and its senses.

When, almost half the year, people walk on snow, political action on the streets takes a different feel. When at last the snow starts to melt and the sun begins to warm bodies, social relations become effervescent. Consider Victor's account of the beginnings of the student strike at Concordia University in February 2012: '*It was really warm over the course of that week, so like, really warm, it was really weird in February or something. And, then at the University level people shut down de Maisonneuve [Boulevard] … It was very much a scene and people like couldn't just wear one red square, but had to cover their entire body in red … How much were you able to exude your implication aesthetically. And it just turned into kind of a party on the street, which was fine, I wasn't against that, but it just kind of made me uncomfortable cause I have a hard time mixing these things, like … eh, it just seems like a very privileged way to protest. Let's have a party in the streets!* (Victor, student who participated in the 2012 strikes). In this description, Victor, who spent part of his childhood in the United States, highlights Montreal's 'privilege' in being able to demonstrate with fun and through aesthetics, unlike in other cities where demonstration inevitably leads to police violence. He also alludes to the importance of the exceptionally warm weather during that week in February 2012. He further emphasizes the embodiment of people's commitment to the cause: '*cover[ing] their entire body in red*'. 'Fun', 'warmth', 'aesthetics', and 'embodiment' are terms we will recurrently use in the following pages. As we will see, demonstrating with fun and through aesthetics is rather deeply rooted in Montreal youth political worlds. Writing about 1970s politics and the rise of the Montreal Citizen's Movements, Timothy Lloyd Thomas (1997, p. 150) points out that '[d]espite the often bitter politics of language and secession, on the street Montrealers do better than survive, they party and they flourish'. Despite his seemingly overly enthusiastic tone, Thomas' interpretation and understanding of the specificity of how political action unfolds in this place resonate with Victor's words.

Importantly, as we have already alluded to, political action in Montreal is coloured by its youthful population. As the largest city of the province, it welcomes many postsecondary students from other regions and countries. In 2010, it hosted 57% of Quebec's students: 264 805 individuals total. Not all young Montrealers are students, of course. While the province of Quebec counted 19% of its population at between 15 and 29 years old in 2011, Montreal counted 20.7% in this age group. There are thus more young people in Montreal as compared to other cities in Quebec. And, as we discussed in the Introduction, beyond these statistics, Montreal is a youthful city because of its lifestyle. Youthfulness, for us, is not determined by biological criteria. It is a state of mind and a way of acting. Montreal's punk scene, for instance, is vibrant. A punk scene is not a prerequisite for youthful political action, but when visible, it is generally associated with youthfulness. Punk (along with hip-hop, perhaps) is the quintessential urban culture. Its closeness with anarchism makes it a particularly important aesthetic trend in activist milieus around the world (Marcus 1989). The fact that many Montreal youngsters adopt punk lifestyles or simply punk looks colours the city's streets with a rebellious feel.

This echoes an observation made by Thomas (1997, p. 150) in reference to the context of 1970s Montreal, where 'social ecologists and anarchists … were far more numerous and influential than in any other Canadian city'. Significantly, the first punk bar in Montreal was opened in 1977 by youngsters who felt excluded from the francophone Québécois nationalist scene and its music (Lamarque 2016). Rather than Québécois hippie culture, industrial London became the cultural reference for these young Montrealers. In the 1980s, with the opening of the bar Foufounes Électriques, a second wave of punk music production emerged, in both English and French. The scene is still very lively today.[3] Lamarque's ethnography emphasizes that because of its bilingualism, the Montreal punk scene is distinct from the New York and London scenes. On the other hand, with its do-it-yourself (DIY) philosophy, punk culture shares affinities with many contemporary youthful political movements (Holloway 2002; see Figure 1.1). One of Lamarque's informants

FIGURE 1.1 Punk culture. In a demonstration against police brutality, a woman carries artwork saying, 'Service porcin violent de Montréal' ('Violent Pig Service of Montreal') – a play on the acronym of the Montreal Police Service (SPVM). *Source:* photo by Marilena Liguori.

notes, '*Today, while this [punk] spirit still exists, during the student strikes for instance, we see that there is resistance, not quite cultural, but an articulated resistance, a vision for another kind of society*'[4] (F. Anderson, 26 March 2015, cited in Lamarque 2016, p. 86).

The development of the Montreal punk scene, somewhere in between Québécois francophone hippie culture and the influences of industrial London, is also evocative of the 'sensations of living among competing codes' (Simon 2006). Montreal politics and culture are influenced by the intermingling of linguistic communities and the spatialization of linguistic differences which have historically been used as markers of racial hierarchies – something that we will elaborate on in the next section.

Historically, the St Laurent Boulevard has played the mythical role of dividing French and English zones. 'The Main' or '*la Main*', as anglophones and francophones would respectively call it, is also characteristically known for the ways in which segments of its built environment along a south–north axis have come to mark the successive waves of newer immigrant communities and their patterns of settlement (see Figure 1.2). Sherry Simon (2006, p. xi)

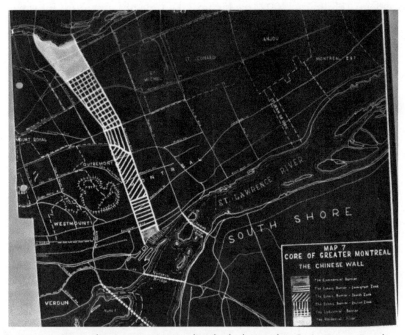

FIGURE 1.2 Map depicting zones divided along the St Laurent Boulevard. *Source:* retrieved from the archives of the Institut national de la recherche scientifique – Centre Urbanisation Culture Société in Montreal. Date and author unknown.

has written about the 'sensibility of the divided city', where linguistic and cultural communities are 'physically close but culturally distant.' In her study of translation practices in Montreal, she attends to the aesthetic difference that living in a city where 'two languages mingle relentlessly' makes. 'Translation is put to the test', she writes, 'it becomes a *condition* – the condition of living in a city with a double history, located somewhere between Paris and New York, and between Iqaluit and Miami' (Simon 2006, p. xi; emphasis in original). Furthermore, she argues that '[w]hat makes Montreal different from other global cities is that immigrant [or Indigenous] languages enter the city's conversations as a 3rd partner, in an always-triangular configuration … Montreal's double language ground, formed of languages unequal in history and authority, is not always an easy space for newcomers to manoeuvre in'.

While the St Laurent Boulevard has historically been the middle ground for the 'divided city', youth urban culture and politics are today characterized by bilingualism and cultural diversity. Here, 'multilingualism, mixed languages, and code-switching are preferred modes of communication, forms of translation specific to its polyglot sensibility' (Simon 2006, p. 10). Research on hip-hop language practices provide interesting windows to see this polyglot sensibility at work. For instance, a research project analysing Quebec rap lyrics used nine distinct linguistic categories for analysis, 'including three varieties of French, three of English, Haitian, and Jamaican creoles, and Spanish' (Sarkar and Allen 2007).

One could argue that living in 'one of the oldest North American urban settings' (Castonguay and Dagenais 2011, p. 2) gives a certain weight to power hierarchies materially inscribed in time and space. Indeed, the urban experience in Montreal is also shaped, in part, by layers of colonization, industrialization, deindustrialization, and brownfield (re)developments, all stratified in the built and unbuilt environment. These layers create stark aesthetic contrasts when one travels through the streets: from the colonial and imperial depot buildings of the old port to the glass, steel, and old grey-stone commercial buildings and skyscrapers of the downtown area; from the upper-class houses and high-rise apartments of the west, to the working-class elongated duplexes and triplexes of the east, to the postwar former suburbs of the north. The weight of the colonial and capitalist historical processes that have produced and are producing this urban space are easily perceived, as they are inscribed in the landscape.

To this day, infrastructure built for the efficient transportation of goods and resources constrains the movement of people across the city: overpasses, highways, railroads, the port, and the St Lawrence Seaway all crisscross space, blocking pathways and forcing people to take detours. From the experience of moving through (above, under, and alongside) this infrastructure, one can sense the supremacy of economic interests and the decision to ensure the efficiency of economic flows over and above concerns for the quality of life of individuals and communities – freight has priority. The ordered displacement of racialized communities to make way for the construction of this infrastructure has deeply shaped the urban space and influenced the political process and formation of political subjectivities in Montreal – not only in the urban political moment of the 1960s and 1970s, where citizen groups formed to protest against the construction of metropolitan highways and private housing developments that destroyed entire neighbourhoods (Hamel 1991; Douay 2012; Economides and MacWirther 2017), but also in the nineteenth-century Kanien'kehà:ka (Mohawk) opposition to railroads passing through the community of Kahnawake (Alfred 1995). We can also see it echoed in Kabisha's words opening the Introduction.

While the temporality of cycles and boom and burst displaces peoples, neighbourhood cultures, and hangout joints (Boileau 1991; Douay 2012; Harel 2014), it also opens fields of possibilities for the rearrangement and creative prefigurations of sociopolitical and sociospatial relations (Lévesque 1999; Sarrasin et al. 2012). The *Champs des possibles*, located in the Mile-End neighbourhood, is a good example. Now an urban park co-managed by the municipal administration and citizens, this area located in between old manufactures and train tracks had been reclaimed by citizen groups through their use of it for a wide range of activities, including urban agriculture and non-institutionalized forms of environmental education (Douay 2012).

This case is also telling of a libertarian culture that shapes Montreal politics and urban youth worlds. Writing in 1997, Thomas argued that 'Montreal's civic culture lends itself to libertarian, even anarchistic, solutions to its current political and economic malaise. Montrealers have learned that if any good is to come to their city they must find their own solutions' (Thomas 1997, p. 150). This attitude is still vibrant today. The active presence of many groups operating on the basis of *autogestion* (self-management) principles attests to it (see Douay 2012; but also Lambert-Pilotte, Drapeau, and Kruzynsky 2007; Sarrasin et al. 2012). They constitute and make visible alternative templates for the organization of professional relations and everyday life, beyond their mediation by the state and municipal bureaucracies.

Montreal's politics and culture are also shaped by the city's tensed racialized spatializations. These are deeply rooted in the political geography and history of settler-colonization. Charmaine Nelson (2016), for instance, notes that the walls enclosing the settlement have historically served to keep the racialized and feared Others out (most notably, Indigenous populations), while keeping the domesticated, contained Others in – those who contributed to the city's economic development through slave labour (Black and Indigenous slaves, mostly). Even if the walls have now been put down, racialized neighbourhoods are still markers of segments of youth populations targeted as being 'at risk' of illicit or illegal activities (Manaï and Touré Kapo 2017) and concentrate immigrant communities facing disproportionately higher rates of unemployment or underemployment – a symptom of systemic racial discrimination.

If fights for language rights moved Montrealers out on the streets in the 1960s and 1970s, for the contemporary generations of young Montrealers, tensions are more visible when it comes to racialization and the complex imbrications of intersectionality. 'Under sexual nationalism's current influence across the West,' writes Bilge (2012, p. 309), 'Quebec's linguistic worries seem to be out-staged (if only temporarily) by gender-justice-oriented ones.' By 'sexual nationalism', Bilge means 'the incorporation of gender-and-sexual normativities into the governmentality of migrant/Muslim integration and the politics of the nation' (Bilge 2012, p. 304). In her analysis of the 'reasonable accommodation crisis' in 2006–07,[5] she brilliantly shows how Quebec's mainstream feminism has become a core civilizational value protecting against 'barbaric' religion, most notably Islam. 'These "other men,"' she pursues, 'not only stand for their alien (and barbaric) religion, but also act as ghostly apparitions capable of drawing Quebec back into horrendous times of pre-modernity, the *Grande Noirceur* (Great Darkness)' (Bilge 2012, p. 310). Bilge reminds us here of the non-urban Quebec of the 1930s to 1950s, home to despotism, anti-urbanism, and domination by the Catholic Church.

The Quiet Revolution (*la Révolution tranquille*), a period of rapid cultural mutations, socioeconomic transformations, and political changes that took place in the Province of Quebec in the 1960s and 1970s, threw away such anti-urbanism and favoured the rise of feminism. The Quiet Revolution's fundamentally *urban* history shapes Montreal's political culture today. It digs racialized, gendered, and generational divisions among feminists and in everyday spaces. It further makes some forms of political action more hearable and visible than others.

In 2016, when an advertising campaign announcing the celebration of Montreal's 375th anniversary included only members of the White, francophone artistic community and star system, it spurred wide protests and denunciations by Montrealers excluded once again from such representations, as well as those shocked by the lack of acknowledgement of the city's diversity (CBC 2017a).

'Race' is a difficult term to utter in Montreal, as elsewhere – but perhaps more so than in Chicago or Los Angeles, for instance. Up until some very recent and highly publicized controversies,[6] it was conspicuously absent from the public debate – although not entirely, as the formation of the Student of Colour Montreal collective demonstrates (Hampton 2012). The city's engagement in organizing a public consultation on systemic racism, called for by citizens through their 'Right of Initiative',[7] also attests to the vibrancy of popular mobilizations and organizations committed to shedding light on the insidious logics of racism (Barbeau 2017). With an ethnography of aesthetical political action sensitive to bodies and nonverbal communication, 'race' is something we need to say out loud.

In the context of the following ethnographies, which cover the first half of the 2010s, we note that while feminism was loudly debated and affirmed within the student movement (Surprenant and Bigaouette 2013), to take one example, racism was mostly absent from the debates that we were aware of. In our interviews with students, however, some mentioned having been shocked by the staging of a giant papier-mâché puppet representing then Quebec Prime Minister Jean Charest (identified by a tag under its head that read 'Sir John James Charest'), carried by students wearing business suits, their faces painted in black.

What were these students trying to say? We did not speak to all of those who took part in this particular demonstration, so we can only extrapolate. As one informant told us, this staging took place in the aftermath of the infamous P-6 ruling (adopted 18 May 2012), which prohibited students from wearing masks in demonstrations (see Chapter 2). Painting one's face in a dark colour was an act of defiance and a political statement regarding tools of surveillance and policing using facial recognition (on a similar use of masks in other contexts of political protest, see Rosi Braidotti's (2015) remarkable analysis of 'the Pussy Riot project' and feminist politics). An informant told us that any dark colouring could have been chosen. The political effects of choosing black, while eluding this person at the time, were shocking to others. They may have been perceived and interpreted through the prism of the cultural artefacts of the Quiet Revolution.

In 1969, Pierre Vallières published *Nègres blancs d'Amériques: Autobiographie précoce d'un terroriste québécois*,[8] describing the plight of French-Canadians within Canada. The Quiet Revolution was also a nationalist revolution, through which the urban Left positioned Quebec as a Third World country to be decolonized from British and American domination. In 2012, this performance referred to Charest as 'British', hence the puppet's highly visible nametag. The intent may have been to refer to him as a dominating colonizer. Beneath him, the students could easily be seen as playing the role of 'White niggers', slaving to transport His Highness. It seems that the students wanted to show how they could resist such domination by referring to *James* Cross, the British diplomat who was killed by the Front de Libération du Quebec (FLQ) in October 1970. Racism, domination, and colonization are complex forces of biopolitics (Foucault 1978). They involve disciplining the body, sensual restraint, performative narratives, 'floating signifiers' (Hall 2012), and the aestheticization of difference. The pervasive persistence of racism, the manipulation of affects related to fear of the Other, and the attraction and appropriation of markers of racial difference all influence Montreal's politics and the intersectionality of oppression.

Montreal's Place in the Global Urban Cultures of the 1960s and 1970s

As we can see, it is important to attend to the deep and lasting influences of Montreal's place in the global urban cultures of the 1960s and 1970s on the shapes and narratives of Montreal urban youth worlds throughout contemporary history.

In recent years, a significant body of literature has emerged on the urban and countercultural movements in Montreal in the 1960s and 1970s (Hamel 1991; Thomas 1997; Warren 2008, 2012; Mills 2011; Austin 2013; Ross 2016; Tayler 2018). Along with this scholarship, Literature scholars have examined the forms of literary expression that emerged over the same period (Coleman 2018). Their studies shed light not only on the spatial imagination of novelists, poets, and their contemporaries, but also on national and urban narratives prevalent at the time, and the ways in which they affected the transformation of political subjectivities. Such scholarship provides relevant insights allowing us to better understand why and how young Montrealers have mobilized to act politically, and how these mobilizations have influenced urban politics and urban youth cultures.

Reading these works through one another, we contend that the affirmation of urban movements connecting Montreal to networks of youthful countercultural ideologies, contestations, and protests in the political moment of the 1960s and 1970s brings to the fore the salience of an urban logic of political action alongside a modern state-centred logic of political action. This, we argue, is partly due to Montreal's youthful population and the ways in which youthfulness has historically shaped urban culture by being used as a location from which to experiment sociopolitical change and create aesthetic appearances, particularly in the urban political moment of the 1960s and 1970s.

Some context: this period was one of imposing state interventions in the establishment of a welfare nation-state that was considered the main tool for the creation of social and economic possibilities for French-Canadians living in the Province of Quebec (who would progressively come to understand themselves as Québécois and Québécoises). The election of the Liberal government of Jean Lesage in 1960 and its successive four-year rule of power marked an acceleration of the pace of state reforms and sociopolitical and socioeconomic transformations, as this government engaged on an agenda of political modernization to 'catch up' economically and socially with 'North American modernity'.

The discourse of modernization was also informing development projects led by the administration of the City of Montreal under the leadership of Jean Drapeau.[9] This was a municipal administration characterized by an authoritarian style of governance seeking to maintain a firm, centralizing grip on power along with a closed-door political culture (Ross 2016, p. 130). Even though Montreal was losing its status as economical capital of Canada to Toronto, large-scale redevelopment projects, led by public and private interests, were conceived as vast operations of urban renovation aimed at building a modern, world-class metropolis, and adapting its infrastructure accordingly (Hamel 1991, p. 121). It is in this context that the first skyscrapers, eleven new bridges, the subway system, the 'Expo 67'[10] pavilions on the Île Sainte-Hélène (see the cover of this book), and the metropolitan highway system were set in place to adapt the urban environment to the demands of mass consumption. 'City planners anticipated a city of seven million by 2000, and built (and demolished) accordingly', underscores Sherry Simon (2006, p. 34). Pierre Hamel (1991, p. 122; our translation) further notes that 'the imperatives of profitability and economic efficiency guided this new modernization of urban space, undeniably giving priority to the one-dimensional logic of capital'.

The language of modernization illustrates well how, during this period dominated by the formation of strong national and municipal states, time was understood in a linear manner, with a clear direction: progress. At the provincial level, the strategic goal was to close the gap between francophones (who had limited opportunities for professional advancement) and anglophones, by developing means to seize control over economic and cultural productions dominated by English-Canadian and American interests.

In the course of only six years, from 1960 to 1966, six new ministries were created, eight state-owned companies were established, and close to 13 000 employees were hired in the provincial public sector (Mills 2011, p. 41). Urban ways of life, rather than rural ones, provided renewed energies and templates for the formation of a modern nation-state. As mentioned earlier, this marked a profound contrast to the anti-statist and anti-urban stance of the Duplessis governments.[11]

What spurred such contrasted political transformations with the turning of governmental administration and governing political party? Keeping the analytical gaze on state-oriented political action, seen and understood through the perceptual fields of party politics, is to tell only part of the story. Distinctive of this period in Quebec (as elsewhere across the Americas and Europe) is a demographic and spatial increase in populations living in urban areas (Pelletier 1992, p. 5). In the period that we today call the *Trente glorieuses* (from the end of the 1940s to the end of the 1970s), Montreal's metropolitan region expanded as a result of increased migrations from the countryside and growing numbers of immigrants diversifying the cultural composition of the population; by the beginning of the 1970s, 45.5% of the Quebec population lived in Montreal's metropolitan region (Pelletier 1992, p. 5). Among them were Caribbean immigrants, bringing new perspectives 'to a long-standing Black Canadian community that during that period amounted to somewhere between 10 000 and 15 000' (Austin 2013, p. 31).

The presence of the Black community is most notable in La Petite Bourgogne ('Little Burgundy'). This neighbourhood, however, soon becomes targeted for sustained urban renovation (demolition) projects, along with other parts of the city where socioeconomically disadvantaged and racialized communities were living. In Little Burgundy alone, a population of 20 000 residents in 1966 dropped to just 8000 by 1976 (Douay 2012, p. 85). All in all, from 1965 to 1975, 140 000 Montrealers were forced to move from their homes due to urban renovation or demolition projects. Such projects spurred the creation of citizens' committees exasperated by the narrow and municipally controlled opportunities for participation offered in planning schemes; matters had to be taken into their own hands. The emergence of these committees marks the rise of urban movements in Montreal (Hamel 1991).

We must also note that between 1968 and 1969, *for the first time*, the majority of the Quebec population under the age of 20 was in school (Mills 2011, p. 171). And, of all university students in Quebec, 60% were studying in Montreal (Warren 2008). In colleges and universities, it was the social sciences and humanities departments that most attracted youth (Warren 2008, p. 241). Students read authors like Marx, who had previously been prohibited in francophone institutions governed by Catholic authorities. They studied key figures of the Frankfurt and Althusserian Schools, as well as French existentialists, but also Mao and Lenin, Fanon, Césaire, Berque, and Memmi. A diversity of theoretical frameworks, schools of thought, and worldviews gradually opened up novel analytical toolboxes for reading the world.

The intellectual and cultural life emerging with new energies in the universities, colleges, associations, cafes, and streets of Montreal led to the formation of politicized and socially involved students, 'an exceptional basin of activism,' as Warren (2008, p. 241) notes. Their role within citizens' committees grew towards the end of the 1960s, increasing the committees' volumes in urban struggles, broadening their reach, and leading them to formulate new ideological and political orientations (Hamel 1991, p. 108).

As many analysts have argued, the Quiet Revolution has a deeply urban history, one that *stems from Montreal's streets* and which continues to shape the

FIGURE 1.3 "For a not so quiet revolution": Recycling advertisement referring to the broad sweeping changes brought by the Quiet Revolution, June 2013. *Source:* photo by J.A. Boudreau.

city's political culture to this day (Figure 1.3). What might we learn from and about this urban political moment if we decentre the gaze of political analysis from state-based reforms and political actions?

In what follows, we present a portrait of the Quiet Revolution that reveals changing relations to time, space, and alternative rationalities affecting the formation of political subjectivities and forms of action.

Changing Relations to Time

In the musical environment of the 1960s, increased speed was noticeable not only in the tempo of the music, but also in the circulation of sound, images, and ideas across space. New media made massive entrances in homes, universities, and store windows. The same is true of television sets, but also of print technologies, which become more accessible and – significantly so – operated by youths.

On the pages of countercultural and underground print media produced by youngsters in Montreal and destined for counterpublics located across Quebec and around the world, collages became prominent. The juxtaposition of images and texts, of both original and massively reproduced content, was evocative of new patterns of rhythmic structures, creative (re)appropriations, and simultaneous temporalities.

In recent years, research has examined the role and influence of Montreal-based countercultural and alternative print magazines on the circulation of ideas and identities that came to give sense to globally connected urban youth worlds in Quebec[12] and elsewhere. In her study of *Mainmise*, Felicity Tayler (2018, p. 2) claims that it 'activated transpositions of identity-based political positions between English and francophone transnational countercultural movements'. She makes the compelling argument that it 'enabled to imagine Quebec as a space within alternative/utopian planetary geographies' (Tayler 2018, p. 2). Her analysis points towards the distinctive aestheticization of difference that could be found in *Mainmise*'s pages: 'within this imaginary state, ethnicity was uncoupled from national identity, just as minoritarian identity categories imposed through the liberal discourse of representational politics were destabilized' (Tayler 2018, pp. 2–3). *Mainmise*'s editors' vision of the future is telling of an urban consciousness sensing the limits of a world of nation-states (Figure 1.4). Tayler (2018, p. 17) writes that

FIGURE 1.4 Issues 7 and 10 of *Mainmise,* used bookstore on Ontario Street, June 2014. *Source:* photo by J.A. Boudreau.

they envisioned '[t]he political geography of the twentieth century [as being] replaced by a "global village" of media-enabled transnational affinity groups [and that] within this new arrangement, print media that emulated electronic effects could produce a counter-environment to the nation-state'.

The countercultural press connected urban youth worlds and provided resources which Montreal youths could draw upon to articulate their situated worldviews. Indeed, for $25, member publications of the Underground Press Syndicate had access to a vast bank of images, texts, and publications they could reproduce freely (Warren 2012). As was frequently the case for Montreal alternative publications, these could be translated and recontextualized through the process (Tayler 2018).

Daniel Ross (2016) similarly evokes the role of printed newsletters in connecting urban movements more specifically, and draws attention to cyclist organizations in this regard. In his study of Montreal's Citizens on Cycles (*Le Monde à Bicyclette*, MAB), a group founded in 1975, he underscores the significance of newsletter sections dedicated to international cycling news: 'These international influences reflected the fact that the MAB saw the vélorévolution [a resistance to car culture and consumer capitalism through bicycle practice grounded in a critique of urban everyday life] as something larger than their own local struggle, consistently linking their own actions to the work of cycling organizations around the world' (Ross 2016, p. 140).

Changing Relations to Space

A changing relation to space also marks the ways in which Left intellectuals and militants were inspired by the geopolitical changes that occurred across the world in the post-Second World War period. They saw great similarities between their living conditions, their sense of cultural and economic alienation, and their feelings of linguistic dispossession and those of Third World countries.

In 1961, the Royal Commission on Bilingualism and Biculturalism revealed that in the Montreal metropolitan area, 56% of workers with higher incomes were anglophones, although this linguistic group accounted for only 24% of the total workforce (Mills 2011, p. 34). There was a 35% gap between the average incomes of francophones and anglophones. This proportion was very similar to the difference between the average income of White and 'coloured' people in the United States (Warren 2008, p. 184). Another study conducted in 1965 revealed that one-third of the population lived in poverty and that about the same proportion lived in substandard housing (Mills 2011, p. 34). Furthermore, the rate of child mortality in francophone working-class neighbourhoods was much higher than in anglophone neighbourhoods on the West Island or in the rest of Canada (Mills 2011, p. 34). The built environment reflected these unequal living conditions, so much so that the municipal administration set up panels to hide the 'slums' of working-class neighbourhoods when world travellers came to visit Montreal for Expo 67.

But the city's uneven geographies remained visible. Separated by the St Laurent Boulevard were lower-income working-class neighbourhoods to the east and higher-income anglophone neighbourhoods to the west. Montreal's Black populations were living for the most part south of the train tracks that link the city along an east–west axis. 'This de facto segregation,' writes Austin (2013, p. 33), 'served as an invisible barrier to social mobility and to the city's more public places. Although these divisions were not absolute, they served to remind people of their place in society, particularly given that English-Canadians largely controlled business in Montreal and their office buildings dominated the downtown landscape.'

Italians and Indigenous peoples were facing living and working conditions worse than those of French-Canadians. Despite these conditions, 'in the minds of many, linguistic dispossession and class alienation amalgamated, giving an enormous intensity to the revolts of the 1960s and 1970s' (Mills 2011, p. 34). For many, these statistics shockingly revealed that institutional reforms to secure greater access to postsecondary education for francophones would never be enough and that structural, material, and countercultural transformations were necessary for the 'liberation' of the oppressed (Warren 2008, pp. 182–183).

As Mills (2011, p. 56) writes, 'given that cultural alienation and marginalisation are embedded in Montreal's urban landscape, one of the most important goals for the urban Left is to transform the city. They think that they will thus be able to transform the whole society. To attain this goal, they will attempt to build a mass movement of political resistance.' Indeed, Donald McGraw (cited in Hamel 1991, p. 109; our translation) observes the emergence of 'new types of citizen associations' from the beginning of 1968 onwards: 'They do not aim so much to claim services from institutions rather than implement groups that seek to solve by themselves problems felt collectively at the neighbourhood level.'

Hamel's history of urban movements demonstrates that citizens' committees did not merely concern themselves with the ideological reinterpretation of their living conditions, but did so by identifying, very concretely, 'new perspectives of action' both within and outside of municipal politics (Hamel 1991, p. 109; our translation). The numerous citizen groups that emerge over the late 1960s and all through the 1970s self-organized to provide community services where the state proved to be inefficient in doing so. Food depots, medical clinics, and tenants' associations were created (Hamel 1991, p. 109). They relied on autogestion or self-management principles and did not tend to target or act upon a limited set of issues of urban struggles (Hamel 1991, p. 103).

Reflecting back on his first encounters with these citizens' organizations and associations in the 1970s, the English-Canadian journalist Malcolm Reid, now known for his ethnographic and literary studies on the period of urban and national revolts that animated Montreal youth in the 1960s and 1970s, mentions that such organizations then appeared to him as 'the local prolongation of *Parti pris* ideas' (quoted in Boutin 2009; our translation). *Parti pris* influentially 'articulated a vision of Quebec's oppression as colonialism, arguing for "independence, socialism, secularism"', as Simon (2006, pp. 28–29) reminds us.

The ideological and interpretive frameworks of the Third World national liberation discourses and anti-imperialism and decolonization theories which travelled across globally connected urban youth worlds found significant echoes in Montreal. In the minds and bodies of many militants and intellectuals, everyday urban experiences became meaningful 'as part of a global scheme of oppression' that connected Montreal in the 'political economy of Empire', as Sean Mills (2011, p. 18) so convincingly argues in *The Empire Within: Postcolonial Thought and Political Activism in Sixties Montreal*. This argument is important to explore further as it reveals a networked conception of space that influences rationalities and modes of political action while transforming political subjectivities. Montreal intellectuals of all ethnic origins were significantly influenced by artists and scholars who had come from Third World countries themselves or who were familiar with the works of Fanon, Césaire, and Memmi. Their lived environments reflected relations of subordination, sociospatial exclusion, and dispossession.

Students from the West Indies brought anticolonial ideas to the Montreal Black community (Austin 2013). They invested already established associations with their thoughts and energies or created new organizations. One of these, the Caribbean Conference Committee on West Indian Affairs, had great influence in studying and producing analyses of structural racism and economic exploitation. It set the groundwork for the emergence of Black social consciousness and the Black Power movement in Montreal (Austin 2013). This movement significantly enriched liberation and anticolonial discourses from Black community members' points of view, revealing the contours and extent of racial oppression and experimenting with new forms of resistance and dissent.

In the aftermath of Martin Luther King's assassination, a march that started at Sir George Williams University (now Concordia University) with 600 people ended at Dominion Square with 2000. The outrage at racist power structures was apparent, vocalized and written out on banners. A few months later, in October 1968, key intellectuals, militants, and community organizers of the global Black Power movement met for the Congress of Black Writers at McGill University (among the speakers were Stokely Carmichael, Alvin Poussaint, Walter Rodney, James Forman, Rocky Jones, and C.L.R. James) – all of them men, even though women had been actively involved in the organization of the Congress, which is illustrative of some of the contradictions of the period (Austin 2013). These leaders had been invited by students and 'discussed problems of everyday life pertaining to discrimination in housing and employment, the lack of possibilities for marginalized people and the social and cultural alienation of Blacks in Canada' (Mills 2011, p. 118). The audience was packed for Stokely Carmichael's speech and the ambiance was electric, the crowd cheering and interrupting him. Many Black militants later affirmed that it was one of the most empowering events of their life, a moment of great emotional intensity and affirmative power, allowing them to understand themselves as political subjects making history (Mills 2011).

Third World national liberation discourses and anti-imperialism and decolonization theories gave meaning to differently perceived experiences of subordination and exclusion. This political climate led to a culture of dissent among urban movements which both questioned and influenced the shape and reach of public and urban policies. Throughout the Quiet Revolution, the urban Left positioned Quebec as a colony. At the beginning of the 1960s, this colonial condition was first conceived and understood in relation to the Conquest of 1759, with the rule and seizing of power of the British people over French-Canadians, who were, as the story goes, relegated to second-class citizenship. As Mills (2011, p. 44) notes, the fact that French-Canadians had themselves colonized Indigenous lands was a 'contradiction that had little weight in the minds of the first architects of Quebec's decolonization'.

Another interpretation of Quebec's colonial condition took shape in the mid-1960s through the prisms of American imperialism's reach over Quebec's natural resources, cultural products, and economy, understood in relation to sociopolitical movements taking place outside of Quebec which were fighting against imperialism and capitalism. Through these lenses, according to Mills (2011, p. 83), 'Quebecers fe[lt] that they [were] participating in a movement with global dimensions ... the ultimate goals and objectives of the movement [were] not merely for Quebecers to establish their cultural affirmation but to liberate Quebec in a quest for universal emancipation'. While such narrative speaks to the intellect, it forcefully plays out on precognitive registers to mobilize and appeal to the affects and sensations of dispossession, marginalization, otherness, and freedom. The seductive effect was felt by the anglophone journalist Malcolm Reid, who, at the time, was stimulated to translate for English-Canadians what appeared to him as 'the most exciting cultural-political movement imaginable at the time' (Simon 2006, p. 28). His book, titled *The Shouting Signpainters: A Literary and Political Account of Quebec Revolutionary Nationalism*[13] (1972) is a story about youth writing for *Parti pris* (Simon 2006, p. 28). 'For Reid, these poets and novelists occupy their moment in history to the full', writes Simon (2006, p. 29). A youthful aesthetic effervescence perceived in and through pregnant moments infuse Reid's writing.

Vallières's (1969) essay, written while he was in prison in Manhattan, had a profound impact in shaping political thoughts and transforming political subjectivities in militant, intellectual, and artistic circles. After its publication by *Parti pris*, many understood themselves as 'white niggers'. Vallières was himself influenced by the concept and movement of négritude, having read Fanon and Césaire. He was also highly stimulated by the thoughts of Malcolm X and Stokely Carmichael and by the Black Power movement in the United States. In 1966, he was arrested by US Immigration, along with his comrade Charles Gagnon, for their month-long hunger strike in front of the United Nations headquarters. They were striking for the recognition of political prisoner status for their imprisoned comrades and attempting to solidify the foundations of a multinational liberation front with revolutionary organizations in the United States.[14] According to Vallières, as Mills (2011, p. 102) mentions, 'just like Black Americans, Quebecers have been brought in America as "valets of the imperialists", "imported to serve as cheap labor", and excepted for their skin, "kept the same conditions"'. Their understanding of négritude consisted in a 'strategic anti-essentialism on the questions of race, by giving to the term "Black" a relational political meaning (not a racial meaning)' (Mills 2011). They used the term 'nigger' as a flexible metaphor that spoke to a borderless class and national consciousness (Mills 2011).

This is very explicit in Charles Gagnon's manifesto, *Feu sur l'Amérique. Propositions pour la révolution nord-américaine*, which connects 'the slums of Mexico, the ghettos of Watts and of Harlem, the hellholes of Saint-Henri and Mile-End' (Gagnon 1968, cited in Mills 2011, p. 102). For Gagnon, the oppressed must recognise themselves as a 'Third World within the empire' (Mills 2011, p. 102) and organise around national liberation movements that were supportive of one another (Carel 2006). The discursive resources of Third World liberation movements and decolonization theories gave Quebecers access to a universal idea of suffering and resistance distinct from that available through the Catholic Church. It played on affective, precognitive registers to provoke, outrage, and harness militant energies.

By employing and adapting the term 'nigger', however, Vallières and Gagnon appropriated for themselves – and the White working-class population of Quebec – Blacks' lived experiences, and thereby marginalized other oppressed groups. They silenced and ignored Indigenous resistance movements and negated structural racism affecting Black populations in Quebec. The contradictions of a movement that aimed at the liberation of all the masses yet relied on patriarchal structures and masculinist cultures led by White intellectuals from the petite-bourgeoisie (Hamel 1991, p. 101) were raised forcefully by feminist groups and Black and Indigenous organizations. Québécois intellectuals were more likely to forge alliances with national liberation movements outside of the province rather than seek alliances across oppressed, subaltern groups in Montreal and elsewhere in Quebec. This, according to Austin (2013), was due to the persistence of racism and the fear of becoming a 'Black nation' through interracial relationships.

The quest for national liberation that took shape in Quebec was inextricably interwoven with the goal of constructing a national, but also an urban identity. The most prominent intellectuals of the time amalgamated language (French) and subordinated social class in a way that blindfolded many to the intersectionality of discrimination and oppression. This is particularly visible in Michèle Lalonde's 'Speak White' poem, which had a profound resonance and agentic capacity to move crowds, harnessing energies. For Lalonde, French language is akin to Quebecers' black skin. This resonated at the time because, as critical race scholar Josée Maropoulos (cited in Tayler 2018, p. 13) has argued, 'some francophones were asked why they did not speak the "White people language", or were simply told to "Speak White"', thereby making language use a marker of racial hierarchy which 'reinforced English as the legitimate "voice" of whiteness in Canada'. The decolonization project was considered one way of overcoming the injustices that were felt in everyday life. Urban Left intellectuals adapted anti-imperialism and anti-colonialism discursive resources to their situations.

These interpretive lenses were not necessarily shared by all Montreal urban movements, even if Extreme Left partisans and sympathizers were to be found among many citizen groups and associations, and attempted to influence political actions in alignment with their assessments of political struggles (Hamel 1991, p. 105). This created sharp ideological debates and dissension on the finalities and appropriate strategies for collective action and nurtured deep, long-standing reflections on the forms, modes, and meanings of activism (Hamel 1991, p. 117).

Nevertheless, such narratives had deep influences on Montreal urban youth worlds during the Quiet Revolution. Aesthetic relations perceived in everyday life transformed political subjectivities and modes of political action. Liberation discourses and strategies evolved in paradoxical, contested, and deeply embodied relationships with the state and its apparatuses, perceived representations, and spatial configurations (Hamel 1991).

This is perhaps no more explicit than in the events of October 1970, when members of the Front de Liberation du Quebec (FLQ) kidnapped the provincial Deputy Premier Pierre Laporte and British diplomat James Cross, leading to the deployment of the Canadian Armed Forces on Montreal streets and the introduction of the War Measures Act. Under martial law, hundreds of Montreal citizens involved in community organizations were imprisoned and their offices, apartments, and gathering places were searched by the police.

Direct action was a mode of organization among many others sharing a repertoire of actions in the globally connected urban youthful movements of the 1960s and 1970s. In Montreal as elsewhere, these included marches and public protests, sit-ins, bed-ins, die-ins, and artistic interventions. These are modes of action that involve the body in urban public spaces, the reconfiguration of sensory dispositions, and the circulation of affect and artefacts through the creation of aesthetic appearances that produce political effects in the here and now.

Consider, for instance, David Ross's (2016, p. 143) account of the mass die-in organized on Ste-Catherine Street by members of Le Monde à Bicyclette (MAB) in 1976: 'At the largest demonstrations, dozens of cyclists covered in ketchup and bandages halted traffic by sprawling across an intersection beside their bikes … Onlookers were encouraged to lie down and participate in five minutes of silence, and some did.' According to one of MAB's key leaders, 'the main goal of these dramas was to show observers an alternative to the current reality; for a few minutes, cars would stop, silence would reign, and cyclists and pedestrians owned the road' (Ross 2016, p. 144). Through such aesthetic appearance that disrupts perceptual fields and sensations by imposing silence and stopping traffic, youth were modifying the perceptual fields of urban rhythms. They acted in deeply embodied ways, putting their ketchup-covered bodies in the middle of the street, to provoke (and seduce, depending on political sensibilities) through a politics of sensations.

Over the urban political moment of the 1960s and 1970s, youthfulness became a position from which to experiment sociopolitical change and sense its intensity, its potentialities. A strong tenet of the Quiet Revolution was the need for all to take part in the modernization of society. The social experimentations and prefigurations of Montreal citizens' committees and urban movements constituted 'fields of experimentations deemed valid' for this purpose (Hamel 1991, p. 107; our translation).

For Hamel (1991, p. 118; our translation), Montreal urban movements allowed 'a new kind of political exploration to take place – on the fringes of political parties and traditional progressive organizations such as labour unions'. We have argued that this marked the affirmation of an urban logic of political action that took shape in relation to changing perceptions of time, space, and alternative rationalities. In the urban moment of the 1960s and 1970s, it was unfolding alongside a state-centred logic of political action. These were not mutually exclusive, but were held in tension: influencing, if not defining, urban and public policies while also, paradoxically, critiquing the class interests defended by the state (Hamel 1991, p. 99).

At the municipal level, urban movements contributed to the creation of opposition parties. One of these, the Montreal Citizen Movement (MCM), won one-third of city council seats in the 1974 municipal elections and would later win the 1986 ones. This party allied a broad and culturally diverse coalition of social actors and movement leaders. It proposed 'libertarian solutions to the urban crisis', local control, and political representation at the neighbourhood scale – something that positioned Montreal municipal party platforms uniquely in the Canadian municipal landscape and is clearly influenced by Montreal's urban culture and politics (Thomas 1997, p. 149). In his study of the MCM, Thomas (1997, p. 30) argues that the party's success was partly a result of the 'unresponsiveness of existing partisan institutions', but also of the 'movement's ability to raise just the kinds of crucial issues that people in cities, not only in Quebec, but elsewhere in North America, are starting to confront: crucial questions having to do with the kind of life that we are to live in our communities and in relation to our fellow citizens'.

The 1970s were also a significant decade for the consolidation of a welfare nation-state at the scale of the Quebec provincial government. Thus, another way of overcoming the injustices of everyday life took shape and affirmed itself increasingly strongly, becoming dominant: it was a neonationalist project that aimed to fill the gaps between francophones and anglophones by using the provincial state as a lever for collective emancipation. Through this project, administrative and political powers were fused together, thereby centralizing interventions within the state apparatus. It was this second venue that came to dominate in the following decades, generating a state-centred logic of political action at the expanse of the Quiet Revolution's urbanity. But then came the 2010s…

Conclusion

There are many similarities between the youth urban worlds of the 1960s and the 2010s. Young people were and are facing rapid processes of urbanization and globalization. They were and are finding themselves facing failed democratic processes, despotic regimes, and a crisis of legitimacy regarding their governments' rule of law. They were and are facing sharp discrimination across racial, gendered, class, and linguistic lines of social differentiation. They were and are appropriating novel means of intellectual and cultural production, making artefacts that circulate rapidly and shape global youth cultures. They were and are adapting to local contexts and discursive resources emanating from and giving shape to a 'common grammar of contestation' (Mills 2011) that echoes and echoed among, across, and between urban youth worlds from the Global South to the Global North. They were and are constructing a clear generational rupture, dreaming of and embodying a 'cultural revolution'. Their mode of urban political action was and is deeply aesthetic. These similarities must not overshadow the sharp differences that are also to be found when we compare the two contexts, however. The most important of these differences is the political economic reality in which these youthful movements operated and operate: the construction of a welfare state in a period of economic boom in the 1960s, and a neoliberal state in a period of severe economic crisis in the 2010s. These differences colour, enable, and constrain aesthetic political action and its multiple potentialities and directions.

With Hamel (1991, p. 94), we note that Montreal urban movements have influenced the expression and contemporary understanding of urban problems. These movements were more numerous, and mobilized more citizens, than in any other cities in Quebec or in Canada. Since the 1960s, thousands of associations, organizations, and groups have been created. They redefined relations between the state and civil society and shed light on the limits to the welfare state's 'mechanical solidarity' through their critiques of bureaucratic management and the approaches that they proposed in substitution of state activities or as an alternative configuration of sociospatial relations (Hamel 1991). It is such a legacy of urban activism that divided the historical imaginary of many French- and English-speaking students during the 2012 strikes (see Chapter 3); the former expressed a sense of grounding and continuity, while the latter often spoke of an anxious strangeness to this legacy. Yet, these libertarian and self-management networks also make themselves visible in the contemporary world of English- and French-speaking urban farmers, as we will see in Chapter 4.

Thomas argues that the history of urban politics in Montreal has given shape to a distinct civic culture. He highlights the frustration that has influenced it:

> More than any city in North America, Montreal has earned the right to be tired of institutionalized politics. It has observed two levels of government, federal and provincial, bickering endlessly with each other at the city's expense. It has lived through the October Crisis, the War Measures Act, two referendums, the Richard and Stanley Cup riots, ever increasing poverty, large language and illegal Canadian unity rallies,

and, recently, electoral fraud. It has also developed as a region unique to Quebec, where, on its streets and in its cafés, anglophones and francophones ignore it all and co-exist happily with mutual respect. (Thomas 1997, p. 159)

The contemporary history and experience of urban politics in Montreal is expressive of an urban logic of political action which can be sensed if we decentre our perceptual and ontological filters from the conventional objects of political analysis.

The history of sociopolitical urban movements is very useful in shedding light on key dimensions of the transformation of the political process. In the spatially and culturally divided city of the 1960s and 1970s, networked conceptions of space gave meaning to local struggles against imperialism, providing protest groups and movements with a shared grammar of contestation. Alternative rationalities, based on Third World liberation discourses, decolonization theories, and counterculture movements, shaped political subjectivities. The language of liberation, decolonization, victimhood, and marginality was shared among artists and intellectuals, uniting protesters in a mass movement (Tayler 2018, p. 72). Actions were embodied, emotional, and globally connected. They consisted in mass protests, occupations of diverse kinds (sit-ins, teach-ins, die-ins, etc.), artistic interventions, happenings – but also kidnappings. Youths were acting through their urbanity, acting through aesthetics. Their youthfulness was understood as a position from which to experiment sociopolitical change and sense its potentialities.

In a very compelling manner, Simon (2006, p. 7) evokes how in the 1980s, 'the discrepancy between (national) ideology and (urban) daily life in Montreal became evident'. Many voices and communities that did not fit within strict linguistic or ethnic categories become increasingly visible and audible in Montreal, bearing on an urban consciousness that exceeded the standpoints of 'francophone nationalists' and 'anglophone opposition'; a consciousness shaped by the historically situated experience of urban life. This was perhaps no more evident than during the unfolding of what became known as 'the Oka crisis', a 78-day standoff between the Kanien'kehá:ka (Mohawk) nation, state police, and the army, after months of resistance for the recognition of inalienable, inherent land and self-government rights at Kanehsatake (for greater perspective, see the documentary film, *Kanehsatake: 270 Years of Resistance*; see also Boileau 1991). But it was also visible in the work of Haitian-born writer Danny Laferrière, who published numerous fiction work exploring the entangling of language and race relations in the 1980s and became a pillar of Québécois literature. In Chapter 2, we discuss his encounter with young writers from the Saint-Michel neighborhood.

In this regard, it became increasingly evident that, as Coleman puts it:

> Montreal's urban stage is not simply a mirror of a 'national space', or what other theorists have called a 'territory': a land to be conquered, mastered and delimited by boundary markers, the objective correlative of a national identity in formation. The city is also and increasingly constitutes a node in a diverse global network of meanings and relationships. It is a decentered, shifting set of paths to be traversed rather than a site of permanent settlement. (Coleman 2018, p. 12)

With the following ethnographies, we propose to traverse some of those paths together and explore their significance in relation to the transformation of the political process. With an epistemology of Blackness grounded in describing the 'universe of operation' built over various generations that have moved, physically and virtually, across various worlds through art and travel, this chapter has discussed the emergence of a certain type of activism and aesthetic critique in which global liberation politics provided the forms through which young Montrealers culturally expressed their sense of dispossession and marginalization. And this, as we have insisted, was sometimes done through colonizing ways, invisibilizing other forms of exclusion.

Notes

1. 'Je vous convie à passer un dimanche au parc Jeanne-Mance / A errer dans cette ambiance où en plein air les gens se mélangent / Et le Possee est assis sur le gazon, en train de "chiller" tranquille / L'atmosphère est aux festivités, revêtu de mon plus beau phrasé / Laissez-moi m'introduire au sein de la masse magmatique / D'un tour de "passe-moi le mic" / Fracasser la glace et faire fondre les différentes classes.'
2. 'se joindre aux tamtams ou au Piknic Électronik n'est pas … synonyme d'entrer en relation avec les inconnus qui constituent la foule. Il s'agit vraisemblablement d'un "gout de l'autre", d'une appréciation mutuelle de la présence d'autrui en des circonstances très particulières. '
3. Lamarque (2016, p. 79) notes that the Facebook page 'Montreal Punk Shows' has 5000 followers.
4. 'Aujourd'hui, pendant que cet esprit [punk] existe encore, à travers les grèves étudiantes par exemple, on voit qu'il y a une résistance, pas tout

à fait culturelle, mais une résistance articulée, une vision pour un autre genre de société.'

5. In March 2006, the Supreme Court of Canada allowed the wearing of kirpan under strict conditions in Quebec's public schools. Heated public debate on 'reasonable accommodations' unfolded in the province as a result. The judicial term 'reasonable accommodation' refers to a legal obligation to accommodate certain minorities' demands, going against the right to equality protected by the Canadian and Quebec Charters of Rights and Freedom. The 'reasonable accommodation' crisis ended with a provincially appointed public commission being set up to investigate the matter (the Bouchard-Taylor Commission, which ended its hearing in December 2007). In the fall of 2013, the newly elected nationalist Parti Québécois (PQ) set another fire with a proposed Charter for the protection of Quebec values, which would have prohibited the wearing of 'conspicuous religious symbols' in public buildings. Reactions were immediately hostile in Montreal, and the PQ lost the April 2014 provincial elections after less than two years in power. Nevertheless, in 2019, the government of the Coalition avenir Québec (CAQ) was able to impose the Law on the Secularity of the State prohibiting public employees in a position of authority to wear religious signs. The law was being contested in court at the time of publication.

6. The opposition to a public consultation that was to be organized by the Quebec Human Rights Commission on systemic discrimination and racism is illustrative of the malaise that the word 'racism' evokes in the Quebec public sphere. In October 2017, the provincial government made the decision to change the mandate of the consultation as a result of several issues, including pressures from opposition parties (Parti Québécois, Coalition Avenir Québec) and voters who claimed that focusing on 'racism' would depict Quebecers as racists and xenophobic (Radio-Canada 2017; CBC 2017b). Public debates and protests took place throughout the controversy and gained renewed energy in the summer of 2018 when members and groups of the Montreal Black communities, along with allies, protested against a theatrical production spearheaded by Robert Lepage, called *SLAV: A Theatrical Odyssey Based on Slave Songs*. The Montreal Jazz Festival was to host the world premiere of this production, described as a journey 'through traditional Afro-American songs, from cotton fields to construction sites, railroads, from slave songs to prison songs' (The Canadian

Press 2018). Protesters publically raised the issue of the lack of Black artists among the show's cast and creative team. The protest spurred heated public debates in Montreal, Quebec, and beyond (Nevins 2018). The Jazz Festival decided to cancel the show in its original format. In the meantime, another theatrical production involving Robert Lepage and the Paris-based Théâtre du Soleil gained visibility in the media, this one entitled *Kanata*, which focused on the history of relationships between Whites and Indigenous Peoples. Indigenous groups and their allies raised concerns about the lack of meaningful consultations with the Indigenous nations and communities being represented in the show and, again, the lack of Indigenous representation in the artistic and creative teams responsible for the production (Hamilton 2018). These highly mediatized and debated events created a public conversation on racism, cultural appropriation, artistic freedom, White privilege, and censorship (for greater context, see Everett-Green 2018) which had far-reaching echoes and deeply uneven consequences for the minority groups involved.

7. The Right of Initiative (*droit d'initiative*) refers to a process and tool of participatory democracy enshrined in the Montreal Charter of Rights and Responsibilities by which any Montreal resident aged 15 or older can request a public consultation on 'any idea, orientation, or innovative project that's important to [them] and others' (Ville de Montréal 2011b). It was first used by citizens and groups requesting a public consultation on the state of urban agriculture in the city.

8. 'White Niggers of the Americas: Premature Autobiography of a Quebecois Terrorist.'

9. Drapeau was mayor during 1954–57 and 1960–86.

10. The 1967 International and Universal Exposition.

11. Duplessis ruled for fifteen years (1944–59), maintaining a firm grip on power through corruption, repression of workers' movement, and collusion with clerical authorities, foreign investors, and liberal professionals outside of Montreal (Mills 2011, p. 36).

12. Warren (2012) indicates that, historically, underground publications in Quebec have for the most part been 'a Montreal affair'. *Parti pris* (1963–68), *Socialisme* (1964–74), *Quebec Underground* (1962–72), and *Mainmise* (1970–78) are just a few of the alternative print magazines created over the period. They reached a wide audience: the distribution of *Mainmise*, for instance, surpassed 26 000 copies at its peak (Taylor 2018, p. 6).

13. It is relevant here to point out, with Simon (2006, p. 33), that '*The Shouting Signpainters* is named for one of Paul Chamberland's most famous long poems, "L'Afficheur hurle" – an angry cry of revolt.'

14. Ivan Carel (2006, pp. 150, 159) points out that Stokeley Carmichael sent out a message in solidarity with the pair while they were imprisoned in the United States, before their deportation to Montreal's Prison de Bordeaux in January 1967.

FIGURE 2.0 'BBQ at the Plan Robert.' Source: illustration by Lukas Beeckman.

Chapter 2

The Urban Political World of Racialized Youth: Moving Through and Being Moved By Saint-Michel and Little Burgundy

It's a nice sunny day and we can smell from the street the sausages being cooked on the BBQ as we enter the Plan Robert.[1] A complex of low-rise public housing in the Saint-Michel neighbourhood, the Plan Robert is home to approximately 200 families (see Figure 2.1). Alain, Malcolm, and Julie-Anne enter the central courtyard. They have been invited by two very popular police officers to attend a picnic jointly organized by them and the *Maison des jeunes Par la Grande Porte*, a youth organization located in the complex. It's 30 June 2011. Paul, a tall White police officer and Rodney, a shorter Black police officer with a contagious smile, are there. They are central characters of the neighbourhood.

Mike was about 24 years old when we met him near the Louis-Joseph-Papineau high school in the northern part of Saint-Michel. *'I have seen police officers speaking to youths, bla, bla, bla … they try to explain to them how to behave, how not to behave.'* Mike doesn't like police officers, *'but me, personally, I never had contact with police officers. In fact, for me it's only Rodney to whom I spoke because we were together at the barbershop. But police officers and I are not really friends because I try to make … I try to find a parallel way with others, like we will never cross them in fact'*[2] (6 April 2011). Rodney meets many young men at the barbershop. One day, as he was enjoying a hamburger at McDonald's with two young men from the neighbourhood, they confided to him about violent acts they were planning to carry out. As Rodney tells Alain and Julie-Anne this story, he makes wide gestures with his arms, smiling out of amazement: *'They didn't remember that I was wearing my shirt!'* Sophie is one of Rodney's young colleagues, white skin, dark hair, she likes biking around

Youth Urban Worlds: Aesthetic Political Action in Montreal, First Edition.
Julie-Anne Boudreau and Joëlle Rondeau.
© 2021 John Wiley & Sons Ltd. Published 2021 by John Wiley & Sons Ltd.

FIGURE 2.1 Plan Robert, Saint-Michel neighbourhood. *Source:* photo by Marilena Liguori, 2013.

the neighbourhood when patrolling. When a young woman ran away from home, Rodney recalls, she sent a text to Sophie: *'Mme Sophie, I am running away, but don't worry.'*

While Sophie is newer to Saint-Michel, Paul's and Rodney's names were mentioned to us by almost all the youths we met there. Paul arrived in the Poste de police 30 (PDQ 30 – local police station) 25 years ago. Before community policing became a formal policy, he changed his own approach to his work. During the violent 1990s, he used repressive measures to try to control gang activities. One day, he told us, a drive-by shooting killed two innocent victims (one a pregnant woman), and he said: *'That's enough.'* He was morally outraged. He sat down and reflected on his work and changed his approach, while maintaining repression when necessary. He began to see youths in their milieu, working with various local partners. Moral outrage is still what drives his action. In a more recent example, he speaks of a young woman who was aggressed by gang members and his reaction: *'And then I went to see the guys and I said: "If I see another one trying that, trying to hit a young girl like that for nothing, I will be the first one to come and get you. He [pointing at the aggressor] is a big idiot and I don't want that anymore." And the guys, they didn't even say a word. They were about 30 guys there, and they didn't even say: "But why [did you arrest our friend]?" It's the prevention we make, the relations we create that enable us, even when we have to do repression, to get the message through. And the message was clear.'*[3]

He gives us another example where one of his colleagues was 'saved' from being circled by 'gang members' when responding to a call because a young man recognized him and stopped his friends from pushing him in a corner. The man remembered that he had come once 'in his living room' to speak with his mother and estimated that this officer deserved respect because of that. Paul remains amazed at the strength of human relations: '*In the long term, you're a winner all the way. This time, he helped us avoid a confrontation because one day we went to sit in his mother's living room. Special, no? No, no, it makes me flip each time. And it's always anecdotes like that that come back...*'[4]

Neither Paul nor Rodney grew up or resides in the neighbourhood, but they are very involved personally beyond police work. They founded a boxing club. They created a nonprofit organization through which they raise money from private sources (foundations, businesses) to fund youth activities on an ad hoc basis. This is an extra resource they created for themselves outside the police institution (but with the consent of their superiors) that enables them to be more flexible in their work with youths.

We can hear laughter and smell the sizzling BBQ as Alain, his son Malcolm, and Julie-Anne enter the courtyard. Paul and Rodney are playing babyfoot with two young men about 20 years of age. Paul and Rodney are winning the game. The two young men decide to grab a hamburger and go back to sitting on the couches they have installed on the grass. Paul explains to us: '*These are tough guys, gang veterans.*' Gilles arrives. He must be in his late forties, a jovial man who works for the Centre Jeunesse (a network of provincially administered centres for youth rehabilitation) and is actively involved in *Programme de suivi intensif* (PSI). Deployed in the Saint-Michel-Villeray-Parc-Extension borough and some adjacent streets, the programme targets individuals aged 15–25 years involved in criminal activities related to street gangs or who present a high risk of criminalization through street gangs' activities. It provides clinical support, employment assistance, and training. For each individual, PSI requires three to four meetings per week between them, stakeholders, and occasionally their family, in addition to 20–40 hours of weekly participation in activities related to the programme (training, volunteer work, job search, leisure activities, etc.). In October 2011, it was monitoring around 20 individuals in Saint-Michel.

Gilles confirms, yes, these are tough guys. He introduces us to Miguel, a tall young man with a ponytail who just won fourth place at the Canadian weightlifting competition. With their nonprofit, Paul and Rodney financed his trip to Toronto to compete. Miguel has a fairly long history of institutional encounters with the Centre Jeunesse. Initially, he hated Gilles. '*I was rebellious,*' he explains to us. '*When they told me Gilles would be my supervisor at the Centre Jeunesse, I didn't want to see him. He tapped me on the shoulder and said, "Everything will be all right", as if he hadn't heard what I had just said.*' A couple of months later, as we meet them during the picnic, Gilles shows him off like a proud dad. Miguel graduated from high school and began to study at Cegep.[5] He found a part-time job and became a youth worker in the Plan Robert. Gilles calls him his son and cracks a few jokes about how they look alike (alluding to their different skin colours). Paul speaks to Gilles about the sneakers they need to buy for Miguel. He needs them for weightlifting. Paul can pay for them. Miguel seems shy as he is receiving too many compliments.

Nathalie arrives. She works with youths here in the Plan Robert. She has organized a handball league, financed by Paul and Rodney's nonprofit. They also financed this picnic, but they don't want that to be known. '*We're not here to gain recognition,*' says Rodney. There are about eight other police officers from the local station, including Sophie. But they interact less with youths and don't stay as long. The local police commander arrives without his uniform. The others are wearing theirs. We briefly speak to them, but quickly move away to meet the cooks. There are about five community organizers and workers gathered near the BBQs.

With a juicy hamburger in hand, Julie-Anne goes back to sitting near the couches occupied by youths. Rodney comes to sit near her. He speaks softly, telling her that eight years ago, he almost got killed here twice. '*The first time, it was exactly here near the couches. A guy pointed a gun at me but he didn't shoot because there were people behind me. The second time, it was in the other alleyway...*' But someone cuts him off and he doesn't finish his story. Julie-Anne asks him if he thinks about this every time he comes here. He shakes his head affirmatively and remains silent for a short while.

Gilles calls Julie-Anne and Alain to introduce them to the 'big boss', as Paul calls her, the 'superior mother'. Madame Paris is the oldest resident here. She knows everybody and resolves any conflicts. She asks us who we are and we explain that we are researchers. She says that she has excellent relations with Paul and Rodney, but not with the other police officers. She shakes her head, pointing at the group of officers around Sophie. '*They hit our youths*', she says. The group of young men and women sitting on the couches are looking at us. They seem on guard and they don't move from their couches, even if they socialize with Rodney and Paul. Paul explains that this is their home, so they won't make any trouble here. There is a young Latina woman among them with a small baby. Julie-Anne asks her how old he is. She says six months and moves away. She obviously doesn't want to speak to us.

A six-year-old boy arrives with a shiny red plastic cowboy hat. He responds to his grandmother, who speaks to him from the balcony on the first floor. She wants him to eat, but he doesn't feel like it. Paul tells the grandmother that he's going to fix him a plate. The boy goes to see his father, sitting on the couches. We see him later, eating with Paul, who whispers to Julie-Anne: '*He's the son of one of the gang leaders. It's obvious that he'll go through that also but we're trying* to *"save" him. He'll be able to make choices. Already he likes me very much. But because of his position, he doesn't have any choice but to be a small "caïd", a school yard leader. After that, we'll do all we can so he can choose something else.'*

As we are leaving the picnic, we feel the urge to speak to some youths. Although we are in their space, their home, we don't have access to their world during this police event. Paul and Rodney are doing work that is much appreciated by community organizations in Saint-Michel. But how do the youths see and live their world?

As Stéphane tells us, '*There are many nuances to make you see, because each police officer, each person, it's different. However, the system as such makes it that heavy trend. And it's also like a group dynamic that police officers live, you see. And there's a real fraternity within the police as such, so many times they will put themselves in a position of strength against us: It's them against us, if you know what I mean.*'[6] Stéphane is 22 years old when we meet him at his house in April 2011. He likes sports, he likes to '*express my ethnicity with for example my hair, my dreads*'.[7] Like most youths in Saint-Michel (as elsewhere, we might add), he does not like the police institution. Yet, he distinguishes between the institution and certain individuals such as Paul and Rodney.

Robyn Maynard, a Black feminist writer and community activist based in Montreal, reminds us that the sociopolitical and geographical effects of state neoliberalization processes implemented in the latter part of the twentieth century have been highly uneven along racial social demarcations. She writes, 'at the same time as neoliberal states have scaled back investments in social services and supports, a significant investment of public funds has turned towards policing and incarceration. In Canada, state abandonment in the mid- to late twentieth century was accompanied by a renewed investment in state surveillance and repression in Black communities' (Maynard 2017, p. 82). In *Policing Black Lives: State Violence in Canada From Slavery to the Present* (2017), she compellingly documents the mutations of racialized bio-political state power and its effects on Black youth and communities. Her work sharply attests that 'Black youth face heightened surveillance and disciplinary measures at massively disproportionate rates compared to their white peers' (Maynard 2017, p. 217). The racist and stigmatizing associations between Blackness, criminality, and danger have prevailed in the discourses, practices, and interventions of politicians, newspapers, and police forces over centuries (Maynard 2017, p. 9). If attempts were made to ban Black people from Canadian cities in the early part of the twentieth century, the power of such associations also shockingly resonates from a very proximate time in space: in the practices of the Montreal police forces, where 'pictures of young Black men [were used] as targets for their shooting practice throughout the 1980s' (Maynard 2017, p. 9).

Saint-Michel is known for its very active web of community organizations. A number of people are locally famous, including Paul and Rodney, as we have already seen, but also Harry Delva, who created the youth patrol programme at the beginning of the 2000s. These patrols are conducted by youths who may have been close to the 'gang' world, but the programme's first goal is to recruit school dropouts or 'pushed-outs'[8] to work as patrollers and help them go back to school or find employment. The mission of the patrollers is to ensure the tranquillity of the area and prevent antisocial behaviour by positioning themselves as representative-mediators to youths, thereby defusing potential conflicts. At first, Harry Delva was working alone on the streets, he tells us, but youths said: *'But you cannot understand us, you're too old.'* This was when he decided to create a team of youths from the neighbourhood in order to get the message across more easily. Youth patrollers play an important intermediary role between youths and police officers, particularly when school ends.

We first began to regularly spend time in Saint-Michel in 2008, when Alain completed an internship at the Maison d'Haiti, one of the landmark neighbourhood organizations. At first, in the context of a ubiquitous public debate on street gangs in Quebec and Montreal in particular, our focus was on understanding why we did not feel insecurity in the neighbourhood, whereas the media was constantly speaking of it as a 'dangerous' place, an 'anthill' (Maunay 2015). Never did we feel Saint-Michel was dangerous, so why does such a representation persist?

How can neighbourhood representations last for so long and differ so dramatically from the aesthetic, the ambiance, and the affective relations of people living there? We began this chapter by describing instances of how such public debate unfolds in local situations. Our intention was not to reproduce the image of a dangerous neighbourhood. Instead, we aimed to describe the context against which the aesthetic of racialized youth worlds develops. In addition to ethnographic immersion in the neighbourhood since 2008, involving spending time in the parks, speaking to youths, spending time with youth patrollers of the Maison d'Haiti, and interviewing key neighbourhood figures and police officers, we draw on material produced by two groups of ten young residents aged between 15 and 25 when we first began to work with them in 2014. With the intention of breaking away from the media, police, or community organizers' views about Saint-Michel and Little Burgundy, the MapCollab project began in 2014 with a first set of intensive workshops in Little Burgundy, followed by another set in Saint-Michel. Through 30 hours of discussion and co-creation over seven weeks, youths produced a multimedia guide to their neighbourhoods (their work is available at mapcollab.org if you wish to immerse yourself in their aesthetic world while walking these places), as well as a print publication (Ateliers MapCollab 2018). Here, we follow them through their itineraries in order to enter their worlds, their neighbourhoods, and the multiscalar connections they trace between Saint-Michel, the rest of the city, and the wider world.

Moving Through Saint-Michel and Little Burgundy with an Epistemology of Blackness[9]

Hola amigos y amigas, welcome to BURGZ.

Hello everybody, un monde plein de surprises vous attend.

Georges Vanier metro is the only metro station that is in LITTLE BUR-GUNDY. It is the main mode of transportation coming in and leaving Little Burgundy.

On ne juge pas un livre sur sa couverture. On ne juge pas une personne sans la connaître, alors on ne juge pas BURGZ sans connaître ses histoires. Bienvenue dans le quartier de la Petite Bourgogne un quartier rempli d'obstacles et un quartier en pleine croissance.

Amour, Haine, Hauts, Bas, peu importe, je reste Burgundy

mapcollab.org[10]

Little Burgundy, like Saint-Michel, suffers from an excess of negative representations. Located south of the highway and the train tracks, it is very close to the central business district. The MapCollab group in Little Burgundy wrote the above introduction to their neighbourhood, emphasizing its various languages and colours, but mostly the need to get to know it before judging it. No matter how difficult its histories may be, or how affectively intense everyday life is for youths, they 'remain Burgundy'. They affirm the power of their aesthetic agency. They chose to present Little Burgundy beginning where one can enter the subway station. Sajib, 17 years old, explains it clearly: '*people really think Burgz is their home. I won't enter your place without saying anything, and nobody can enter without asking permission.*'[11] Indeed, for youths in Little Burgundy, the neighbourhood is clearly defined. They know where it starts and where it ends, and they feel it is theirs.

From the metro station, Tivon suggests we go to a Black youth organization called DESTA: Dare Every Soul to Achieve. Located inside a small church, this is where we held the MapCollab workshops. It is a welcoming and warm place, offering help with schooling and job hunting, and it includes a very cool youth café. Imad then brings us to walk the rue des Seigneurs, where we can appreciate a striking blue mural depicting the great jazz legends of the neighbourhood (see Figure 2.2). '*On rue des Seigneurs, too many things occurred. Brothers disappeared and others crashed – crime, their mentality because society abandoned them. Dreamers, youth full of ambition slowed down by a bad reputation; double efforts for the same congratulations. We start from the bottom, the route is thus longer here, at our place. Or we hold hands, or we eat our nails!!!*'[12] (mapcollab.org). With his slamming words, Imad brings forth painful memories about the neighbourhood, memories about sadness and fear. With the image he chooses to represent this street, he calls to mind the glorious musical history of the neighbourhood. If these jazz legends made it, he says, it's because they worked '*double for the same congratulations*'.

The words chosen by Little Burgundy youths in their spoken and written texts constantly refer to binaries: love/hate, highs/lows, obstacles/growth, danger/potential, or, as Chris says, '*from fun to tears*' (mapcollab.org). Sometimes this is expressed through a longer temporal process of neighbourhood change; other times, it reflects situational fluctuations in feelings towards specific places and moments. But youths always emphasize safe spaces. For Chris, '*luckily the park is near*' (mapcollab.org). At the end of the rue des Seigneurs, we enter Jessie-Maxwell Smith Park. Nearby, we can see the École de la Petite-Bourgogne, a French-speaking primary school identified by Louisa as a safe place where she met her friends and found support. The video clip she produces during the workshop is very nostalgic of these childhood years. She laments how friendships change as she grows up. Many others in the group speak of childhood memories to emphasize how the neighbourhood has changed. '*Before*', says

FIGURE 2.2 Mural rue des Seigneur, Little Burgundy neighbourhood, 17 May 2014. *Source:* photo by Imad Chowki and Colin.

Sajib, '*people didn't have a choice but to fight. But today, it's a choice for them.*'[13] As Tom puts it: '*The name holds weight ... People want to test us.*' Even if violence is less intense on Little Burgundy streets than it was in the 1990s and early 2000s, when people had to fight for their protection, as Sajib explains, the neighbourhood's reputation still has a strong hold. Even today, this reputation is felt by youths as a threat. '*People want to test us.*'

Indeed, the neighbourhood went through a long period of violence in comparable ways to what happened in Saint-Michel. Street violence is still associated with these two neighbourhoods in popular representations. At the beginning of our workshops in Little Burgundy, we asked youths to draw a map of their neighbourhood. We gave them an 11 x 17' blank sheet of paper and asked them to draw what they felt best represented it. Maria used gang-related representations in drawing her map. She divided important places into four categories: youth places in yellow, her home in pink, and Bloods and Crips places in red and blue, respectively (see Figure 2.3). The youth places she identifies are community organizations and her school. In red are specific residential buildings: the one with the jazz legend mural, the building where her best friend lives, and the Lionel-Groulx metro station, which is also circled with blue as it is a contested territory. Also in blue are the Georges-

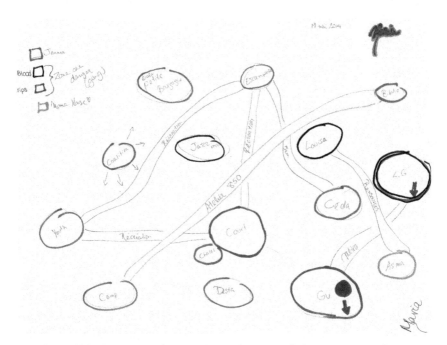

FIGURE 2.3 Maria's mental map. *Source:* mapcollab project, Little Burgundy, May 2014.

Vanier metro station and neighbourhood parks. These places are linked by lines representing the activities she does there: recreation, art performances, mobility.

If such history still weighs on Little Burgundy as Tom suggests, things have changed now. Everyone agreed in the workshops. Others in the group, such as Tatiana, insisted on safe places and a positive image of the neighbourhood without representing negative aspects. In her map, Tatiana wants us to '*Meet [her] kind of Burgz!*' (see Figure 2.4). Featuring prominently in her drawing is the Canal Lachine, where '*Everyone fix their problems their own way & the Canal Lachine is a place that enabled me to escape from my problems*'[14] (mapcollab.org). This is how she presents the next place on the MapCollab itinerary for the Little Burgundy visit. The Canal Lachine is, for her, a place for all social classes. It was built when Montreal was the main industrial hub of Canada. It no longer serves for major industrial freight, and has been transformed into a green recreational space. Tatiana also represents the two metro stations (Lionel-Groulx and Georges-Vanier), her school, and the sports center.

Bringing the visitor from the Canal Lachine to the Théâtre Corona and the Jazzmen Park, Maria writes, '*This neighbourhood is like an attraction park. When we enter, we don't want to leave!*'[15] (mapcollab.org). After a corner store called Dépanneur Bob, where many youths met as children, Kabisha brings us to her home in a public housing complex on rue Saint-Antoine. Her slam forcefully criticizes the gentrification process the neighbourhood is going through, because it only superficially changes the facades of her building, erasing the pain she lived inside: '*Our home has been transformed into yet another residence that matches the posche-lookin', condominium-stylin' and high-end places in Burgundy ... The external no longer reflects the internal. Our building was once a reflection of us. The outside once whispered the stories of us people. Stories of pain, but also, stories of bloody battles won ... We are the people of Burgundy. Our building on Saint-Antoine is now merely a show, inviting passer-bys into an evolving neighbourhood that doesn't include us broken folk in the picture*' (mapcollab.org).

From Kabisha's cosmetically repaired home, the MapCollab group wants us to end the visit at the Oscar Peterson Park, where they offer us a joyful video clip about the importance of this place for children and youths.

Before moving to Saint-Michel, let us pause a moment to reflect on the co-production of these multimedia guides to these neighbourhoods. This short visit through Little Burgundy gives a sense of the affective relations producing the neighbourhood beyond media coverage of gang activities. The aim was to rethink the tourist guide, to resist Lonely Planet's monopoly and give voice to the people living there. By offering a visual, textual, and audio scape to visitors who download the guide on their mobile phones, the idea was to visit the neighbourhood *with* youths.

Why revisit the tourist guide? Because we began this project believing that in order to understand local places, we need to break from essentializing their spatiality. A neighbourhood is mapped differently by different people; it doesn't always have clear boundaries, and most importantly, it is constantly in affective, physical, representational movement. To use Gilroy's (1993, p. 4) words, it is a 'living, micro-cultural, micro-political system in motion'. In *Black Atlantic*, Gilroy argues that Blackness was not constructed through fixed boundaries, but instead through the circulation of ideas, activists, and key cultural and political artefacts such as tracts, books, gramophone records, and choirs, across various cities on the Atlantic. Gilroy (1993, p. 19) writes: 'The specificity of the modern political and cultural formations I want to call the Black Atlantic can be defined, on the one level, through this desire to transcend both the structures of the nation state and the constraints of ethnicity and national particularity. These desires are relevant to understanding political organizing and cultural criticism.'

Similarly, for the MapCollab project, we wanted to work with the imaginary and material importance of the moving video artefact. Gilroy

FIGURE 2.4 Tatiana's mental map. *Source:* mapcollab project, Little Burgundy, May 2014.

uses Benhabib's notion of transfiguration to explain the importance of Black music in the constitution of political social relations: 'This politics exists on a lower frequency, where it is played, danced, and acted, as well as sung and sung about, because words, even words stretched by melisma and supplemented or mutated by the screams which still index the conspicuous power of the slave sublime, will never be enough to communicate its unsayable claims to truth' (Gilroy 1993, p. 37). Black music is a powerful political tool that has a long history in Little Burgundy, home of great jazz players. Music was also omnipresent during the MapCollab workshops in Little Burgundy and Saint-Michel. Youths came with their voices, their guitars, their slams, their dances. Towards the end of the workshops in Saint-Michel, such musical intensity created discomfort for one of the young women whose religious beliefs prohibited her from entering this performative musical aesthetic. We will come back to these different aesthetic relations later in this chapter.

What we wish to emphasize at this point is that like the exiled Black intellectuals and artists studied by Gilroy, the MapCollab youths of Saint-Michel and Little Burgundy constantly challenge state centrism through a transnational critical race politics and consciousness. Youths in Saint-Michel are much more mobile than their counterparts in Little Burgundy: they constantly travel back to Haiti or North Africa, to Western Canada or Miami, and they are likely to have changed houses many times. In an interview conducted by Colin from Little Burgundy with Marc-Kendy from Saint-Michel during an oral history workshop in December 2015, Colin asks:

COLIN   *Is four years the most time you lived in the same place?*

MARC-KENDY   *Yeah, yeah, yeah. And I can tell you this was really a change, a real change really. I don't know how to say, you know when you're so used to change all the time, but you know when it has been two years in the same house, I was like 'damn, mom, this is not us all this', I am like tired of it, you know.*[16]

When Marc-Kendy asked the same question of Colin, he responded:

COLIN   *I grew up in Little Burgundy. I've lived there ever since I was born. I've been living in the same house on the same street pretty much like ever since my parents moved in with me when I was a baby so … uhm yea, I've been just in Little Burgundy.*

In Saint-Michel, not only do youths regularly change houses or cities, but the neighbourhood itself has a different morphology compared to Little Burgundy: it is much larger, and thus not entirely walkable (see Figure I.0).

Yet, in Burgundy, youths also participate in the constant creation of what Simone (2010) calls the epistemology of Blackness. Simone suggests that Blackness is 'a means of tying together the various situations and tactics that have been at work in the long history of African people moving out into and around a larger urban world' (2010, p. 268). Because Black people have historically moved across various cities, through their 'multiple and discrete sojourns and implantations' (Simone 2010, p. 280), such as in Little Burgundy and Saint-Michel, they have invented a 'universe of operation' (Simone 2010, p. 297). Whether Saint-Michel and Little Burgundy youths actually move physically or not in the present is not as important as the legacy of movement by their ancestors, who learned to 'bring an increasing heterogeneity of calculations, livelihoods, and organizational logics into a relationship with each other' (Simone 2010, p. 279) as they implanted themselves in specific neighbourhoods. This perspective engages with Blackness as 'a device for affirming and engaging forms of articulation amongst different cities and urban experiences that otherwise would have no readily available means of conceptualization' (Simone 2010, p. 279). The epistemology of Blackness enables us to see the arbitrary instead of essentializing and fixing social, racial, and spatial boundaries. Rather than assigning Burgundy and Saint-Michel youths identities and stereotypical representations based on their skin colour and where they live, the epistemology of Blackness invites a focus on their gestures, on what they do, where, when, and how. Instead of solely looking at Black subcultures (music, clothing), the MapCollab project aims to describe how youths organize their daily environments and daily lives.

Élisabeth's post on the mapcollab.org website synthesizes wonderfully how many youths wish to speak of Saint-Michel (see Figure 2.5). It captures with a simple image – that of the subway line – and a simple number – 67, the bus line running on Saint-Michel Boulevard – the importance of mobility for this neighbourhood. Élisabeth also mentions other important neighbourhood sites: Louvain Street, the McDonald's near the subway station, the two French-language high schools (Jean-François Perreault-j.f.p and Louis-Joseph-Papineau-l.j.p), the Maison d'Haiti, and the local police station (poste 30).

Unlike with the Little Burgundy tour, in Saint-Michel it is very difficult to walk to all of the places identified by youths; distances are too important. This is why the 67 bus is so central to the neighbourhood's identity. In her mental map, Élisabeth, who is 21 years old, connects everything with the number 67 (see Figure 2.6). She also identifies Harry Delva and the Maison d'Haiti, as well as poste 30. Note that Harry Delva is connected to her high school, Louis-Joseph-Papineau (Louis-Jo). Indeed, in her video clip, she stages herself in an interview with an unidentified social worker (played by one of

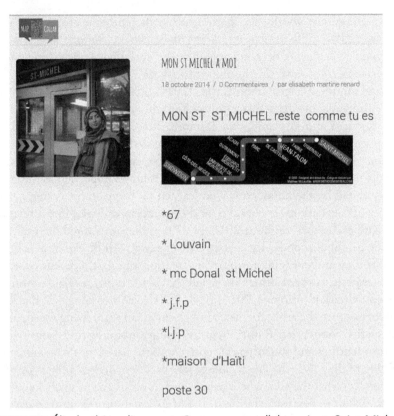

FIGURE 2.5 Élisabeth's online post. *Source:* mapcollab project, Saint-Michel, October 2014.

the community youth workers involved in the MapCollab workshops). She speaks of an incident that happened in her school on 25 October 2005. A young White man hit another student with a sharp instrument. *'He stabbed him'*, she says. But because he was White, he only got a few days of suspension from school. *'They didn't even call the police!'*[17] Had it been a Black man who had done this, the school would have immediately called the police. She is outraged at such injustice, a perfect example of racialized punishment disproportionately affecting Black youth (Maynard 2017, p. 219). She further expresses frustration about the media that keeps soiling the neighbourhood's name. It came to the school and *'We felt like lab rats! We were no longer students, just lab rats.'*[18] She forcefully denounces representation imposed on the neighbourhood, stripping youths of their agency. From active students, they became passive lab rats. When Joëlle saw Élisabeth's video at the public launch of the mapcollab.org website, she could not hold back tears coming from an unexpected feeling of injustice moving from and through her gut.

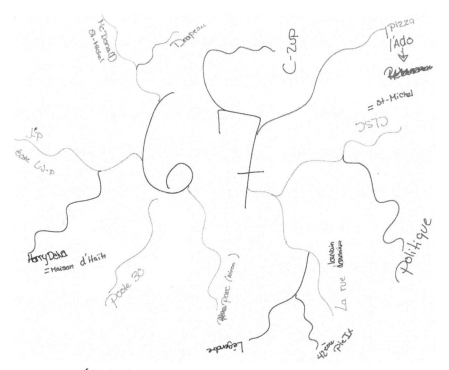

FIGURE 2.6 Élisabeth's mental map. *Source:* mapcollab project, Saint-Michel, October 2014.

Years later, she still vividly remembers the images and this pregnant moment. Élisabeth's video is powerful – she chose to stage and perform her own part in a collage of temporalities. In telling her experience of this past event *anew*, she is both unmasking the racial prejudices that she and her peers were forced to contend with as youths denied innocence and societal protection, and at the same time dubbing over[19] the past experience, repeated to expose and interrupt a cycle of violence that screams for accountability and response-abilities in shared pasts, affecting and still living in shared presents.

Élisabeth has a beautiful toddler. This is why the CLSC (Centre local de services communautaires, a local social and medical centre) figures on her map. She links the CLSC to the word 'politique'. When explaining her map during the workshop, she links politics with media stereotyping and the politicians who came to her school to promise a new basketball court in order to win votes. For her, poorer neighbourhoods are victims of more 'politics' than richer ones. She has a strong sense of power relations and speaks out strongly against injustices.

For Salma, who is 16 years old, Louis-Jo falls victim to too many rumours. '*Times have changed*', she says in her video clip. She presents a very positive image of her school. Her approach contrasts with that of Élisabeth,

FIGURE 2.7 Giulio's mental map. *Source:* mapcollab project, Saint-Michel, October 2014.

who prefers to express outrage. Salma chooses to emphasize the beautiful. For her, she entered the school as a girl and recently graduated as a young woman who has *'learned how to have a voice that counts'*.

For Giulio, who is 23 years old, Louis-Jo is not as important as the adjacent park, Parc Champdoré. This is where he regularly plays basketball. His video clip similarly plays with childhood memories and present attachment to the place. *'Finally … the bell rang'*, he writes. *'Finally… I can escape. Finally I can express myself.'*[20] Giulio was studying to become a school teacher when he participated in the workshops. His mental map expresses some of the rumours that plague Louis-Joseph-Papineau school. He draws the school with its windows crossed out (see Figure 2.7). In 2009, a journalist from La Presse got permission to spend three days in Louis-Jo. Her first article begins as follows: *'Louis-Joseph-Papineau high school looks like a cement block washed up in the middle of a field. A bunker without windows, dirty white'*[21] (Ouimet 2009). It produced much anger. Louis-Jo students reacted promptly, writing letters to her. While narrating this anecdote to us, Rodney concludes:

> *You know, it is a journalist that I respect very much. She had a strategy. I knew her conclusion and she chose her way to denounce a situation: there*

is a need for more resources in those milieus. This was her conclusion: 'Stop thinking that everything is so easy.' But the way she chose did more harm [to her relationship with youths]. But at the same time, I was surprised by youths' reactions.[22]

This anecdote illustrates well the clash of two types of logic: strategic on the one side (the journalist portrays the neighbourhood with pity in order to politically ask for more resources), tactical on the other (youths feel betrayed by the trust they gave her, insulted at the negative stereotype she conveys about their neighbourhood). Rodney positions himself in between these two logics in this specific anecdote: he understands what the youths didn't appreciate (the journalist's strategy) and he empathizes with their feeling of betrayal, but he was still surprised by the force of their reaction.

On his map, Giulio also draws the McDonald's, the Petit Maghreb section of Jean-Talon Street (represented by the Algerian flag), a group of multiethnic youths, and, in the centre, the hexagonal park adjacent to the other high school and the metro station.

From Louis-Jo, the Saint-Michel multimedia guide continues with Marc-Kendy, who brings the visitor to a boxing club where Ali Nestor has created a safe space for youth to get rid of their excess energy or rage, but also to finish their high school degree, which he developed through alliances with the school board. Marc-Kendy wishes to study the prevention of delinquency. He believes in the power of community organizations and wishes to contribute by working in this field. He emphasizes the power to act.

The MapCollab project sought to give youths the power to produce representations of their neighbourhood. Giulio's video capsule begins with close-ups on the faces of his fellow workshop participants. There is no sound, except his masterful beatboxing. After a joyful tour through the François-Perrault Park (represented as a hexagon on his map), it ends with the following message: *'There is nobody else but me who should decide the face of St Michel, not even statistics.'*[23] Salma, Élisabeth, Giulio, and Marc-Kendy have taken a strong voice to represent Saint-Michel.

François-Perreault Park is where Ouali, who is 20 years old, decided to bring the visitor. Ouali arrived in Canada from Algeria only 11 months before we began the workshops in Saint-Michel. His slam describes how *'Arabs, Haitians, Québéckers, and South Americans play together.'* He speaks of Saint-Michel as a *'quartier libre'*, a free neighbourhood. *'It's like medication,'* he says, *'my neighbourhood is my life'*.[24] For him, Saint-Michel is a *terre d'accueil*. He feels at home, particularly because of the Petit Maghreb, a portion of Jean-Talon Street formally called as such because of its concentration of North African businesses (for a detailed history of how this appellation came about, see Manaï 2015). The Petit Maghreb also features prominently on Salma's map, represented in colour by North African flags. Salma also includes the 67 bus and Tim Horton's, a doughnut chain restaurant (see Figure 2.8).

Nico, who is 20 years old, chooses to present the visitor another aspect of Jean-Talon Street: houselessness. Nico arrived in Montreal from Haiti in 2010. He is a singer and a slammer, regularly performing in the neighbourhood and beyond. Working full time in a warehouse, he managed during the workshops to finish his high-school degree. On 17 October 2014, a Walk Against Misery (*marche contre la misère*) was organized in the neighbourhood by community organizations as a protest against poverty. Many MapCollab youths participated. Nico wrote a slam about injustices and inequalities. It was performed in various places in the neighbourhood. It tells the story of a houseless man who falls in love with a young woman. '*Neither for the Left, neither for the Right*', sings Nico. He plays the role of a man who is '*not really*

FIGURE 2.8 Salma's mental map. *Source:* mapcollab project, Saint-Michel, October 2014.

autonomous', isolated but '*in love even without an identity'.*[25] The slam is a message of love and solidarity.

Patrick, who is 25 years old, also expresses a message of glee, hope, and tenderness. Accompanied by his guitar, he brings us to the Gabrielle-Roy School, serving young adults with the aim of finishing their high-school degree. Patrick arrived from Haiti after the earthquake in 2010. The guitar is central to his life. He regularly plays at his church, and he brought it to almost every workshop. After his arrival from Haiti, he quickly changed to the Gabrielle-Roy School. This was where we met him. He liked how the school opened space for him to perform and play music. During the workshop, he began to write. Patrick speaks good French, but still does not always feel perfectly fluent. Writing the poem 'L'espoir' for the multimedia guide was important to him. During our oral history workshop, he explained this in the following words:

> *We began working together at MapCollab. It enabled me to write a text on hope. And from day to day, I continued writing. It makes my brain and my memory exercise. Always writing. Sometimes, when I am at work, and something comes to my mind, I write it. So, I say, it's a good way to really speak of your trajectory, to know who you are, to know what you want to be in life, and it can, it can remain an example for the future generation. And myself, it's like, I also want to be a model for my brothers. I don't know how, but I want to be a model for my brothers.*[26]

Patrick's, Nico's, and Ouali's videos in the multimedia guide include scenes where we see hands writing. Being able to write, to slam, to sing, to dance was central to youths' feeling towards the workshops. This is the theme of Felipe's contribution. A soft-spoken young man of 23 years old, Felipe speaks French and Spanish. He chose to bring the visitor to the space where we held the workshops, a community organization called Go emploi. Felipe likes to draw. He filled the white board with abstract and joyful lines, and had the whole team join him in an improvised beatboxing and dancing.

The Saint-Michel MapCollab group lives translocally. Mobility at the scale of the neighbourhood is as important as their constant travels to Haiti, the United States, and North Africa. In his fabulous book about how Haitians 'remade Quebec', Sean Mills (2016) traces these connections back to the 1930s. Undoubtedly, as Austin (2013) beautifully expresses in the excerpt quoted in the Introduction, Caribbean cultures are central to politics in Montreal. The epistemology of Blackness is strikingly relevant to understanding racialized youth worlds in Saint-Michel and Little Burgundy.

Being Moved: Representations and Affective Aesthetic Relations

The visual, audio, and textual scapes produced by Saint-Michel and Burgundy youths constitute much more than a tourist guide to their neighbourhood. They are intensely affective. The idea of co-producing an audioguide with youths came from Steven High, who was co-researcher on this project. This quickly evolved into more than an audioguide, because the youths decided to expand the media they used to express themselves. High has produced a number of in situ audio tours to present his oral historical work. The great advantage of such tours is that they force the walker to slow down, immerse themselves in the visual, textual, and audio scapes digitally produced, and connect themselves to the physical urban moments and spaces they need to negotiate. Thompkins (2011, p. 237, cited in High 2013, p. 75) puts it beautifully: 'the disembodied voice and the embodied walker [are] stitched together via the city, its map, its history, our collective histories and futures, and, perhaps most importantly, the affect that is so associated with the headphones'. But this is an uneasy relationship, producing some dissonance between listening and being in the city in a specific moment and place. In an article analysing such experiences, High (2013, p. 82) recalls: 'In one scheduled walk in March 2012, we even had to negotiate through hundreds of student protesters dispersing after a huge assembly. We felt like salmon swimming upstream. Even when we walk as a group, we are not a group. We share an auditory space, but are separated by our headphones. Nor are we quite in sync, building tension into our forward journey.'

The multimedia guides produced in the MapCollab project were different from the one analysed by High in that they used a different technology, enabling the walker's mobile phone to detect their location and thus initiate the multimedia content when they arrived on site. This way, there were no problems of pacing the sound with the walk. These technologies evolve rapidly. In the next chapter, we will briefly discuss another experiment with walking affective expressions during the student strikes that swept Montreal in the spring of 2012.

What was important to us in the MapCollab project was to break from the stereotypes that so painfully affect youths and enable them to produce their own representations of their neighbourhoods. As a major producer of representations, the media describes a place or a group of people through words and images for those who cannot or dare not physically go there. The multimedia guides produced by MapCollab remain in the realm of representations, in that they work with images, texts, and sounds that appeal to cognitive understanding. And yet, because these images, sounds, and texts are meant to be seen, heard, and read *while physically being in the neighbourhood*, they also appeal to affective and embodied communication through asynchronous, curated, yet open-ended and spontaneously interconnected aesthetic experiences. In analysing these disembodied and embodied forms of communication, Simone's (2016, p. 7) epistemology of Blackness is insightful, because, as he puts it beautifully, Blackness 'has learned to mine the city for beats and polyphony that reverberate across generations and nations, so as to attune bodies to each other from Rio to New Orleans to Luanda'. And, we might add, to Montreal.

Blackness may not belong exclusively to Black people. The social construction of Blackness and its sociopolitical history are inseparable from the discursive formations and systems of representations, knowledge, and power that were invented by Europeans to justify the transatlantic slave trade (Maynard 2017). The association of phenotypes and physiological traits – black skin, hair, and so on – to pathologizing attributes is a social construction that has linked Blackness and Black 'cultures' to criminality, danger, threat, lower intelligence, subhumanity, and inhumanity in ways that have continuously been used to legitimize the devaluing and unequal treatment of Black lives, to this day. This is the operative power of *anti*-Blackness and why Blackness, for Black artists, activists, and communities, constitutes such a productive and empowering site to contest and 'unmask' race (Acampora and Cotten 2007) and disidentify its encoded meanings by 'working both with and against representational norms' (Lax 2014, p. 15). Based on his analysis of live work, queer cultural critic José Esteban Muñoz describes disidentification as a performative, aesthetic political process: 'Disidentification is about recycling and rethinking encoded meaning. The process of disidentification scrambles and reconstructs the encoded message of a cultural text in a fashion that both exposes the encoded message's universalizing and exclusionary machinations and re-circuits its workings to account for, include, and empower minority identities and identifications' (Muñoz 1999, p. 31).

We see disidentification at work in the representations (media products) that MapCollab youths have produced against the background of their experiences of their urban worlds. Both in and beyond their performativity on a representational level, they move us to engage with Blackness inscribed and recircuited in the urban (spatially contingent, temporally continuous) fabric of their neighbourhoods and beyond. To borrow words from Iain Chambers's (2017, p. 92) insightful analysis of postcolonial artworks, we may say that the multimedia guides produced by the youths disassemble and reassemble 'the languages and techniques of what is transmitted' as their neighbourhood and its history, creating a repetition (along the landmarks of the walks) that 'dubs the past to mark the difference in the present [and] elaborates a critical cut across and within an inherited … discourse.' It 'occupies our time attending a reply', Chambers (2017, p. 92) concludes.

In this sense, we find it analytically rich and meaningful to engage with Blackness as a way of living the city which builds on what Black people have constructed in the neighbourhoods where they have sojourned. It is from this perspective that Blackness may not belong exclusively to Black people, as it can be about following tracks and paths, enabling us to sense and perhaps even to say 'something about the city that nobody else can [say], and if we are really prepared to listen, we could not rest at ease with the theories of the city being put into play today' (Simone 2016, p. 217). Hip-hop has been approached and theorized in similar ways in relation to Blackness and urban knowledges (Rose 1994; Recollet 2010; Alsalman 2011, pp. 34–37). These are profound challenges to the institutions producing authoritative knowledge on the city and the world. Indeed, most academic and mainstream knowledge about the city, the people inhabiting its spaces, and its history rests on controlling what is said by certain people (racialized youths) and showcasing what is said by others (academics, mainstream artists, journalists).

In her study of urban narratives, Finnegan (1998) compares the academic, planner, and personal tales of the city. She shows that texts and stories about the city cannot be understood without ethnographic sensitivity to their performance, circulation, and enactment. It is not only what is being written or said, but how the story is told – with what embodied gestures and affective communication. More than capturing how racialized youths imagine and represent their urban worlds, with the MapCollab project and the multimedia guides we sought to articulate the text with its performance, the disembodied voice, and the affective and embodied experience of walking through their neighbourhoods in their youth urban worlds.

The MapCollab guides to Saint-Michel and Little Burgundy seek to move visitors not only with a physical tour of the neighbourhoods, but also (and mostly) by appealing to a range of aesthetic experiences (affective, sensory, cognitive, and noncognitive). Analysing these youth worlds as 'antisocial' or 'at-risk', as the media and public policies do, blinds us to what is being constructed on a daily basis. Allow us to borrow Gilroy's (1993, p. 38) words on transfiguration again: 'The bounds of politics are extended precisely because this tradition of expression [transfiguration] refuses to accept that the political is a readily separable domain. Its basic desire is to conjure up and enact the new modes of friendship, happiness, and solidarity that are consequent on the overcoming of the racial oppression on which modernity and its antinomy of rational, western progress as excessive barbarity relied.' Just like disidentification, transfiguration refers to a means of communication in 'lower frequency,' or to put it in the language used in the Introduction, to letting an aesthetic appearance affect you beyond what it may have come to represent or be recognized for, beyond what it says to your cognitive capacities. This is what the rhythm of Kabisha, Imad, and Nico's slams is doing. This is what the subtle tear on Asma's face as she enters the Dépanneur Bob as a child and exits as a young woman means. This is what Louisa's profound voice or Giulio's beat-boxing performs.

It is not only through artful performances that transfiguration and aesthetic appearances are produced. We heard an anecdote concerning a new local police officer. The freshly graduated officer, who did not know Montreal very well, let alone Saint-Michel, was patrolling on Jean-Talon Street. He suddenly put in a call for backup. Panicking, he said: '*There's a huge crowd of Arabs taking over the street!*' He was afraid the crowd would get out of control and that he would not be able to contain it alone. He had no clue why the street was suddenly flooded by joyful bodies. As we were told this story, Paul and Rodney were quietly smiling: '*It's the end of the Ramadan! It's normal, don't worry.*'

Their objective in recounting this story is to emphasize the need to learn about Saint-Michel's diverse population in order to be able to do good police work. This involves human relations, cultural sensitivities and knowledge, and constant embodied engagement. But beyond this message, the anecdote illustrates the power of an aesthetic appearance which speaks to the new police officer's affects more than his cognitive capacity to analyse the situation. He felt afraid and overwhelmed by the appearance of the crowd on the street in celebration of the end of Ramadan. The circulation of artefacts such as North African flags, the chattering noise coming from the numerous cafés on Jean-Talon Street, the smell from the feast, all provoked intense effects on the officer, unaware of the custom. He could not cognitively make sense of what was happening beyond what he spontaneously identified as 'a huge crowd of Arabs' appearing, but the aesthetic appearance of the situation, with its circulating affects, certainly called for a protective, defensive response for him. In this moment, we see the power of a racialized regime of perceptibility and recognition at play in mediating the sense and meaning that this novice police officer (unfamiliar with the temporality and forms of these celebrations on Jean-Talon Street) made of his sensations and how they generated fearful emotions in him. Even though Saint-Michel is known as a multicultural neighbourhood, the aesthetic experiences of cross-cultural encounters call for aesthetic finesse and cultural sensitivity in understanding situations and recognizing the organization of signs and sensations that govern fields of perceptions and actions, and which have differentiated political effects depending on one's intersectional positionality (a White police officer gazing nervously and fearfully at young people cheering from the cafés as he reaches for his radio transmitter, or the youths in these cafés receiving this gaze and anticipating what might be coming).

To understand youth worlds, we need to be attuned to such transfigurative or affective aesthetics, as this allows us to look for politics in different places. The Little Maghreb sector is a portion of Jean-Talon Street, officially designated as such under the initiative of the borough mayor. She focused on this sector as it has witnessed a number of youth-related complaints in the past few years: crowding, hanging out on the street. When there is a soccer match, as at the end of Ramadan, the cafés become very dynamic social spaces that overflow on to the street. This creates apprehensions. The Maison d'Haïti hired a youth patroller specifically for this area in 2011.

During the 2011 World Cup, 7000 people celebrated on the street, and only four police officers were posted. For the Morocco–Algeria match on 4 June, youths sat with flags on police cars, chanting, having fun (see Figure 2.9). Police officers and the mayor walked around, saying hi to everyone, a little like a politician on a campaign.

Things became tenser at the end of the match, when a group of Algerian youths began to throw bottles and rocks at Moroccan youths on the other side of the street. The few police officers there (Rodney, Paul, and two colleagues)

FIGURE 2.9 On Jean-Talon Street, before the end of the Morocco–Algeria match, 4 June 2011. People are gathered near the window of a café transmitting the match. Police officers are in the background. Youths sit or lean on their car. *Source:* photo by J.A. Boudreau.

entered the crowd, in between the two groups, along with a youth patroller and Harry Delva. They were simply breaking up fights or arguments, trying to calm things down. Business owners of both origins entered the crowd and began to take aside the most problematic youths, screaming at them like parents would: '*Why did you do this? We were having fun. And now things are over. What will they think?*' and so on. We were standing just behind the group of Moroccan youths, in front of a Moroccan bakery. The owner came out and spoke to them, asking them to call their friends and meet further down the street. Phones began to work and they slowly moved away. In the meantime, the riot police arrived. They stood in line with their full gear, without advancing. They didn't do anything and remained at about 50 metres from where the youths were. In the end, both groups of youths walked hand-in-hand with both flags towards the riot police chanting '*Go Habs Go!*' and the party continued calmly ('Habs' is the nickname for the Montreal hockey team, the Canadians). By chanting this, the Moroccan and Algerian (and Tunisian) youths were attempting to establish connections with the police officers through cultural closeness and a form of transfiguration (thinking that hockey is for police officers the same as soccer is for them, and aesthetically attaching the familiar 'Habs' signifier to the signs signified by their Algerian and Moroccan flags, thereby also spatially connecting Montreal in aesthetic continuities with the countries significant to their senses of belonging in their youth urban world).

In this situation, many political gestures were made: youths asserting their identity with flags, speaking to international journalists from Algeria and Morocco in both Arab and French; youths gathering to celebrate on the streets, sometimes against their parents' will; young women entering cafés that are generally frequented mostly by men; youths lifting Rodney out of joy… This was a fun, warm, and joyful afternoon. These *political gestures* became *political acts* when tension began to arise. But more clearly, they became political acts when the youths began to join hands while holding Moroccan and Algerian flags, chanting a hockey slogan to communicate with the wall of riot police shields. The chant appealed to specific cultural representations of White Montrealers as hockey lovers. The flags, the joined hands, and the smiles appealed to embodied aesthetic communication.

The effects of this political act and these political gestures were multiple. At the scale of neighbourhood governance, the borough mayor and the local police station – along with community organizations – persisted in their community prevention work. At the scale of the local North African community, leaders and local businesses maintained their pressures for formal recognition of the Little Maghreb. At the global scale, the after-match was discussed in the Moroccan and Algerian media.[27] For the youths who were there, the effects may have been multiple, ranging from arguments with their parents and extended family back in North Africa to a lasting sensation of thrill, fear, anger, or excitement. But, most importantly, this political act must have impacted their sense of identity and political subjectivity. Indeed, public spaces take on a different role during sportive encounters. As Viot, Pattaroni, and Berthoud (2010) suggest, such encounters are agonistic: visual and sound expressions of membership and identity are welcomed in ways that break with everyday requirements for more discretion in public spaces.

Racialization: Disembodied Profiling Entangled With Embodied Racist Encounters

If we entered these youth worlds with a spatial lens – the neighbourhood – we quickly realized we needed to grow out of this spatial entry to reflect on a central factor shaping the contours of these urban worlds: racialization. We saw with Simone how an epistemology of Blackness based on the legacy of Black mobilities and their ability to create a 'universe of operation' in the neighbourhoods where they sojourned enables us to see the arbitrary, the unexpected ways through which people articulate their daily lives in complex environments. Racialization, by contrast, seeks to constrain and limit, curtailing the movements and signification of certain bodies, by *imposing* patterns and predictability through which 'races' are produced and legitimized (while being made to appear natural), in order to sustain social hierarchies of dominance and inequality (Andersen 2014; Maynard 2017).

Prevention measures, ranging from community policing to public subsidies for community projects aimed at keeping youths away from street gangs (in the 2000s) or religious radicalization (in the 2010s), are based on practices of racial profiling. They work with an actuarial logic. On paper, profiling means using probabilistic calculations to establish risk factors. Through this approach, youths are conceived as statistical aggregates; their behaviour is 'predicted' by their concentration of risk factors, including their skin colour, ethnicity, and place of origin (what is usually referred to as 'race' in this context). In our interviews, we constantly heard local actors appropriating the risk factor discourse to describe their neighbourhood or their own social work. For instance, the local police commander exposed youth vulnerability, while hesitating to use the actual words: *'They are youths who unfortunately have fewer means, more challenges. So, they are youths … I don't want to say they are at-risk, but they are youths who weren't unfortunately … spoiled by destiny, I don't know.'*[28]

If we ethnographically examine what local civil and police actors actually do with youths, or ask them how they perceive them, responses are not always coherent with the risk factor discourse. They speak less in terms of vulnerability and more in terms of empowerment, although this distinction is more or less intense according to who is speaking. For instance, there was a gendered and job distinction between the more maternal discourses of community relations police officers, who (in Saint-Michel) are female, and the more respect-driven discourse of police patrollers such as Paul and Rodney, who are mainly male. Compare these two excerpts, the first by Julie, who was the community relations police officer at the Saint-Michel police station, and the second by Paul:

JULIE   *It's all true, it's disadvantaged, yes, in comparison to another neighbourhood, but this does not mean there is less potential. We need to give these youngsters confidence [in a maternal tone, she sometimes speaks of 'my' youths], the possibility to do other things. This is the opportunity: when they do sports, when they are engaged in projects.*[29]

PAUL   *They [youths] will respect the individual; they will respect you. You know them well and you are going to say [to gang youths]: 'Me, guys, it's me who organizes this thing, please.' The guys will say: 'I respect you, no problem, you can do what you want, nothing will happen.'*[30]

The contrast here cannot simply be explained by gender, but also by the mandate corresponding to each position. Community relations police officers work exclusively on prevention, mainly in schools (elementary and secondary). They work with youths in general, and not so much with criminalized youths. Police patrollers have a repressive as well as a preventive mandate. They work with older criminalized youths (many older youths have children, who are now the target for prevention work, such as the little boy with the red plastic cowboy hat we described at the beginning of this chapter). These criminalized youths are not really seen as vulnerable. Rather, the relationship developed between Paul, Rodney, and gang 'veterans' is one of equal forces and mutual respect.

Despite these differences, the logic of prevention based on profiling techniques (identifying risk factors) remains racialized. Although the police keep insisting that criminal profiling and racial profiling are not the same thing, on the ground, these profilings are generally amalgamated and have important effects on youths.

Racial profiling has been publicly contested since at least 2003, when a working group on the issue was created locally, followed by various consultative commissions at the provincial level. A grassroots group, *Mères unies contre le racisme*,[31] began to make pressure to fight discrimination. Young men from the Plan Robert were repeatedly ticketed for sitting on the fence at the entrance of their complex: '*And this can bring catastrophic effects for life, for what will happen next for these youths. So, and one of these youths was arrested, etc … a tough arrest. And there was, I remember, there was a press conference on the Plan Robert with two of these youths and their families, etc. And there was a judiciary pursuit that, by the way, led to the condemnation of the SPVM [City of Montreal Police Service]*[32] (interview with local elected official, 6 May 2011).

Following the 2008 revolts in Montreal-Nord, a neighbourhood adjacent to Saint-Michel, the Montreal police service began a public reflection on racial profiling. With the death of a young man of Latino origins named Freddy Villanueva, murdered by a police officer, the Montreal police needed to explain the controversial anti-gang operations of its Eclipse Squad. This is when, in conjunction with a shift of priorities at the federal and provincial levels, the term 'street gang' gradually disappeared from the public scene (Ville de Montréal 2011a), to be replaced by 'radicalization'. If certain measures were taken, such as awareness workshops for police officers, racial profiling techniques persist at the local level, while the provincial public debate is openly targeting racialized youths with its radicalization prevention programmes.

In short, profiling relies on the statistical identification of patterns. Racism, on the other hand, involves embodied and affective relations of attraction and revulsion, based on evaluations both socially and historically engineered. '*So we are going through the parking lot,*' recalls Stéphane. He was returning home from the Cegep with two friends, '*and then there was an old lady there in her car and everything and she says: "Hey hey hey, we're not in Africa here. We don't eat on the street." You know what I mean/situation you see … very very eeeh … that … racism that expresses in and of itself, you see.*' Stéphane hesitates to use the word 'racism' in this conversation with Alain, who is also of Haitian origin. '*So we are three youths, you see: I'm smiling, the other one runs and tries to hit the car, and the other one doesn't do anything.*'[33]

Stéphane is describing a situation of racism (revulsion based on certain bodily characteristics 'to establish *forms* of difference through which evaluations between humans are drawn'; Andersen 2014, p. 15) and racialization (generalizations about someone's expected behaviour based on stereotypical understanding of race – as in the affirmation that in Africa, people eat on the street) that had an effect on the three friends. They engaged in different political gestures in response: smiling, hitting, freezing. The woman's comment about Africa and eating habits had the effect of excluding them from Montreal's 'civility'. As Maynard (2017, p. 212) writes, 'Black children [and youth] are often the receptacles of the negative projections of a society mired in the fear of Black bodies. Societal hostility is often woven into everyday life for Black persons; everywhere they go [and often in places where they expect it the least], they encounter psychological violence in terms of systemic disregard, surveillance, suspicion and the presumption of guilt.'

In a collective book edited by Frantz Benjamin (2012), a local elected official in Saint-Michel, writer Dany Laferrière, describes a similar situation:

> *In the neighbourhood of Saint-Michel. A small group of six youths are talking in front of the corner store ... I come out of the store with a newspaper under my arm. Tell me Dany, are you Québécois or Haitian, asks one of them laughing. Tricky question.*
>
> *However, it should have been a simple question for someone like me who has lived in Quebec for 30 years ... Why this question, I say. Suddenly, six cold faces. You were born in Haiti, and despite of that you're considered a Quebecois writer. We were born here and we are Haitians. How do you explain that?*
>   (Laferrière in Benjamin 2012, p. 1718; our translation)

Somehow, because Laferrière was able to mark the Quebecois literature scene in the 1980s with his *Comment faire l'amour avec un nègre sans se fatiguer* (1985) and many other critically acclaimed works thereafter,[34] his Blackness and his Haitian origins do not seem to matter as much anymore as do those of this group of young men in Saint-Michel. Mills (2016) describes how Laferrière 'discovered himself to be a writer in Montreal, and it was also in Montreal where he had the surprise "of discovering that I was Black". "A Black person," Laferrière explains, "only exists in the presence of a white person. Before, in Port-au-Prince, I was only a human being. This bowled me over into a new universe. I had to account for all of this, and to do this I had to become a writer"' (Mills 2016, p. 213).

Laferrière's widely successful first novel took a frontal approach to racism and racialization in the context of rising French-speaking nationalism in Quebec. As briefly explained in Chapter 1, this cultural movement was inspired by ideas about *négritude*. Speaking French was racialized, as Michèle Lalonde so aptly captures in her poem 'Speak White'. This points to Whiteness and markers of racial differentiation as situated social constructions with powerful political effects. Mills highlights how Laferrière's novel, showcasing a young Black man who has sex with English-speaking White women, plays on various levels to criticize processes of racialization and racism at play in Montreal. If the novel was criticized by Black feminists for its heterosexual and male normativity, its entry in the gallery of unavoidable readings for someone interested in Quebec literature had the effect of modulating the significance of Laferrière's origins and Blackness on his inclusion in Quebec's national identity and polity. By writing a book about racism and racialization, Laferrière stopped being racialized in the same ways that the six youngsters in front of the corner store are.

In similar ways, Patrick's and Nico's relationships with writing and music are central to their being in Montreal, and to making sense of the racialized subjectivities wrongly attached to them. In his oral history, Nico recalls:

> *My biggest pride since I arrived in the neighbourhood is the texts I've started to write. I started to write texts for Haiti – I was speaking of Haiti. When I arrived here, it was other causes that I had to defend [laughing], you see? When I started to defend this cause and when I write texts and when I arrive somewhere to say that I, I come from Saint-Michel, I write this or that text ... Everybody: Wow! Good Job! Because when you see someone is positive in a neighbourhood where everyone ... because he's Black ...*[35]

To find a place in his new city, Nico wrote. He made sense of Saint-Michel in this way, and he also, as Laferrière says, discovered he was Black in Saint-Michel. '*We can't stay there – like receiving only bullets like ta-ta-ta-ta-ta-ta – they're spraying us with bullets, with machine guns. We're trying to say many things ... to insult with words. When I speak of machine guns – It's words that I mean – They're striking us with that.*'[36] Nico speaks of the embodied pain and violence that racialized representations provoke. He describes the words transmitting negative representations as bullets having very real, harmful effects in his body.

Through the MapCollab project and in their daily lives, Saint-Michel and Little Burgundy youths constantly navigate race, class, and gender with aesthetic tools such as writing, singing, and drawing, but also by expressing outrage or fear – like Élisabeth did in her video, or like Stéphane's friend did when he hit the racist woman's car. Only with an epistemology of Blackness can we be attuned to the unexpected effects of these performances. Because, youths tell us, race is what we do, what we interpret and say about our sensations, not what we have.

Conclusion

In *Killing Rage: Ending Racism* (1995), bell hooks narrates how she felt like an exile in her social circles when she began to stop being ashamed of her rage, 'using it as a catalyst to develop critical consciousness, to come to full decolonized self-actualization' (bell hooks 1995, p. 16). Indeed, she notes, 'we pondered whether Black folks and white folks can ever be subjects together if white people remain unable to hear Black rage, if it is the sound of that rage which must always remain repressed, contained, trapped in the realm of the unspeakable ... Perhaps then it is that "presence", the assertion of subjectivity colonizers do not want to see, that surfaces when the colonized express rage' (bell hooks 1995, p. 12).

In her work, bell hooks constantly repeats this message, this call to open spaces for affective expressions, for the aesthetics of political relations. This chapter is a modest attempt to answer this call with the voices and performances of racialized youths in Saint-Michel and Little Burgundy. Race is crucial to any understanding of urban aesthetic political relations. We had three objectives here. First, we wanted to explore how the epistemology of Blackness can work with and against racialization, to transcend its logics. Emphasizing what is constructed in these neighbourhoods can attune our sensitivity to the unpredictable, rather than the actuarial logic of racial profiling and patterning. If we limit ourselves to an analytical reading of situations of subordination and subjugation (which are enforced by policing institutions), we cannot capture the complexity of aesthetic agency and transformative aesthetics (using disidentification and transfiguration) performed in everyday life. Tivon explains this brilliantly: '*This is the south side of Elgin Terrace. The two blocks surrounding these backyards are rammed packed with low-income housing project buildings and houses. I used one camera to take these two pictures. While taking these pictures I was being watched by six different cameras. Due to past crime in the area, the city and the police decided to secure Little Burgundy with over 50 surveillance cameras. The areas you see in the pictures above have approximately eight cameras alone. Privacy is not your backyard*' (mapcollab. org). So, who is watching who? Tivon's use of the camera is personalized and expresses his world in all its arbitrariness and messiness, his gaze on those set on keeping his movements and behaviours in check, on those surveillance cameras that work more like scanners: looking for patterns and regularity. The epistemology of Blackness works with Tivon's camera, Kabisha's spoken words, and Giulio's beatboxing 'lower frequency'.

Second, we attempted to play with the difference between stigmatizing representations appealing to the cognitive and communicative forms appealing to affective and precognitive registers. On the one hand, we contrasted negative media representations and policies requiring profiling and actuarial calculations with their micro-local deployment in specific ethnographic encounters such as the BBQ, the end of Ramadan, and the Morocco–Algeria match. On the other, through the MapCollab project, we sought to explore affective and aesthetic communicative forms such as the multimedia guides that invite visitors to articulate their cognitive and affective experiences of the neighbourhoods.

Finally, we explored the politics of the aesthetic gestures produced and performed in these contexts by underlining the modalities of power at play in racist encounters. We focused on ways in which racism works through seduction and attraction (or its opposite: revulsion). We saw with the White woman's comment on eating habits in Africa, uttered to exclude

Stéphane and his friends from Montreal's civility, that beyond conscious will or interest, such political gestures (the woman's comment) have concrete painful and harmful effects. In her raging critique (in bell hook's sense) of the lack of punishment for the young White man who stabbed someone at school in 2005, Élisabeth expresses injustice: '*We cannot be teen-agers because of the neighbourhood.*'[37] Why, she asks, is the media immediately here when something happens, transforming the neighbourhood into an '*affaire de clowns*' (a clown's thing)? Because of stigmatization, youths cannot be transgressive like they should be. The historically and socially constructed pathologizing racist associations attached (beyond their control) to their skin colour and spatialized in the dominant representations that circulate around their neighbourhood are always used to explain their youthful behaviour, curtailing their movements. Robyn Maynard echoes Élisabeth when she remarks, along with historian Robin Bernstein, that youthful innocence is 'raced white'. As she points out, 'Black youth are often treated as suspects instead of as the children they are, in the very place where children get socialized and educated. Experiencing this typecasting and demonization is deeply harmful to Black youth who are in their formative years' (Maynard 2017, p. 217).

How are racialized youths political? How do they assert their political agency? By mobilizing various 'frequencies' through their performances, by intensifying their rage (bell hooks 1995), by constructing unexpected 'universes of operation' (Simone 2010, 2016), by transfiguring, disidentifying, and playing with modalities of power that are accessible to them. If, as we will see in the next chapter, direct forms of protest are much more available to White students than to racialized youths, the youths of Saint-Michel and Little Burgundy are nonetheless fundamentally political, even if perhaps less visibly. In order to hear, see, and feel such politics, one needs to walk and ride in the neighbourhoods with an epistemology of Blackness.

One of the modalities of power available to racialized youths is seduction. How to dress, how to respond to police officers; youths are not submissive, but strategically seductive. Marie is 19 years old. When we asked about her thoughts on police officers, she explained: '*It all depends on how you are with them, your behaviour. If sometimes I am arrested and I know I'm not legal ... So the way I speak: I am nice, I don't argue, I'm not arrogant. Suspicion will be suspended because you were nice today, I give you a chance. It is settled this way. You don't have to be really arrogant. Police officers act according to you, the way you get at them, if you're an asshole, they will be assholes.*'[38]

Another example before we move to the urban world of student strikers; let us hear how Xavier empowers himself through seduction, exercising aesthetic agency by being acutely aware of aesthetic judgements that will affect how he is perceived and the possibilities afforded to him: *'I can avoid wearing jeans, like I wear my jeans low. When I lower my jeans people, the first image they will have of me is: he's a badass. But if I wear my jeans normally, I wear normal shirts also, everyone will say this is someone, is someone good. They will learn to know me, but if they see I have low jeans, they will say: Oh this one, it's a bastard and I don't want to know anything about him.'*[39]

As Élisabeth so aptly explains, transgression is not available to racialized youths because when they do visibly transgress mainstream norms, the media transforms the neighbourhood into a circus and their actions are explained with actuarial profiling and embodied racism. However, political action manifests itself through various registers (the affective and the cognitive), channels (performance, emotions, ways of being and doing), and modalities (seduction, domination, authority, coercion, manipulation).

Notes

1. The following is based on excerpts from our field notes. Dialogues were not recorded and are presented from memory, except where they are explicitly translated based on subsequent recorded interviews.
2. 'J'ai déjà vu que les policiers sont en train de parler aux jeunes bla bla bla… Ils essaient de leur expliquer comment faire comment ne pas faire. Mais moi personnellement, j'ai jamais eu de contact avec les policiers. En fait, moi c'est juste Rodney à qui j'ai parlé parce qu'on était dans un barbershop ensemble, mais les policiers et moi, on n'est pas trop amis parce que moi j'essaie de faire… j'essaie de trouver un chemin parallèle avec les autres, comme on va jamais se croiser en fait.'
3. "Si y en a un autre qui veut essayer ça, essayer de battre une petite fille de même pour un rien, je vais être le premier à venir vous chercher. Ça c'est un gros épais et je ne veux plus ça.' Puis les gars-là ils ont même pas dit un mot. Ils sont une trentaine de gars-là, y avait plus 'Mais pourquoi' là. C'est la prévention qu'on fait, les liens que l'on crée qui nous permet quand on a une répression à faire d'aller passer le message comme ça. Puis le message était clair.'
4. 'Sur le long terme t'es gagnant sur toute la ligne. Cette fois-là, il nous a évité une confrontation juste parce qu'un jour on a été s'assoir dans le salon avec sa mère. Spécial, non? Ça me fait capoter ça à chaque fois. Puis c'est toujours des anecdotes ça qui ressortent…'
5. A collège d'enseignement général et professionnel (known in English as a general and vocational college) is a postsecondary education institution, generally attended at 17–19 years old. Cegeps grant Diplomas of

College Studies in preparatory pre-university education programmes, as well as professional and technical education programmes.

6. 'Y'a beaucoup de nuances à faire tu vois, parce que chaque policier, chaque personne c'est pas la même chose. Mais par contre, le système en tant que tel fait que y a certaines tendances qui sont lourdes. Puis aussi, c'est aussi un genre de dynamique de groupe que les policiers vivent en tant que tel tu vois. Puis y a une vraie fraternité aussi de la police en tant que telle. Donc beaucoup de fois, ils vont se mettre en rapport de force : c'est eux contre nous, tu vois ce que je veux dire? '

7. 'exprimer justement mon appartenance ethnique, disons avec mes cheveux par exemple avec mes dreads.'

8. Maynard (2017, p. 222) notes that the concept of 'push-out' has been developed by Black activists and researchers as a corollary to the term 'dropout', which 'disguises the structural racism both inside and outside of the education system that impacts Black children's ability to remain in school'. She explains that, as a result, '"dropping out" or "low academic achievement" can more accurately be described as the result of a concerted "push out"' (Maynard 2017, p. 222).

9. The following youth voices are taken from the mapcollab.org website, as well as recordings of conversations made during the workshops. Each youth decided whether they wanted us to use their real name or a pseudonym.

10. 'Hola amigos y amigas, welcome to BURGZ. Hello everybody, a world full of surprises awaits you. Georges Vanier metro is the only metro station that is in LITTLE BURGUNDY. It is the main mode of transportation coming in and leaving Little Burgundy. We don't judge a book by its cover. We don't judge a person without knowing her, so we don't judge BURGZ without knowing its stories. Welcome to the Little Burgundy neighbourhood, a neighbourhood full of obstacles and a growing neighbourhood. Love, hate, ups, downs, whatever, I remain Burgundy.'

11. 'le monde sentent vraiment que Burgz c'est leur maison. Je vais pas rentrer chez toi sans rien dire pis, personne ne peut rentrer sans demander.'

12. 'Sur la rue Des Seigneurs, » writes Imad, « trop de chose sont arrivées. Des frères se sont envolés et d'autre se sont écrasés le crime, leur mentalité puisque la société les a délaissé. Des rêveurs, des jeunes plein d'ambition freiner par une mauvaise réputation; double effort pour les mêmes félicitations. On part du bas, la route est donc plus longue chez nous soit on se donne la main ou on se ronge les ongles!!!'

13. 'les gens avaient pas le choix de se battre. Mais là aujourd'hui, c'est un choix pour eux.'
14. 'Chacun règle ses problèmes à sa manière & le Canal Lachine est un lieu qui m'a permis de m'échapper de mes problèmes.'
15. 'Ce quartier est comme un parc d'attractions. Quand on y rentre, on ne veut pas en ressortir!'
16. '- Est-ce que quatre ans c'est le plus de temps que tu as été comme installé dans un endroit? - Ouais, ouais, ouais. Puis je peux te dire que c'est quand même un changement, c'est comme un changement vraiment. Je sais pas comment te dire, tu sais lorsque tu es tellement habitué de changer tout le temps, mais tu sais arriver à ma deuxième année dans le même house. Là j'étais comme 'damn, mom c'est comme pas nous, tout ça.' Je suis comme tanné, tu sais.'
17. 'Il l'a poignardé, ils ont même pas appelé la police!'
18. 'On se sentait comme des rats de laboratoire. On n'était plus des élèves, juste des rats de laboratoire.'
19. We analytically explore the performativity of this aesthetic strategy in depth in the next section. The notion of dubbing over past temporalities in temporal collages is from Iain Chambers (2017, p. 92).
20. 'Enfin … la cloche a sonné … Enfin … je peux m'évader. Enfin … je peux m'exprimer.'
21. 'L'école Louis-Joseph-Papineau ressemble à un bloc de béton échoué au milieu d'un champ. Un bunker sans fenêtres, blanc délavé.'
22. 'Tu sais c'est une journaliste que je respecte beaucoup. Je savais qu'elle avait une stratégie. Je connaissais sa conclusion et elle a choisi son chemin pour dénoncer une situation, un besoin de ressources dans ces milieux-là. C'était sa conclusion: « arrêtez de penser que tout se fait facilement ». Mais le chemin qu'elle a pris ça a fait du tort, puis en même temps j'ai été surpris de la réaction des jeunes.'
23. 'Il n'y a personne d'autre que moi-même qui devrait décider du visage de Saint-Michel, pas même les statistiques.'
24. 'Arabes, Haitiens, Québécois et Sud-Américains jouent ensemble … C'est comme un médicament … mon quartier, c'est ma vie.'
25. 'Ni pour la gauche, ni pour la droite … pas vraiment autonome … amoureux même si pas d'identité.'
26. 'On a commencé le travail ensemble à MapCollab, ça me permet aussi d'écrire un texte sur l'espoir. Et puis au jour de jour, je continue aussi à écrire, ça fait travailler mon cerveau et ma mémoire. Toujours écrire, ça se peut que je sois au travail quand quelque chose te viens à la tête tu l'écris. Donc, je dis, c'est une bonne façon vraiment de parler de ton parcours, de savoir qui tu es, de savoir qu'est-ce que

tu veux être dans la vie et ça peut, ça peut rester comme un exemple pour la génération future. Et moi c'est comme, je veux aussi, je veux être un modèle pour mes frères, je sais pas de quelle manière, mais je veux être un modèle pour mes frères.'

27. For a video transmission of the afternoon, produced by Mtélé.ca, but which ends before the *'Go Habs Go!'* chanting, see https://www.youtube.com/watch?v=pEJnodGOi5k.

28. 'C'est des jeunes qui ont malheureusement peut-être moins de moyens, plus de défis. Donc, c'est des jeunes, je veux pas dire qu'ils sont à risque, mais c'est des jeunes qui n'ont pas été malheureusement euh … gâtés par le destin, je ne sais pas trop.'

29. 'C'est ben beau, c'est défavorisé oui, par rapport à un autre quartier mais ça fait pas en sorte qui a moins de potentiel là. Il faut leur donner la confiance, la possibilité de faire d'autres choses à ces jeunes là. C'est ça la possibilité quand ils font une activité sportive, quand ils sont impliqués dans les projets.'

30. 'Ils vont respecter l'individu; ils vont te respecter toi. Toi tu connais bien, tu vas dire "Moi les gars c'est moi qui organise telle affaire s'il te plait", les gars vont dire "Je te respecte, pas de problème. Tu fais ce que tu veux, il ne se passera rien".'

31. Mothers United against Racism.

32. 'Et ça, ça peut avoir des incidences catastrophiques sur la vie, pour la suite des choses pour ces jeunes là, donc, et un de ces jeunes-là a fait l'objet d'une arrestation, etc … assez musclée. Et il y a eu, je me rappelle, il y a eu une conférence de presse qui avait été donnée sur le Plan Robert avec deux des jeunes, leurs familles, etc. Et il y a eu une poursuite judiciaire qui, en passant, a conduit à une condamnation du SPVM.'

33. 'Donc là on passe par le parking, et là il y a une vieille madame qui est là dans sa voiture et tout là et qui dit "Hé, là là, hé on n'est pas en Afrique ici. On mange pas dans les rues." Tu vois qu'est-ce que je veux dire/situation tu vois … très très hum … qui … un racisme qui qui s'exprime en tant que tel, tu vois. Donc on est trois jeunes tu vois: Moi qui sourit, l'autre qui court puis qui essaie de frapper la voiture, puis l'autre qui fait rien.'

34. It is noteworthy to mention that Laferrière was elected to the Academie Française in 2013 and has received many prestigious prizes and honors in Quebec and in Canada, including Officer of the Ordre de Montréal, Officer of the National Order of Quebec, and Officer of the Order of Canada.

35. 'Ma plus grande fierté depuis que je suis arrivé dans le quartier, c'est que les textes que j'avais commencé à écrire … j'avais commencé à écrire des textes pour Haïti – je parlais d'Haïti – quand je suis arrivé ici, c'est une autre cause que je devrais défendre (en riant) tu comprends? Quand je commence à défendre cette cause-là puis quand j'écris des textes et puis quand j'arrive quelque part aussi pour dire que moi, je viens de Saint-Michel, j'écris tel ou tel texte … tout le monde: Wow! Good job! Parce que quand tu vois quelqu'un qui est positif dans un quartier où tout le monde … parce qu'il est noir …'

36. 'On ne peut pas rester là – comme à recevoir juste des balles comme ta-ta-ta-ta-ta-ta – on est en train de nous mitrailler avec des mitraillettes. On est en train de dire plein de choses … de s'insulter avec des mots. Quand je parle de mitraillettes – c'est comme des mots-là – on est en train de nous foudroyer avec ça là.'

37. 'On ne peut pas être ado à cause du quartier.'

38. 'Tout dépend de la façon que t'es avec eux, pour ton comportement. Si des fois je me fais arrêter et je sais que je suis pas légale. Mais la façon que je parle, je suis gentille, je donne pas d'argument, je suis pas arrogante avec. Les soupçons seront suspendus, puisque t'a été sympa aujourd'hui, je te laisse une chance. Ca s'arrange comme ça. Tu n'es pas obligé d'être vraiment arrogant. Les policiers ils agissent selon toi, la façon tu arrives envers eux, si tu es chiant ils vont être chiants.'

39. 'Je peux pas porter des jeans comme je descends mon jeans. Quand je descends mon jeans les gens, la première image qu'ils auront de moi c'est un petit voyou mais quand je mets mon jean normal je mets mes chemises normales aussi puis tout le monde va dire que c'est quelqu'un, c'est quelqu'un de correct. Ils vont apprendre à me connaître mais quand ils voient que j'ai des jeans qui sont bas ils vont dire que oh lui là, c'est un bâtard je veux rien savoir de lui.'

FIGURE 3.0 'Pots and Pans.' *Source:* illustration by Lukas Beeckman.

Chapter 3

The Urban Political World of Student Strikers

Quincy is a tall sporty blond man. He is very spiritual: he practices meditation, he searches for alternative ways of knowing. When we met him in 2013, we went on a long walk that began at Place Émilie-Gamelin.[1] As we passed the Cegep du Vieux-Montreal, he reconstituted for Julie-Anne his memory of being there during the 2012 student strikes, known as the Maple Spring. He vividly described the barricade that blocked the college entrance and how he felt all this metal was aggressive and violent. The Cegep du Vieux-Montreal sits right in front of the social housing complex Habitations Jeanne-Mance. When Julie-Anne met him again a week later to watch the video they had co-produced during this walk, he expressed the following as the apartment complex appeared on screen, ignoring the Cegep du Vieux-Montreal which was the focus of the frame:

QUINCY   *And as we were walking to one of the apartments, I realized it was right in front of the spot. So I started talking about like space, and I started talking about the violence that I fear being out in that regard, or people knowing that I came out and that I'm not in a monogamous relationship. But that you know I'm open to same-sex interactions. And then we ended up like going to their apartment and dancing and I was a little bit high. I smoked some weed. And then my friend, another guy, he had been very interested in what I was saying, and I started getting the impression that maybe he, like he and I had a connection. So that maybe he was going to like reveal something to me about how he felt about me, but I didn't really feel ready for that so as we were leaving we were having this sort of conversation but not really, you know? It was kinda like beating around the bush and there was a palpable tension, like sexual tension. And as he left a van came by and they yelled, 'fucking faggots'.*

JULIE-ANNE   *Ahhhh.*

Youth Urban Worlds: Aesthetic Political Action in Montreal, First Edition.
Julie-Anne Boudreau and Joëlle Rondeau.
© 2021 John Wiley & Sons Ltd. Published 2021 by John Wiley & Sons Ltd.

QUINCY   *Yeah.*
JULIE-ANNE   *And this happened how long before we met here?*
QUINCY   *This was, no this was, yeah this was about a week before we met.*

In this excerpt from our second interview, Quincy interprets his biometric data. The peak occurred when we were standing in front of the college. The first time, Quincy spoke about how ambiguous he felt towards the use of violence in political action. Standing there provoked a strong affective charge, which, as we learned in the second interview, was not explicitly related to what we were talking about (the violence of the barricade), but rather to this specific place, where he had experienced an intense moment just a week before we met. However, his sexual and political experiences were intertwined in his analysis:

QUINCY   *Yeah, and I ended up chasing after them on my bike, and this is where all of this was like playing in my head: the idea of like, I was being victimized, I was being othered, I was being hurt, trying to be hurt, and how am I going to answer to that? You know? But I like became enraged and I started to chase after the van. They were stopped at a red light and I pulled up next to the window passenger, and I looked in and I probably looked kind of nuts (I had a big beard at this point). And I looked in and I saw this sixteen-year-old boy, you know, and when he saw me looking in the window he went like: ah aha ah [making distress sounds]. And he went like: 'It's the guy on the bike, it's the guy on the bike' [imitates terrified voice]. 'It's the guy on the bike, it's the guys on the bike, it's the guy on the bike.' And like I saw his soul, you know, I was still a bit high, but I could see like that I had totally inverted the like. . .*
JULIE-ANNE   *Power relation? . . .*
QUINCY   *Like, so like all this has been going on through my head. So you know when we talked about this, and like just the idea of like, you know, when you said it now: the violence can be a peaceful act, it was like pfft [imitates crashing sound or two things hitting each other]. Wow! Violence, a peaceful act. I don't know, you know, but like having just come out of this experience, it's like well what's violence, and you know, do we need to stand out? And how do we do it skilfully? How do we do it respectfully? Peacefully? You know? Yeah.*

Quincy's spiritual experiments make him very sensitive to power relations and the political use of violence during episodes of political contestations such as the strike. He consistently analyses 'Politics' in Rancière's purist definition of a rupture with established power relations, in relation to his very personal political gestures – in this case, chasing the teenager who had called him 'faggot'. For him to reveal this story during our second interview, as he was interpreting his biometric data, was a political act: by putting words on his political gestures, he constituted himself as an actor 'coming out' of the closet, both sexually and with regards to his stance on violence as a 'peaceful act'.

The intertwining of the intimate and the political can be explained by the feeling of living in a suspended time and space, in a sort of rupture with the past. Studies on carnivals illustrate this very well. The strike city was felt as a moment during which rules no longer mattered. What mattered was the empowering feeling of the here and now. In February 2012, Montreal was swept by the massive mobilization of students opposed to a 75% tuition fee increase announced by the provincial government of Jean Charest. What came about was the longest and largest student strike in the history of Quebec, which quickly evolved into an unprecedented 'social crisis' (Chiasson-LeBel 2012). More than 300 000 students were mobilized into a struggle against the government that lasted more than eight months. In Montreal, hundreds of demonstrations, rallies, and economic disruption activities were held daily between February and August 2012.

Although the protest events were mainly organized by the three largest student unions in the first weeks of the conflict, this rapidly became a more horizontal and bottom-up movement. Facing a stubborn government, students turned to confrontation and direct action (Savard and Cyr 2014). Their repertoire was diversified, including artistic expression and active appropriation of urban spaces and the imaginary (Labrie 2015). Police reaction was brutal, leading to 3500 arrests – a record number, some three and a half times more than in any of the previous 20 years (Dupuis-Déri 2013).

In this chapter, we return to this specific moment of Montreal's history.[2] As opposed to other chapters in this book, here we focus on an explicitly political event. Yet, we do not want to analyse it using the traditional sociological tools measuring power relations, strategies, and organization. As valid and useful as they are, they do not help in teasing out the aesthetic elements of this political historical moment. Instead, we work with emotional mapping, life narratives, biometric data, and video to analyse strikers' urban trajectories and their emotionally charged places.

Quincy expresses his ambiguity towards violence and his efforts to supersede his aggressiveness. In other words, he is acutely conscious that whatever we do, intentionally or not, it has an effect in the world. Following his example, this chapter explores the question of political effects. We consider the effective reach of different modalities of power – and of seduction in particular – when agency is distributed among various actors and objects in specific situations. When analysing the hundreds of stories we heard during our interviews with strikers, we seek to highlight the role played by their mode of orientation towards the future (Munn 1992, p. 106). How important is the future to them? Are they casual about it? Anxious? Do they anticipate it? Do they speak of a near or an indefinite future? We also want to characterize their conception of change. People normally decide to be politically active because they want to affect the world around them; they want to have political effect. How do the strikers conceive of the effects of their acts, and on what scale do they view them? Do they focus on personal changes? Group change? Social transformation? We highlight the sequence of these gestures in situations of action. How did the strikers act and react? What was the role of strategic thinking and planning?

Becoming a Striker: Pregnant Moments 'Breaking the Real'

> We are living alienated lives and striking moments, with my friends we call these: breaking the real. Because we are breaking a certain order of things, an affective relationship to the world . . . A striking movement is like a liminal moment. Things are undetermined, rules aren't as clear as during productive everyday life. Anything can happen. You can wake up one day and end up at the end of the day in this or that action making this or that banner, getting to know this or that person, consoling this or that person you don't know. It's like a social body came to exist instead of a multitude of atomized individuals.[3]

Fred has been living in the Rosemont neighbourhood for about a decade. He was very involved in the strike. Like Quincy's carnavalesque intertwinement of personal political gestures and collective political action, he describes here a pregnant moment. 'Breaking the real' in these 'liminal moments' constitutes a nondirectional conception of temporality. We do not know where it will lead us, we simply feel it and let ourselves go with the flow of moments articulating themselves.

We began our interviews by asking strikers *why* they decided to get involved in the movement's activities. In their responses, they insisted on friendship, the confirmation of their identity ('*I had leftist tendencies*', '*I used to be involved*'), self-realization ('*it is empowering*', '*to acquire a kind of strength*'), pleasure, excitement, and hope (see Figure 3.1). These are essentially positive motives: strikers emphasized an affective relation to their commitment more than a rationally developed ideological discourse. They described their involvement as an intuitive intertwining of situations, where

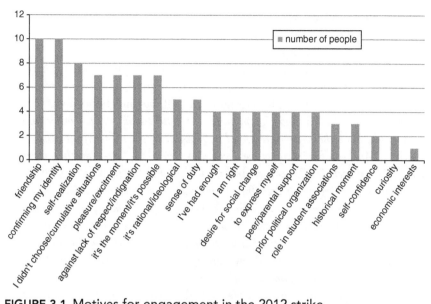

FIGURE 3.1 Motives for engagement in the 2012 strike.

they did not 'decide' at one specific point to become active, they just did so. In other words, we were asking the wrong question. They were not explaining *why* they got involved, but *how*.

Friendship, pleasure, self-realization, indignation, hope. . . These are the reasons evoked by strikers to justify their involvement. Walking with them throughout their personal 'city on strike' during this project has given us a much richer sense of *how* they became strikers. They became strikers because they could constantly rely on embodied, tiny political gestures. Kim remembers one time she was trapped by the police on Ste. Catherine Street: *'I will always remember this girl. I don't remember her face, but she took my hand, everyone was holding hands to help calm ourselves to avoid running, for walking slowly, to avoid hurting ourselves. And it's that, this feeling . . . and I'm not someone who touches, I'm somewhat misanthrope as a person, I say this humbly . . .'*[4] Or again, Sarah poignantly remembers as we stand in front of the building they occupied on the McGill campus: *'So none of us knew what to do . . . and I remember telling to one of my friends who had done so much work and everyone really respected him, and I remember being like "Look like, I really think that if you were to go and say what you thought was best" – like he's more experienced in this stuff – "like, I really think people will listen to you" . . . And he did and he said we should all hold arms and that's what we did. It just gave people something to do. Who knows if it was effective, but it was like so much more calming when you're standing there and you have like two people on either side of you and everyone is bracing themselves for you don't know what, but . . .'*

Touching, holding arms: these are affective pregnant moments that gradually transform youths into strikers. More than simply individual strikers, these pregnant moments constitute collective subjects. Ivan remembers the first time he went out on his balcony in the Villeray neighbourhood to bang on a casserole: *'It was more a moment, we would look at each other and we were proud to be there, we were proud to be together, even if we didn't know each other . . . And you know, when we decided to take to the street together, when we were leaving each from a corner and we would meet in the centre of the street, to continue walking afterward. But it was a little spontaneous, it happened by a simple look, there were no words from someone who would say to the other: let's do it. It was spontaneous like this. We were all on the same wave length, and that, you know, there was something happening that was . . . like that was out of just words or something like that. It was really going towards something that came to get us inside, our values, who we really were.'*[5]

Pots and pans are central artefacts of the strikes. When people began to bang on them every night at 8 p.m., strikers mingled with neighbours. Ting tang bang . . . a concert of pots and pans began to fill the hot summer air. There were no words, just neighbours on their balconies and on the street, out and making improvised music to tell the Quebec provincial government that its law restricting the right to demonstrate was unacceptable. In the meantime, hundreds of students had gathered downtown at Place Émilie-Gamelin for another 'illegal' demonstration against the rise of tuition fees. It was May 2012. They had been on strike for four months and, despite violent confrontations with the police, nightly demonstrations were consistent. Like every other night, the police took to their megaphones and declared the demonstration illegal. They asked the students to disperse. To this, the students responded as ever: *'We go forward, go forward, not backward!'*[6]

Artefacts downtown were different from Villeray's pots and pans; the sounds were different, too. Roger gives a glimpse of another pregnant moment during a nightly demonstration on Ste. Catherine Street: *'and then, there's a moment when people began to scream: "A united people will never be defeated!" And I was looking towards the east . . . The only thing we could hear apart from people's screams was the echo of these screams on the buildings. It must have lasted about ten, twelve seconds. There were three slogans that really hit in well. Everybody was synchronized and everything . . . And then there was a move, really, ehh, not a move but a moment of . . . nothing was moving, there was only the sound of people, and they pushed a grenade on the crowd, ten feet over my head, and, and then I remember that something broke in me . . . that, maybe it's naïve but if there are ten thousand people screaming that, and that this is the only thing you hear, that's it, the guts, the balls and the arrogance to fucking throw a grenade on them, it's . . . you know, it's like: "OK, that's how it's going to be".*[7]

Roger's pregnant moment was imbued at first with a strong feeling of empowerment and solidarity, but when the police threw grenades at the crowd, it was rage and indignation that began to circulate on the street. As strong as these affects were, when we ask Roger and the others why they participated in specific activities where they risked being arrested or hurt by the police or the fearful crowd, they tend to use a publicly acceptable and rationalized justification. Ivan, for instance, says: *'there was also a hyperrational process behind all of this, in the sense of how can I get involved, where do I get involved, and where is the limit. I don't mean limit in the sense of "limit", but it was my way of defining myself at the moment.'* They similarly evoke a sense of duty (*'against an unjust state'*).

Ideological explanations come more forcefully when explaining their participation in risky activities than when they are asked to speak more generally of their involvement. Here again, however, peer support is central: *'I knew I wasn't alone. We were collectively risking something'*; *'it was not as scary because you're there with people'*. Even when they feel the need to justify their engagement with publicly acceptable motives (duty, rational political arguments), affective relations remain important. When we speak about 'risks', Christine highlights her intuitive skills in detecting them: *'We were walking and we were saying: "Ok, this really smells likes a trap, a gang of small kids who never demonstrated, who doesn't know anything". You know, because you become, you develop demonstrator's aptitudes.'*[8] Pascal similarly explains that this experience of risk, these intuitive skills, are much more important than preparing in advance. In short, he emphasizes being in reaction rather than preparation mode: *'Let's say I was seeing there was trouble. Well I would try to stay a bit on the side. I didn't feel like throwing myself between the police and the guy he wanted to hit, things like that. I would think a little about what I was doing, but it wouldn't go further than that . . . It would also depend if I had reasons to think it was imminent, I don't know, when the police were charging hitting on their shield, well the risk seemed more imminent than when there were just walking normally looking at us. It was going and coming, I was thinking, and then I wouldn't be thinking anymore.'*[9]

Intuition comes with experience, and as the Maple Spring unfolded, experience accumulated and tolerance to risks became augmented. Christine pursues this: *'Probably at the beginning there are things I wouldn't dare doing, but as I was getting involved in the conflict, and in the sort of increase of pressure and tension, I ended up boosting myself and accepting probably to increase my risks. I accepted going to demos where I would probably not normally go. At the same time, this curb went down again from the moment when, I think there are consciousness moments where, ok, there's really a risk I will get hurt violently. You know when you have seen big cases of injury, completely at random, then I think there is a bit of questioning like: Am I ready to go there? You know. I was ready to get arrested, I was ready to be peppered, but you know, but am I ready to be physically hurt, permanently? I think that at that moment, I stepped back a little. I think that, in fact, I realized at that time that I was afraid for real, which I probably had not felt before.'*[10]

It is through experience that reflection emerges. Strikers did not evaluate much before acting; they were not predominantly acting strategically. On Facebook and Twitter, a colour code circulated, rating the risk level of each action. But most strikers did not care much about risks. Gina says it all: *'you risk stepping outside the status quo and you risk starting things on, in a direction that changes.'* As Wajdi puts it, they were more sensitive to the consequences of inaction than action:

JULIE-ANNE   *Were you thinking about the consequences of your participation?*

WAJDI   *In a way, we would say we were only thinking about that. Because we live in a world that is self-destructive in many aspects. If we don't do it, personally, if we don't ask the question of what will be the consequences of staying with our arms crossed or the consequences of taking the risk to do something uncalculated, blurry, chaotic, but that can really have a considerable social impact, or environmental, well I was thinking only of the consequences of what I was going to do [laughter].*

JULIE-ANNE   *Were you thinking at your personal consequences?*

WAJDI   *Well, personal consequences, I have trouble dissociating the personal from the collective. The old feminist slogan says that the personal is political. It remains true everyday. Yeah, I really have difficulty in untangling these two things. On the other hand, I made many friends in this and there are many positive personal consequences.*[11]

The strikers' feelings towards risks are more experiential, intuitive, and perhaps transgressive. They do not emphasize planning and strategies. They speak more of tactics – which implies immediate reactions in situations – than of planned gestures. They further emphasize a strong feeling of improvisation during actions. Umberto puts it this way: *'I don't feel like it was out of control, like it was chaotic and I feel like decisions were always being made so it was never like, random. It wasn't like a riot out of control. I don't want to suggest that, but I don't feel like there was a clear plan and we were following that plan. I feel like most things were like "now we're going to do this thing; it's kinda . . . it's pretty spontaneous" and then you would develop a habit around that.'*

It is not that the strikers did not spend hours organizing various actions: teach-ins, economic perturbation actions, marches, artistic performances, and so on. Some actions were genuinely spontaneous, but most were organized by someone. But what most strikers retain from their city on strike is a strong feeling of improvisation. When an action was launched, no one had control over its unfolding. Spontaneity became habit. This was not chaos, but rather a nonlinear conception of time whereby cumulative situations were intertwined, whereby actors adapted and improved.

This lack of centralized control was extensively criticized by the media. It was the basis of the government's refusal to recognize the student actions as legitimate. But many students valued it highly. Let us consider Wajdi's words:

WAJDI   *For me, it's crystal clear that if things had been under control, we would have fucked up. In the sense that we had a moment of collective strike. It was a moment when we gave ourselves the means to be asocial in all respects, through the actions we were taking as much as through the ideas we were juggling. There were many people who dared to think, and say, and do things they wouldn't have done otherwise. And these things, if they had been under control, if they would've had to report to someone, it wouldn't have happened.*

JULIE-ANNE   *When you say asocial, you mean outside of society?*

WAJDI   *Yes, I mean etymologically. So to my view, it is controlling. Yes, I think that people had an ethic, a morality, so many things were controlled in that sense. But in the sense of institutional control, no, it was really a moment of chaos. I'm really happy because it opened many possibilities. I saw more stars in people's eyes during this strike than during all my university studies.*[12]

These 'stars in people's eyes' were associated with a sense of fulfilment during the strikers' experiences in specific moments and places. We wanted to see whether such situational stories would be balanced by more linear temporalities. We carefully analysed their feelings towards risk-taking, because the notion of 'risk' implies an evaluation of the consequences of an act (and thus a linear temporality, a projection of the future as the consequence of the present). A career plan is an example of linear temporality, whereby a future is conceived over the long term, resulting from the successive achievement of predefined steps (like climbing a ladder). Most students never mention their careers when we ask them about the impact of the strikes. Others laugh at these 'risks'. Sarah says, '*and if classes don't happen, finals don't happen . . . you know, it will affect the rest of your life and bla, bla, bla.*' Or, again, Alain is finishing his Cegep when we meet him. He has beautiful curly hair and is very passionate when speaking of the strike. His parents disapproved of his involvement, saying he should do something with his life. He would respond, '*But I am doing something with my life!*' Comparing the fact that he had to wake up at 5:30 a.m. to organize this or that action to his brother's sleeping in as he was still going to classes, he is adamant that political work is a good thing for his 'career': '*But when they will read about the Spring of 2012, well they will say, they will feel like this energy of happiness: "Hey! You did something with your life." You didn't do anything at the same time. You know, even if a demo is not commodifiable, in the sense that you cannot receive a salary because you participated in a demonstration, at the same time, man, it's like, while you were sleeping or you were doing something, there was a historical moment happening just next to you.*'[13]

Students value the 'here and now' because this is where and how they self-realize. These moments come to define their whole life, without consideration of the future. They are totalizing. As we walk on University Street, Sarah tells us about a conversation she had with a friend. She had bought new shoes over the weekend, as had her roommate. When they realized they had both bought the same ones, Sarah said to her friend: '*What is our life like?*' '*Our life,*' she concludes, '*can be synthesized by demonstrations. Even during weekends we're preparing our protests.*' When we meet Sarah one year after the strike, she explains to us how difficult it was to fit back into linear time: '*And, I like had pretty bad anxiety about just about everything and about being on campus and doing school work and meeting deadlines and like . . . I just didn't have that ability anymore, whereas before the strike it had never been a problem. I was like a perfect student kind of thing and like . . . but afterwards I really struggled getting back into it and like, I think a lot of it was because we never really made a lot of time to deal with stuff, like . . . go home to sleep, get up and go to work.*' The strike was totalizing, totally in the here and now.

Béatrice similarly laughingly expresses this totalizing involvement in the here and now. She speaks of the '*sharp strikitist syndrome: you're always humming demonstration slogans . . . you are dreaming of Gabriel Nadeau-Dubois,*[14] *when you are walking on the street you evaluate the risks of being trapped by the police . . .*'[15] Ivan insists on his aversion to 'tomorrow': '*You know, we go downtown, do we go or not, do we go sleeping, do we work tomorrow morning, you know it's [pause], you know, it's boring at the same time to ask these questions. It's boring not to say, not to believe . . . [pause] not to be totally immersed finally in what we are doing, in what we believe. You know, not, aaaarrgh, tomorrow tomorrow no, look, right now, in the present, this is not what I believe in. I believe we should continue, we have to fight to demonstrate, we have to do that, we have to continue.*'[16]

When the future is mentioned, it is closely related to what they are doing in the here and now. They speak for instance about how they felt the urge to 'be there' in order to be able to talk about this presence to their future children. Roger says, '*I was 30 years old and it was important for me to be there, simply because in 20 years, I don't want to say I sat on my ass during this time, you know . . . I have the impression that next time, it will come very soon. We will not wait 35 years before it happens again.'*[17] Their future is thus embodied in the present.

Roger, Sarah, Fred, Ivan, Wajdi, and many others describe their involvement in the 2012 strikes as a series of totalizing pregnant moments. They emphasize certain artefacts: pots and pans, the police megaphones, grenades. They describe how at certain moments they experienced an aesthetic appearance: the united song of the crowd, the musicality of the pots and pans, the arms braced in fear of the police. To express this in Marcotte's (1997, p. 150) words: 'On the one hand, the "spectacular" [the aesthetic appearance] stops, freezes, glorifies the present time; on the other hand, the importance given to look, fashion, dating, periodization, makes of time a pure succession of moments that evidently has nothing to do with what we call a historical movement.' It is only as they experience these pregnant moments that youths gradually constitute themselves as an acting subject: the striker.

Walking the City: Space During and After the Strike

> in this space of mobility, in this time freed from the duty of orientation, action unfolds as a vital activity, game, party sometimes. (Marcotte 1997, p. 151)

If we were to identify a collective actor for this period, it would be the 'walker', because 'walking is demonstrating, but it is also marching towards change' (Fortin 2013, p. 518; our translation). The street was predominant on the mental maps produced by the youths at the beginning of our first meeting. The street served to relate significant places and composed a reticular conception of space.

Matt draws a very affective map, where streets are predominant (see Figure 3.2). He indicates that the Palais des Congrès is a 'dangerous labyrinth'. He strikes away Chinatown, which is adjacent to the Congress Center, where violent confrontations with the police took place in April 2012. He draws the Berri underpass as a hexagon. As we are walking beneath the tunnel, Matt's biometric activity goes up: *'What is fun is the view we have from up there, that's why we go up there. It's significant mostly because the street is wide and long. It goes all the way to the square. It's symbolic you know, you see the central bus station, the square, and everyone who is there.'*[18] The 'tunnel' is in fact an overpass on top of a small hill where marches with thousands of people would walk. Protesters were able to look back and admire the size of the crowd as

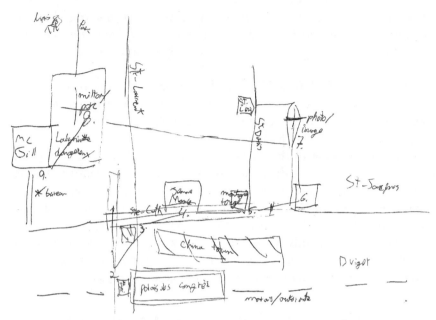

FIGURE 3.2 Matt's mental map – a reticular conception of space.

they climbed the hill and feel the vibration of their exhilarating screams when passing through the tunnel.

The vast majority (19/27) of the mental maps produced by the strikers we met depict a reticular conception of space. The experience of walking the city during demonstrations and other activities helps them 'connect' their significant places into a network. Béatrice expressively remembers how, as she was walking so much during the strike for various marches and activities, she came to connect the dots: '*It's like a big puzzle with pieces of different colours. It's really full of small closed worlds that touch each other, that sometimes cross, and others that really don't touch each other.*'[19]

This reticular conception of space is also typically very temporally dynamic. For instance, Hubert expresses how various moments and places hold relative significance: '*I think that it is a candid observation to realize how much everything is superimposed and continues simultaneously, you know. That as some people are thinking they are going to die from the tear gas, others are buying Pop-Tarts. There is no universal cohesion where everything occurs at the same time. Nothing stops because something is happening. The earth continues to turn. Fukushima continues to send radioactive substances in the ocean. There is no rupture, just never.*'[20] Although he was participating in a historical political event, Hubert does not see the same ruptures as Rancière would.

Instead, in this superposition of moments and places, strikers construct some *'activist mental maps'*, to use Alain's words. Or, as Christine would say, '*It is super interesting to see the city become a sort of map for, you know, guerilla strategies [laughter]. I'll use the term "guerilla", I don't know what else to use. But you know, observe the city through an angle.*'[21] Space is valued strategically according to its risk potential – or, more often, according to the feeling of belonging or the ideological value to which it is associated.

With the biometric data collected and the interpretation provided by the interviewees during our second meeting, we mapped the most significant places in Montreal for students, using colour coding associated with specific emotions (friendship, empowerment, solidarity, fear, feeling of rejection, safety). These places are concentrated in four areas of the city. Near the Place Émilie-Gamelin (a small plaza adjacent to the militant French-speaking University of Québec in Montreal, UQAM), most students felt strong positive emotions: empowerment and friendship (see Figure 3.3). The plaza was, and still is, the main gathering point for marches and protests in Montreal. The second important zone is the downtown business district and the Congress Centre. Here, students expressed fear and insecurity because it was the site of violent confrontations with the police. However, empowerment and solidarity were also commonly expressed in reference to this zone. The third zone is near McGill University, Montreal's most well-known English-speaking university. The distribution of emotions there is similar to what we see near the Congress Centre, but participants felt much less fear and more solidarity. The experience of students who supported the strike at McGill was marked by important interpersonal conflicts with students who rejected the strike. They expressed significantly negative experiences on picket lines for that reason. The last important area is concentrated on the Berri tunnel, as mentioned by Matt.

These places were significant to the students because they are where they felt their engagement most strongly, but also because they frequently went there over the eight months of the strike. These spatial routines – for instance, the 'illegal' demonstrations every night for more than 100 days, starting at Émilie-Gamelin at 8 p.m., or the daily sound of pots and pans on the balconies of residential streets, also at 8 p.m. – were efficient disturbance strategies. Many news articles evoked business owners' and other economic actors' worries about the temporary functional displacement of the city's economic spaces. Restaurant owners, for instance, complained about reduced business during the strike.

However, beyond the efficiency of these spatial routines, what Matt, Alain, Quincy, and Kim reveal is how the intensity of feelings in these places still affects their relation to the city even a year after the strike. It affects how they move about the city, preferring to walk, avoiding subway cars when

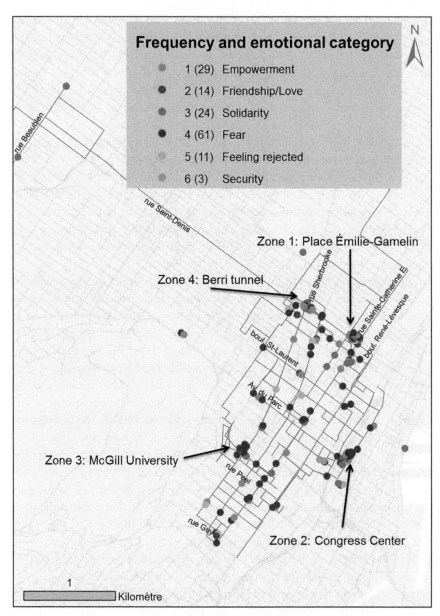

FIGURE 3.3 Affective spaces of the city under strike. *Source:* map by Mathieu Labrie.

they see police officers because they still feel '*traumatized*' or '*angry*'. It affects where they go and how they get there. Most feel it affects their feeling of belonging to the city. For instance, as we are walking near the Place des Arts, we ask Roger how he feels about the fact that many tourists are now there for the Montreal Jazz Festival, without a clue about what had happened there a year ago. He responds without hesitation:

ROGER   *Yeah, it's mine.*
JULIE-ANNE   *Montreal is yours, this is what you were saying about appropriation.*
ROGER   *All the more when you see police officers, often they describe . . . it's not people who know Montreal, and then they were getting out of their neighbourhoods and . . . and you could see they were arguing: 'no, Sherbrooke is that way, and no, Sherbrooke is the other way!' [imitating comic voices]*[22]

We ask them whether they see themselves building their lives in Montreal and whether their involvement in the 2012 actions plays a role in this decision. Most say that this connection confirms their desire to stay in Montreal. As Christine says: '*It just reconfirmed, it just reconfirmed that Montreal was my, my headquarters. It was my headquarters and I will always come back [laughter].*'[23] With this question, we wanted to encourage respondents to speak about urbanity, to articulate through words what we had been exploring differently throughout our meetings (time, space, affect). They responded in three ways: 'Yes, I want to live in Montreal, without a doubt'; 'I want to live in a large city but I don't know which one'; and 'I want to live in the countryside while being in Montreal'.

Most strikers want to live in 'the city', in Montreal or elsewhere. But eight express a desire for the 'countryside', without leaving the 'city'. The 'country-side' as described by these interviewees is urban because it is lived reticularly with the city, on a nonlinear temporality and through an affective relation to the world. Fred expresses this as follows: '*No doubt that Montreal will always stay at the core of my life. But it is just that we need a relief valve because it has become a little hard. Rapid gentrification, too many cars. It's stressful you know. But at the same time, I am involved at the community level. It's just that there's space outside of the city where you can breathe a little. At the same time, I see myself in a co-op in Montreal for instance, with friends. Getting into that kind of thing.*'[24]

Fred rejects urban planning and its problems, but not urban living. He desires urbanity even if he wants to '*work the land*' and '*have chickens and pigs*'. Fred, Ivan, Wajdi, and Hubert envision an alternative urbanity. They speak of a world in which the 'city' and the 'countryside' are strongly connected to their political, cultural, and social practices. Urbanity for them has '*something wild, which is not domesticated you know, which you can't put in a park with a fence and that will stay there, you know.*'[25] In this excerpt, Hubert speaks of skateboarding as a metaphor to describe his political engagement and his worldview. We could say that he is also describing urbanity. We will come back to Hubert's skateboarding in Chapter 5.

Urbanity, borrowing Marcotte's (1997) description of the 1980s novel in Montreal, means action 'within a dilated space, without boundaries or with very thin boundaries, a space that in itself invites crossing, displacement'. The street is the most graphic example of such reticular space. It is also filled with specific artefacts. The sound of pots and pans and the vibration of ecstatic screaming under the Berri tunnel show how these aesthetic experiences have changed the students as much as the streets of Montreal. When Quincy and Julie-Anne walk under the underpass a year after the strike, Quincy's body is still shivering: '*Like, what's really awesome about this is when you go into the tunnel, I mean, you can hear yourself. I think we can cross through. Um, we hear it amplified . . . Like, I remember feeling ecstatic, like totally ecstatic, like going through the tunnel and hearing like, just like the vibration of it right? It's just like how loud is it? And people started screaming right? It makes me emotional [weak tone as if he is going to cry].*'

The striking city is a city of walkers; it is a profoundly aesthetic city. If we were to analyse these eight months of intense student presence in the street with a focus just on the organization of the movement, its strategies, its resources, we would miss this aesthetic intensity. It is striking how this political period was dominated by the logic of the street. If we compare the number of governmental political acts with those of the students, we see a clear imbalance and disconnect (see Figure 3.4). Loic describes the dynamics:

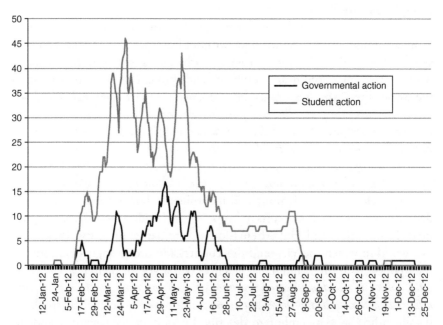

FIGURE 3.4 Comparison over time of student and governmental actions. *Source:* produced by Denis Carlier.

'*Until 22 March more or less, the political agenda was controlled by the CLASSE [the main student organization]. It was during the CLASSE's congresses that things happened, where everything was voted, where perturbations were voted and all of that. Whereas the night demonstrations were really decentralized nobody had control, nobody took the lead of the demonstration. It was political confrontation at its purest.*'[26]

Indeed, the government reacted for the first time to student mobilization after the first big demonstration of 22 March 2012. The following month, it refused to negotiate with student organizations. This is when the street became the preferred space of action. When the Charest government announced its Plan Nord, a huge demonstration was raging outside the Palais des Congrès. This was the first violent confrontation with the police, and it was to be followed by even more violent events in Victoriaville. It was also when night demonstrations began. In reaction to this intensifying logic of the street and the retreat of the student organizations, the government voted in Bill 78 in mid-May, restricting street protest, demanding that itineraries be approved in advance, and prohibiting the wearing of face masks. And then began the pots and pans. This all ended on 23 May with massive arrests.

Strikers were acting on the street. They were not following formal student leadership. The movement was self-organized and highly decentralized. If we compare governmental acts with formal student assemblies and student communication, we see, however, that in this formal institutional space, government and student organizations followed and responded to one another (see Figure 3.5).

Figures 3.4 and 3.5 show how the logic of the street is much less progressive than governmental and formal student organizational action.[27] It is more intermittent, with very intense peaks. In other words, it is composed of multiple, simultaneous, and cumulative situations. Students did not always react to governmental action. They were not solely state-centred. They followed their own logic, which was more urban. As Hubert puts it: '*If you're in the present moment, if everybody is, we adjust to each other, we adapt. The control of the road safety code is forgotten; it's another form of control that comes into being, a sort of self-management.*'[28]

The Political Effects of Seduction and Provocation

What were the political effects of this self-management and mutual adaptation on the street? How did it all work? Deliberately avoiding saying the word 'leader', we asked the strikers whether they wished to identify 'dominant figures' of the movement. A synthesis of their responses is given in Figure 3.6.

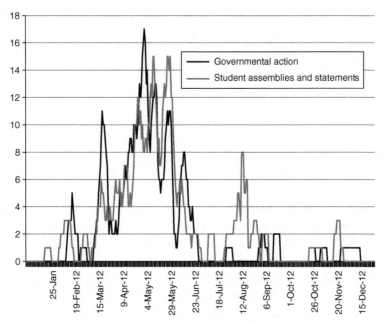

FIGURE 3.5 Comparison over time of actions initiated by the government and by formal student organizations. *Source:* produced by Denis Carlier.

'The crowd' is by far the most common response, followed by the three spokespersons (Gabriel Nadeau-Dubois, Martine Desjardins, and Luc Bureau-Blouin); however, these were generally mentioned only to discredit them or diminish their importance, with the insistence that they were designated to speak to the government, not to represent the crowd. The most critical strikers would call them 'rock stars' or insinuate they had a 'Che Guevara complex'. Loic expresses very well what many others meant by the crowd being the dominant figure: *'I think that the nature of this decentralized, popular movement partly explains why I can't really name icons because it wasn't a movement of leaders; it was a movement belonging to everyone. There were no differences between a CLASSE executive and the average student in Drummondville or Saint-Laurent and . . . eh, I think we will mostly remember that, this aspect. In fact, I hope we will remember that and we won't remember GAB [Gabriel Nadeau-Dubois] as the saviour of the masses.'*[29]

According to Wajdi, *'the movement's resilience to repression is that there was no head. Because there were no heads to cut, it was more difficult for the powers in place.'*[30] But this is not always easy to accept. Sarah explains how she had to get rid of her 'leadership reflex'. She describes being destabilized when her university dean did not act as a leader who could control a crisis: *'I was very*

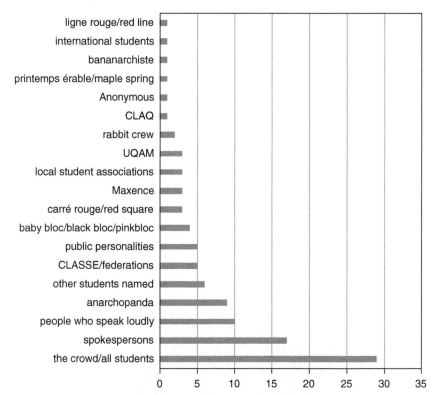

FIGURE 3.6 Dominant figures of the Spring 2012 strikes – synthesis of responses by 27 participants.

like naive I think at the time about like what administrators want and what they were there for and like, I was like, why won't she come down? It's like this horrible thing happened right here, and she like . . . Why wouldn't she come talk to the people who she's here to lead or whatever.' The absence of an authority figure during an intensely affective moment was difficult for Sarah at first. But then she learned to get rid of this quest for authority. Many strikers further described how leadership and authority would morph according to the situation. Hubert explains, *'I was not sure like who was up front. Sometimes it was like anyone would take the lead.'*[31]

Strikers describe the crowd's shared knowledge and their appreciation of non-human actors. The symbols most appreciated are those that remain anonymous, those that are not human, like Anarchopanda (even if we knew a real person was hidden behind the mask) or the red square. Anarchopanda and the red square share agency with the strikers. They are profoundly important because they work through seduction. Being non-human, they are not intentionally seductive. But they have clear political effect. They are affectively attractive. As we were walk with Gary towards the Chinatown lion gates, we pass in front of a mural depicting the panda facing a police officer (see Figure 3.7). Gary laughs: '*I know Anarchopanda is pretty. . .*' He does not finish his sentence and pauses to think. '*I don't know, it's actually really impressive how meaningful it is. Like it's not just a funny costume, you know: he was a symbol of the mask bylaw [P8] and the fact that I can't remember. . .*' His tone changes inquisitively: '*he was a philosophy professor or a psychology professor, the guy who was inside? . . . Anyway he would be like [does not finish sentence] . . . He would be arrested and [does not finish sentence] . . . I feel like he wore the mask to his trials I think.*' Gary is emphasizing here Anarchopanda's bravery and provocation. Nathaly, on the other hand, insists more on seduction: '*I mean, in terms of important figures, I mean Anarchopanda is really lovable, I mean there is nothing like getting a hug from a giant plush man on a demo. So I think,*

FIGURE 3.7 Anarchopanda wearing a red square and facing a police officer. Mural painted in August 2012 by Kosséça !?! (K6A) during the Under Pressure festival. *Source:* photo by David Widgington.

I think that was a very clever symbol throughout, because it was anonymous.' The comfort of a big plush hug is indeed seductive. Nathaly imagines Anarchopanda as a paternal caring figure: *'So I think Anarchopanda was like: "These are children! I'm going to dress like a panda and I can do it, I'm going to be anonymous and I'm also a Cegep prof, secretly." I don't, I thought that was a really, really beautiful gesture of solidarity and risk-taking that took some stress off the students. I don't know . . .'* She is grateful for the comfort he provided. She was seduced by him, despite disagreeing with some of his ideas: *'I really did love Anarchopanda. I think that was really great, although I have his Facebook feed and sometimes he sends out stuff I don't support at all. [laughter] So it's like, Anarchopanda, those are protesters against gay marriage! It's like, dude! Everybody posted stuff on his Facebook, 'cause he's got a Facebook wall, it's like Anarchopanda kind of like tweets.'* Seduction wins over rational argumentation.

Gary and Nathaly are attracted to Anarchopanda, seduced by his care and risk-taking. Demonstrations are important for that, Nathaly goes on: *'demos aren't the things that does stuff, it's more like getting in the streets and having a party and like, you know, hug each other, and do fun shit and like, then we go back and do the work. We still have to do the work and I think that's the thing that the media doesn't understand, they don't understand what that means. I remember one demo, like I had a reporter coming and being like "What do you think you are doing today, what do you think you're accomplishing?" [mimicking voice] And it was a demo that we did specifically in solidarity with some international students. And he just didn't understand what a demo does, and I was like "Well I'm taking a break!"'* Demos are seductive, they are central even if they don't 'accomplish' anything visible or rational.

Distributive agency, in the sense of analytically incorporating all forces at play in political action, from red squares to megaphones, from Anarchopandas to the Berry tunnel, from strategic student organizers to the occasional walker, does not mean that political acts have no effects. What matters in the exercise of power is our experience of its effects. Allen (2003) distinguishes between different modalities of power – seduction being one of them. Each modality has a distinct effective reach. Strikers constantly describe how seduction (even if this is not the word they use) was central to experiencing victory. They define political change as a series of 'experiential victories' grounded as part of various individual daily rhythms. Nonlinear, cumulative, and simultaneous change is associated with liberation and power. The strikers' orientation towards the future is defined by intense and embodied experiences in the present that have effects in the short term. They do not exhibit an abstract vision of the future as a linear set of steps needed to accomplish a predefined goal.

They insist on the effects of being a striker on their personal life: self-realization, self-confidence, awareness, skills, new friends, new lovers. . . They have the sense that victories go beyond their personal lives, but cannot evaluate things at that scale. Alain says, '*It's always difficult to know . . . eeh . . . what gesture will have a positive, negative impact. Total effects, so I . . . I wouldn't put this completely on a pedestal, but I wouldn't make it a thing . . . completely, eeh . . . how to say . . . completely unimportant.*'[32] However, they insist on less 'totalizing' victories (to use Alain's words again); victories that one experiences more than measures. Fred is the most eloquent here: '*The victory, there were many. It was that many people were politicized, many people saw that everything is rotten and that we should never trust politicians. And that people can self-organize. This, it was an experiential victory you know. That's why I find strikes are cool, because they're moments when collective knowledge is developed. Because if we see social movements in terms of "On 4 November, we obtained this gain. . ." [in a news commentator's voice]. Well, we will just be depressed because it almost never happens this way.*'[33]

Social change, for the strikers, is about individual rhythms that accelerate during moments of freedom such as the strike. When they decided to vote to end the strike in various student assemblies, Wajdi remembers, '*It was a difficult situation because we knew we were leaving the movement behind, that it was the end of a historical movement. Well, that's it, it's a feeling of loss, not in the sense of defeat necessarily, but the loss of a certain power that we have to mobilize, not necessarily to change society or to make people move, because everyone decides to go at their rhythm, but a loss. It was a liberty that we were giving ourselves being on strike.*'[34] Umberto follows this interpretation as we walk near Concordia University:

UMBERTO   *This doesn't feel like the same city anymore. And you want and I want that city . . . to be back. I want Spring 2012, you know? And that's not gonna happen. Yeah hum so it's this passage of various speed, right?*

JULIE-ANNE *Uh-huh.*

UMBERTO   *The very intense speed of Spring 2012 to a much slower speed of social transformation at a much smaller scale.*

Future benefits are measured only after experiential victories, after action. Ivan reflexively concludes our walk by saying, '*But sometimes when we think about it more in the longer term, in the moment we want change, for sure, but it will come in the short, medium, or long term.*'[35] Acting on the spot, in the moment, before thinking about the effects, before making any social assessment involves, as Ivan explains in generous details, individual sacrifices for the collective good. He speaks of physical, temporal, psychological sacrifice. Involvement was sustained, despite sacrifice, by experiential victories. As we walk in front of an anarchist bookstore with Wajdi, he warmly remembers seeing a young woman wearing a hijab buying an anarchist book:

WAJDI   *Well, I found that very interesting. Yeah, there were many small moments like that one that were quite sympathetic.*

JULIE-ANNE   *But it gives the impression that it has a sense? No? That it gives hope.*

WAJDI   *For sure, it gives the impression that things are changing. But at the same time, I can't know and I don't want to judge either how and what this young woman thought before and after the strike, what is her identity or whatever. I think she can certainly be very politicized and wear the hijab if she wishes.*[36]

This specific situation did not have a clear impact on the strike as a whole, but every striker experiences such 'small sympathetic moments'. It is these multiple simultaneous situations that make up the experiential Spring 2012 of each striker and influence their involvement. Social change and political effects are thus described as an unpredictable imbrication of situations, of present moments. These are sometimes cumulative (they add to one another to produce change) and sometimes simultaneous (they are neither coordinated nor directly related, but create a collective narration of the movement). Fred, again with clarity, synthesizes what many others express in similar words: '*It was difficult to understand what we were doing or where we were going because every day new things happened that gave another sense to the movement or to what we were going to do the next day.*'[37]

Classical social movement analysis will discuss political effects in terms of political gains, in terms of winners and losers in an ideological conflict, in terms of a conflict between opposing interests. This is a valid mode of political analysis. For the student strike, the ideological core of the conflict resided in an antagonism between two distinct social projects: a neoliberal and a social justice project. Strikers spoke to us about the problems associated with neoliberalism and capitalism, about the stubbornness of the government, about misinformation in the media, about feminism, anarchism, racism, individualism, state repression, about the Left and the Right, about those who have '*a big house in the suburbs*' and a '*big job in the government*', about bourgeois and reactionaries. They mostly insisted on the need to demystify '*the system*' in order to construct a better, more equal, more just world. They spoke of the need to '*avoid living as the system dictates*'. They valorized their own combat and convictions, valorized '*the cause*'.

But this type of analysis is not the one we wish to highlight in this book. Instead, we want to zoom in on less visible, more experiential political effects; that is, on the aesthetic dimensions of politics. The strikers we met only briefly spoke of ideological conflicts. They insisted much more on the creation of new spaces of political action. Étienne, for example, when he was speaking of his English-speaking friends, described their political practice as much less confrontational and antagonistic: '*I find that the Anglo way to be an activist is super interesting. They are much less in confrontation and gains, or to claim something to whatever authority, but really more into creating spaces and solidarity and you know "we will create our things ourselves", you know like for instance People's Potato at Concordia, this is crazy.*'[38] We will come back to People's Potato in the next chapter.

Opening such new spaces of political action is something we have witnessed beyond English-speaking youths. The motor of political action would be best described as impulsive. More than antagonism, it was through the intensification of multiple daily encounters and experimentations that strikers got involved. A quick quantitative snapshot of the conversations we had with strikers shows that the most common conflict they reported to us was confrontation with the police. They next spoke of interpersonal conflicts, and only then of ideological conflicts. Spring 2012 was experienced by youth in their daily lives; it was not an abstract ideological confrontation between neoliberalism and social justice. In fact, they do not speak in terms of 'resistance'. This word appears only 30 times in our 54 interviews (27 respondents × 2 interviews each) – less than 0.01% of our corpus. The iconography of the movement does represent resistance, but this is not how strikers remember and speak of it (see Figure 3.8). Instead, they insist on how this social conflict was transposed in their personal lives. Kim remembers that '*I didn't feel I was resisting and I was hot. I had a feeling of . . . terror. It was really horrible that we were there, that we couldn't demonstrate quietly in the street.*'[39] Victor insists that '*like it's a feeling, like, less than an intellectual opinion*'. Loic synthesizes this as follows: '*there is often a false political flavour, but in the end, it was really a question of personality conflicts. There were many people who simply didn't get along.*'[40]

What remains from the Maple Spring is not the ideological conflict but the pain of interpersonal conflicts: conflicts with students who did not support the strike on the picket lines, family conflicts, conflicts with professors, the feeling of being negatively judged or insulted by passersby. There were tensions, the break-up of relationships, of friendships, of family ties. Sometimes, conflicts with police officers would take a very personal turn, beyond the institution involved. Quincy remembers how during a naked demonstration he accidentally crashed into a female police officer, who reacted '*Uuuuh! Ostie tabarnak calisse!*' He recalls, '*and she thought I was such a fucking degenerate*'.

The strike was not felt primarily as ideologically antagonistic, it was aesthetically experienced as a network of sometimes tensed interpersonal relations. This passage from ideological antagonism to situated impulsion does not equate to a lack of conviction. It rather indicates that conviction is as affective and situated as it is rational and ideological. Conviction works

FIGURE 3.8 Iconography of resistance. *Source:* photo by J.A. Boudreau.

through seduction. In this sense, seduction is not a conceptual equivalent to the concepts of resonance or salience in the sociology of social movement. It does not speak of the reception of a specific framing of the political problem, which can be strategically designed. Seduction works through bodies and affect before working through discursive framing.

Seduction generates political effects through affective forces of attraction, remembered by the strikers in terms of care, solidarity, comfort, and sexual desire – but also interpersonal conflicts, the feeling of being too visible or too invisible, of being empowered in a specific situation or being completely rejected. The effect of these affective forces becomes visible when they sustain involvement over time despite constraints.

Very close to seduction as a modality of power is provocation. Spring 2012 is also notable for the way provocation operated. In the introduction, we briefly mentioned 'Fuck toute!' as a provocative figure born in the 2012 protests, but which emerged clearly in the 2015 mobilizations against austerity measures. From an ideological fighter against tuition fee increase in 2012, the student protester had become by 2015 a fighter of 'everything', because, as the Collectif Débrayage (2016) so beautifully puts it, 'totality excludes magic'. In 2016, when the banner became viral on Facebook, 'Fuck toute!' was not only a striker, it had become an entire generation that didn't vote and felt the urge to destroy everything. Fuck toute!

Because youthfulness is a political form based on experimentation, exploration, disorganization, incoherent messaging, or leaderless spontaneity, it is provocative. Spring 2012 is a clear manifestation of such youthfulness. Already in 2012, before 'Fuck toute!', many scandalous subjects had emerged, introducing unanticipated agency on the streets. Perhaps the most visible example is the black blocks. Black blocks are not unique to Montreal. They are a protest tactic invented in West Germany in the 1980s to defend urban squats from eviction. They were closely associated with the punk movement of the time, and have anti-fascist and anarchist sensibilities. They consist of using violence when necessary, mostly during confrontation with the police. They apparently became visible in North America in the 1990s during demonstrations against the United States' war with Iraq.

Black blocks are demonstrators who dress in black, cover their faces, and march as a group with black flags. They provoke by their mere presence, because people know what they stand for: the use of violence if it is politically necessary. Most of the time, they simply walk calmly, provoking only by their dress and their formation as a block. They are not an organization, they are a way of acting. Black blocks do not exist before or after a demonstration. They become black blocks by marching. They are the perfect example of an emerging and situational subjectivity that can only exist in the specific place and moment of a demonstration.

As provocative as they are, black blocks do not constitute an aesthetic appearance, because their provocation is effective only because we can rationally represent their possible violent action. An aesthetic appearance occurs when we cannot use words and cognitively process what is surprising our senses. But this does not make them less provocative. Specific artefacts – black clothes, masks, and flags – serve to produce provocation, but what is most effective in their political action is that they disseminate a specific message: Sometimes it is legitimate to express anger and be violent in order to counter the state's and capitalism's systemic violence.

Provocation is a way to reveal what does not work within social norms. By disrupting what has become invisible and normalized, provocation suddenly makes the norms visible. Through their use of violence, black blocks direct our attention to the violence of 'the system'. This scandalous intrusion produces agency for the troublemaker. Provocation works by consciously trying to trouble the way things are. It goes beyond confrontation and antagonism because it seeks to instil strong feelings: disgust, fear, admiration. The

Manifeste du Carré noir, published on social media in March 2012, says: '*We are angry. We don't recuperate the strike . . . We don't infiltrate demonstrations, we help organize them, we make them alive.*'[41] Provocation is what makes demonstrations alive.

The political effects of black blocks were hotly debated within student associations, on social media, and among the general public. Strikers had contrasting opinions about whether they were helping or constraining the movement. But beyond this strategic discussion, because all strikers have experienced strong feelings through their involvement, the visibility of black blocks provoked self-reflection. We began this chapter with Quincy's spiritual reflection on the use of violence within the movement and in his personal life. Barricades, like black blocks, work through provocation as a modality of power.

Conclusion

This chapter has explored how young Montrealers, most of them students, became strikers. How, in other words, they got involved in the Maple Spring and how they sustained this involvement over an eight-month period despite many constraints in terms of interpersonal conflicts and the risks of being physically or emotionally hurt, of being arrested, of losing their semester, and, for international students, of being expelled from the country. With the analytical tools of the sociology of social movements, we began this research project in 2013 by asking *why* they got involved, looking for their motives. But youths kept bringing us to the *how* of their involvement, more than the ideological *why*.

What the students describe is a series of pregnant moments in specific times and spaces. These moments gradually 'sucked' them into the movement. This is how they became strikers. In short, they describe a situational and performative subjectivity, not an essentialized actor. More than a strategic decision to participate, they describe the sequence of their political gestures in specific situations. They speak of tactics more than planning and strategy. Discussing their relationship to risk-taking, they clearly illustrate that they do not have a linear rapport to the future. Instead, they speak of the liberating power of the 'here and now'. In doing so, they draw a reticular conceptualization of their city in strike – a reticular space that subsists in their spatial urban practices after the strike has ended. This is visible in their discussion about the urbanity of the countryside. The core element of this reticular political space is the street.

In their description of their city in strike, youths emphasize political effects that are oblivious to the sociology of social movements. Instead of speaking of political gains, of battles lost or won, they speak of experiential victories. They emphasize the various rhythms and scales of social change.

Even if political action is for them unfolding through shared agency with artefacts, the materiality of the street and the Facebook wall, and various human
actors, they are acutely aware of the way distributed agency has political effect.
We began this chapter with Quincy's intricate analysis of the effect of the
political on personal and public registers. We heard many such stories during
this research project. What is striking to us in the visual, textual, and bodily
descriptions the students produced is how seduction works as a modality of
power. Unlike other modalities (e.g. the police use of coercion), seduction's
spatiotemporal reach is situational. One is seduced in a specific moment and
space; one feels this seduction in one's body as it is moving in a specific place
at a specific moment with a specific set of objects and material conditions.
Situatedness makes seduction a different concept to resonance or salience.
Nathaly was seduced by Anarchopanda because he hugged her in that specific
demo, where police officers were particularly threatening. In contrast, as a
modality of power, coercion has an ampler spatiotemporal reach. It works
through the threat of force to exact compliance. Thus, the threat of arrest
may work to coerce a striker to stay at home. Threats can work 'at a distance',
like the criminal code. With the state holding the monopoly over the use of
violence, we know at a distance that if we do something illegal, we may get
arrested. Threats can also work at the situational scale. When Nathaly heard
the synchronized sound of the anti-riot squad, she felt the threat of force (being arrested, or being subject to physical violence). This could have led her to
retreat from the demonstration and go back home.

Other modalities of power were visible in this historic episode in Montreal. In Chapter 1, we mentioned the young men who marched with their faces
painted black while holding a Jean Charest puppet. In its racism, this political
gesture mobilized domination as a modality of power. Domination is the in-
strumentalization of inequality in order to restrict choices and close down possibilities. It is exercised at someone else's expense. The young men's staging in-
strumentalized racist inequalities, reaffirmed White supremacy, and excluded
racialized youths from participating in the strike. The spatiotemporal reach of
domination is much more expanded than that of seduction, or even of coercion.

Another modality discussed in this chapter is authority. When Sarah felt
lost because her university administrator did not manage the crisis as a 'leader'
should, she became scared. She explains how she gradually managed to get rid
of her search for authority. The negation of leadership within the movement
and the ridiculing of formal student representatives spoke to a rejection of
authority as an organizational modality of power. Authority is something
specific actors can instrumentalize to induce certain behaviour, but unlike
domination, it cannot lead to submission. It relies on the recognition of the
source of authority: the father, the political leader (some students rejected the
'Che Guevara complex'), the teacher, the law, the ideology. Authority has a

TABLE 3.1 Spatiotemporal reach of different modalities of power.

Modality of power	Spatiotemporal reach	Mechanism of action
Manipulation	Individual	Strategic
Seduction	Situational	Aesthetic
Coercion	Situational and institutional	Threat
Authority	Institutional	Respect
Domination	Structural	Submission

spatiotemporal reach comparable to that of coercion in the sense that it has institutional reach. Domination, in comparison, has structural reach.

Finally, Spring 2012 illustrates the spatiotemporal reach of manipulation. As a modality of power that implies the concealment of intent, manipulation is often attributed by strikers to the mainstream media. Because it relies on concealment, manipulation is necessarily strategic. It is something that one wilfully does. Its spatiotemporal reach can be considerable, such as the influence of the media on public opinion. But because of its strategic and intentional functioning, we can place it at an individual reach (see Table 3.1).

Our focus in this book is the aesthetics of political action. We have thus highlighted how seduction worked in the pregnant moments of Spring 2012. With the examples of the black blocs and 'Fuck toute!', we pointed towards how it does not only work with attraction, but also sometimes through provocation. Both attraction and provocation instil strong affects. This is why they are fundamentally situational: they rely on distributed agency.

Notes

1. The project Trajectoires printannières consisted in two extensive interviews with 27 young people who had participated, to various degrees, in the spring 2012 student strikes in Montreal. We asked each interviewee to choose a meeting point in a place that was significant to them. We sat there for about 30 minutes talking about why they had decided to participate in the movement. We asked them to draw a mental map of their 'city under strike', identifying the places that were most important to their participation. We then began an improvised walk through the city, lasting roughly two hours, during which the interviewee would recall anecdotes and situations as we were visiting the various sites that they had identified. They wore sunglasses which filmed what they were seeing, and Q-Sensor biometric bracelets which translated their

emotional activity into graphic data by measuring electrodermal activity. The interviewer also had a GPS tracker in their bag. After the walk, we produced a video montage synchronizing the audio-video images, GPS, and biometric data. We did not want to interpret the data ourselves (as psychologists would do), and we did not assume that there was a direct relation between electrodermal activity and emotions and affects. Instead, we met with the interviewee a second time to 'give' them back this data. During this meeting, they would see their data synchronized and they would comment on their biometric activity.

2. Parts of the analysis were previously published in Boudreau and Labrie (2016).

3. 'On vit des vies aliénées et les moments de grève, avec mes amis on appelle ça: briser le réel. Parce qu'on brise un certain ordre des choses, un rapport affectif au monde . . . Dans un mouvement de grève, c'est comme un moment liminaire. Les choses sont indéterminées, les règles ne sont pas aussi claires que dans la quotidienneté productive. Tout peut se passer. Tu peux te réveiller un matin et te ramasser en fin de journée dans telle ou telle action à faire telle ou telle bannière à connaitre telle ou telle personne, à consoler telle ou telle personne que tu connais pas. C'est comme si un corps social venait à exister au lieu de plein d'individus atomises.'

4. 'Je me souviendrais toujours de cette fille-là, je sais pas c'est quoi son visage, qui m'avait pris la main, tout le monde se prenait la main pour s'aider à se calmer pour pas qu'on coure, qu'on marche tranquillement, pour pas qu'on se blesse déjà nous-même. Puis c'est ça, ce sentiment là . . . et puis moi je suis pas quelqu'un qui touche, je suis assez misanthrope comme personne, je dis ça assez humblement . . .'

5. 'C'était plus un moment, on se regardait pis on était fiers d'être là, on était fiers d'être ensemble, même si on ne se connaissait pas . . . Pis tsé, quand on décidait de prendre la rue tout le monde ensemble, qu'on partait chacun des coins pis on se ramassait dans le centre de la rue. Pour après ça continuer à marcher, mais ça se faisait un peu spontanément, ça se faisait par un simple regard, il y avait pas de paroles de quelqu'un qui devait dire à l'autre ben tsé, on le fait. Ça se faisait spontanément comme ça. On était tous sur la même longueur d'onde, pis que, tsé il y avait quelque chose qui se passait et qui était de l'ordre. . .tsé qui sortait de juste des paroles ou de quelque chose comme ça. Ça allait vraiment vers quelque chose qui allait nous chercher en dedans. Nos valeurs, qui on était vraiment.'

6. 'On avance, on avance, on recule pas!'

7. 'Pis là il y un moment quand les gens se sont mis à crier: "Un peuple uni jamais ne sera vaincu", pis moi je regardais vers l'est . . . Tout

ce qu'on entendait entre les cris des gens c'était l'écho des cris sur
les buildings. Ça dû durer peut-être une dizaine, une douzaine de
secondes, il y en a eu trois slogans qui sont vraiment bien rentrés; que
tout le monde était synchronisé et tout . . . Pis, il y a eu un mouvement là vraiment . . . euh, pas un mouvement, mais un moment
de . . . y a rien qui bougeait, il y avait juste le son des gens pis ils ont
poussé une grenade au-dessus de la foule, dix pieds de ma tête, pis,
pis là, moi je me rappelle qu'il y a quelque chose qui m'a brisé dans
moi de . . . c'est peut-être naïf, mais s'il y a dix mille personnes qui
crient ça, que tout ce que tu entends c'est ça . . . le guts, les couilles
et l'arrogance de leur crisser des grenades dessus, c'est . . . tsé, c'est
comme, "Ok that's how it's going to be".'

8. 'On marchait pis on se disait ok ça sent tellement la trappe, ça sent
tellement la trappe, un bande de petits kids qui n'ont jamais manifes-
té, qui ne connaissent rien. Tsé, parce que tu deviens, tu développes
des aptitudes de manifestant.'

9. 'Mettons que je voyais qu'il y avait du grabuge, ben j'essayais de me
tenir un peu à l'écart, ça ne me tentait pas de me mettre entre le
policier pis le gars qu'il veut taper, des choses comme ça. Je réfléchis
quand même un petit peu à ce que je faisais, mais ça n'allait pas plus
loin que ça . . . ça dépendait aussi de, si j'avais des raisons de penser
que c'était imminent, je ne sais pas moi, quand les policiers chargent
en tapant sur leur bouclier, ben le risque parait plus imminent que
quand ils font juste marcher tranquillement en nous regardant. Ça
allait, ça venait, j'y pensais j'y pensais plus.'

10. 'Probablement qu'au début, il y a des choses que j'aurais pas osé
faire, mais prise dans l'engrenage du conflit, pis dans l'espèce
d'augmentation de la pression pis de la tension, tu finis par te crinquer
pis j'ai accepté probablement d'augmenter mes risques. J'ai accepté
d'aller dans des manifs où j'aurais peut-être pas été normalement. En
même temps cette courbe-là a redescendu à partir du moment où je
pense que, il y a des moments de prise de conscience ou ok, j'ai vraiment un risque de me faire blesser violemment. Tsé quand on a vu
des gros cas de blessures, complètement aléatoires, là je pense qu'il y a
peu de remise en question de: Est-ce que je suis prête à aller jusque-là?
tsé. J'étais prête à me faire arrêter, j'étais prête à me faire poivrer, mais
tsé, mais est-ce que je suis prête à aller jusqu'à avoir des dommages
physiques, permanents? Je pense qu'à ce moment-là j'ai eu un peu un
recul. Je pense que, en fait, j'ai réalisé qu'à ce moment-là j'avais peur,
j'avais peur pour vrai, ce que j'avais probablement jamais eu avant.'

11. 'Est-ce que tu pensais aux conséquences de ta participation?' / 'D'un
certain point de vue on pourrait dire qu'on pense juste à ça. Parce

que on vit dans un monde qui est assez autodestructeur sur beaucoup d'aspects, si on ne le fait pas, personnellement, si on ne se pose pas la question ça va être quoi la conséquence de rester les deux bras croisés par rapport aux conséquences de prendre le risque de faire quelque chose d'in-calculé, de flou, de chaotique, mais qui pourrait vraiment avoir un impact social considérable, ou environnemental, ben je pensais qu'aux conséquences (rire) de ce que j'allais faire.' / 'Pensais-tu aux conséquences personnelles?' / 'Ben les conséquences personnelles, j'ai de la misère à dissocier le personnel du collectif. Le vieil adage féministe qui dit que le personnel est politique, ça reste vrai à tous les jours. Ouain, j'ai vraiment de la difficulté à démêler les deux. De l'autre côté, j'ai vraiment forgé beaucoup d'amitiés là-dedans pis il y a beaucoup de conséquences personnelles qui sont positives.'

12. 'Pour moi, c'est clair et net que si quelque chose était sous contrôle on aurait vraiment foiré. Dans le sens que, ça été un moment de débrayage collectif qu'on a fait. C'était un moment où on s'est donné les moyens d'être asociaux à tout point de vue, tant par les actions qu'on faisait que par les idées qu'on brassait. Il y a vraiment beaucoup de gens qui ont osé penser, pis dire et faire des trucs, qu'ils n'avaient faits autrement. Pis ces choses-là, si ça avait été sous contrôle, si ça avait été, s'il y avait eu des comptes à rendre à quelqu'un ça ne se serait pas fait.' / 'Quand tu dis asociaux, tu veux dire à l'extérieur de la société?' / 'Oui, je l'entends au sens étymologique du terme. Donc à mon avis, c'est contrôler. Oui je pense que les gens avaient une éthique, une morale, donc il y avait beaucoup de choses qui étaient contrôlées dans ce sens-là, mais sans ce contrôle institutionnel, non ça vraiment été un moment de chaos. Pis je suis très content. Parce que ç'a ouvert beaucoup de possibilités. J'ai vu beaucoup plus d'étoiles dans les yeux des gens dans cette grève-là que pendant toutes mes études universitaires.'

13. 'Mais je fais de quoi de ma vie! . . . Mais quand ils vont lire le printemps 2012, ben ils vont dire, ils vont sortir cette énergie-là genre de bonheur: Aye! tu as fait de quoi dans ta vie. Tu as rien foutu en même temps. Tsé même si ce n'est pas monnayable une manif, où tu n'avais pas de salaire parce que tu participais à une manif, mais en même temps, man, c'est comme, pendant que tu dormais où que tu faisais de quoi, il y avait un moment historique qui se passait juste à côté de toi.'

14. A spokesperson of one of the student unions.

15. 'syndrome de la grèvitiste aigüe : tu es toujours en train de fredonner des slogans de manifestation . . . tu rêves à Gabriel Nadeau-Dubois, quand tu te promènes dans la rue tu évalues les risques de souricière . . .'

16. 'Tsé, on descend au centre-ville, on y va tu pas, on va tu se coucher, on travaille demain matin, tsé, c'est . . . [pause] Tsé, c'est plate en

même temps de se poser ces questions-là. C'est plate de ne pas se dire, de ne pas croire . . . [pause] de ne pas être totalement immergé finalement dans ce qu'on est en train de faire, dans ce qu'on croit. Tsé de pas, ahrrrk, demain demain non. Regarde, pour le moment, dans le présent, c'est à ça que je crois. Moi je crois qu'il faut continuer, il faut faire la lutte pour manifester, il faut faire ça, il faut continuer.'

17. 'J'avais 30 ans et c'était important pour moi d'être là, simplement parce que dans 20 ans, je ne veux pas dire que j'étais resté assis sur mon cul pendant ce temps-là, tsé . . . Moi j'ai l'impression que la prochaine fois . . . ça s'en vient dans pas si longtemps aussi. On va pas attendre 35 ans avant que ça arrive.'

18. 'Ce qui est le fun c'est la vue qu'on a en haut, c'est pour ça qu'on monte ici. C'est significatif surtout parce qu'elle est large, elle est longue a va jusqu'au square. C'est symbolique tsé, tu vois l'Îlot voyageur, le square pis tout le monde qui est là.'

19. 'C'est comme un gros puzzle avec des pièces de différentes couleurs, c'est vraiment plein de petits mondes clos qui se touchent, qui se croisent des fois et y'en a d'autres qui se touchent vraiment pas.'

20. 'Je pense que c'est surtout, je pense que c'est une observation assez candide de juste constater à quel point toutes les choses se superposent et continuent en simultané tsé. Que pendant qui en a qui pensent qui vont mourir sous les bombes lacrymogènes, ben il y en a d'autres qui sont en train d'acheter des Pop-Tarts. Il y a pas de cohésion universelle où il se passe tout en même temps. Il y a rien qui arrête parce que d'autres choses se passent. La terre continue de tourner, Fukushima continue d'envoyer des substances radioactives dans l'océan. Il y a pas de rupture vraiment jamais.'

21. 'Donc ça c'est super intéressant de voir, tsé, la ville devient une espèce de map de c'est quoi les stratégies de . . . tsé de guérilla [rire], je vais utiliser le terme de guérilla, je ne sais pas lequel utiliser, mais tsé, d'observer la ville à travers un angle.'

22. 'Ouin, c'est à moi.' / 'Montréal c'est à toi, c'est ça que tu disais sur l'appropriation.' / 'Surtout quand tu vois encore les policiers, souvent ils décrivent . . . c'est pas des gens qui habitent à Montréal, pis là ils sortaient de leurs quartiers pis . . . pis tu voyais qu'ils s'obstinaient: non, Sherbrooke c'est plus par-là, pis non, Sherbrooke c'est plus par-là!'

23. 'Ça juste reconfirmé que, ça juste reconfirmé que Montréal était mon, mon, siège social, c'était mon QG. Je vais toujours y revenir [rire].'

24. 'C'est sûr que Montréal restera toujours au cœur de ma vie. Mais c'est juste que ça prend une soupape, parce que c'est rendu un peu dur. La gentrification est rapide, y'a trop de chars, c'est agressant tsé. Mais en même temps, je m'implique au niveau communautaire. C'est dire que t'as un espace en dehors de la ville pour souffler un peu. En

même temps, je me vois avoir une coop par exemple à Montréal avec des amis, rentrer dans ce genre de truc là.'

25. 'Quelque chose de sauvage, d'urbain. Qui est pas domestique tsé, que tu peux pas mettre dans un parc avec une clôture pis qui va rester là tsé.'

26. 'Jusqu'au 22 mars environ, l'agenda politique était contrôlé par la CLASSE, les fédérations étudiantes suivaient. Mais ça restait très organisationnel. C'était dans les congrès de la CLASSE que les choses se passaient où tout était voté, où il y avait des perturbations qui étaient votées tout ça. Alors que les manifs de nuit étaient vraiment décentralisées; personne n'avait le contrôle, personne ne prenait la tête de la manifestation. C'était la confrontation politique à l'état pur.'

27. These chronograms were constructed using multiple databases of micro-events that occurred during 2012. We categorized the 1298 acts gathered for the period between 1 January and 31 December of that year according to the main actor involved.

28. 'Si t'es dans le moment présent, que tout le monde l'est, on s'ajuste les uns avec les autres, on s'adapte. Le contrôle du code de la sécurité routière il prend le bord là, c'est une autre forme de contrôle qui s'installe, soit un genre de, une autogestion.'

29. 'Je pense que la nature de ce mouvement décentralisé, populaire, explique en partie le fait que je puisse pas vraiment nommer d'icône parce que ce n'était pas un mouvement de leader, c'était un mouvement qui appartenait à tout le monde. Il y avait pas de différence entre un exécutant de la CLASSE et l'étudiant moyen à Drummondville et à St-Laurent et . . . euh, je pense qu'on se rappellera surtout de ça, de cet aspect-là. En fait j'espère qu'on s'en rappellera et qu'on ne se rappellera pas de Gab comme le sauveur de ses masses.'

30. 'la résilience du mouvement face à la répression, c'est qu'il n'y avait pas de tête. S'il n'y avait pas de tête à couper, c'est plus dur pour les pouvoirs en place.'

31. 'j'étais pas sûr comme qui justement était en avant. Des fois c'était un peu n'importe qui qui prenait le lead.'

32. 'C'est toujours difficile de savoir. . . euh. . . quel geste aura un impact positif, négatif. Les portées totales, donc je . . . je ne mettrais pas ça complètement sur un piédestal, mais je n'en ferais pas non plus un truc . . . complètement . . . euh . . . comment dire . . . complètement dérisoire.'

33. 'La victoire, il y en a eu pleins. Ça a été que plein de monde se politise, que plein de monde voit que tout est pourri et qu'il ne faut jamais faire confiance aux politiciens. Pis que les gens peuvent s'auto-organiser. Ça, c'était une victoire expérientielle tsé. C'est pour ça que je trouve ça cool les grèves, parce que c'est des moments où il y a un savoir collectif qui se développe. Parce que si on voit trop les

mouvements sociaux en termes de "Le 4 novembre, nous avons réussi à obtenir ce gain. . ." Ben on va juste déprimer, parce que ça arrive quasiment jamais.'

34. 'C'était une situation difficile, car on savait qu'on laissait le mouvement là, que c'était la fin d'un mouvement qui était historique, ben c'est ça, c'est un sentiment de perte, pas dans le sens de défaite nécessairement, mais de perte d'un certain pouvoir qu'on avait de mobiliser, pas nécessairement pour faire changer la société ou de faire bouger les gens, parce que tout le monde décide d'aller à son rythme, mais d'une perte. C'était une liberté qu'on se donnait en étant en grève.'

35. 'Mais quand même des fois quand on y repense plus aussi, c'est dans une optique aussi à long terme, dans une optique que sur le moment on veut des changements, c'est sûr que ça va arriver à court, moyen, long terme.'

36. 'Ben je trouvais ça assez intéressant. Ouain, il y a eu beaucoup de petits moments comme ça qui étaient assez sympathiques.' / 'Mais ça donne l'impression que ça sert à quelque chose? Non? Ça te donne une espèce de lueur d'espoir.' / 'C'est sûr que ça donne l'impression que les choses sont en train de changer. Mais en même temps, je ne peux pas savoir et je ne veux pas juger non plus de comment, de qu'est-ce que cette jeune femme croyait avant et après la grève, c'est quoi son identité ou quoi que ce soit. Je crois qu'elle peut très bien être très politisée et porter le hidjab si ça lui tente.'

37. 'C'est sûr que de comprendre ce qu'on fait, où on s'en va c'est dur à contrôler parce que chaque jour il y avait des choses qui arrivaient et qui donnaient un sens tout autre au mouvement ou à ce qu'on allait faire le lendemain'

38. 'Je trouve que la manière anglo de militer est super intéressante. C'est-à-dire qu'ils sont beaucoup moins dans la confrontation pis dans les gains, pis dans demander des gains à une quelconque autorité, mais vraiment plus dans la création d'espaces pis dans la mobilisation solidaire pis dans le, tsé, "on va créer nos affaires nous-mêmes", tsé comme mettons le People's Potato à Concordia là, c'est malade là.'

39. 'j'avais pas un sentiment que je résistais et que j'étais hot. J'avais un sentiment de . . . terreur. C'est vraiment horrible qu'on en soit là, qu'on ne puisse pas manifester tranquillement dans la rue.'

40. 'il y a souvent une fausse saveur politique, mais au fond, c'est vraiment une question de conflits de personnalités. Il y a plusieurs personnes qui ne s'entendaient juste pas.'

41. 'Nous sommes en colère. Nous ne récupérons pas une grève . . . Nous n'infiltrons pas les manifestations, nous aidons à les organiser, nous les rendons vivantes.'

FIGURE 4.0 'Encounter with Earwigs'. *Source*: illustration by Lukas Beeckman.

Chapter 4

The Urban Political World of Urban Farmers: 'It's Not Just Growing Food, It's a Lot More Than That'

'*It's not just growing food, it's a lot more than that*' says one of City Farm School's trainers to Joëlle in describing his understanding of agriculture. A Montrealer in his late twenties, Ben has been involved in what we would call the city's agriculture scene for more than a decade now. This tall anglophone man has worked as Collective Garden Animator and Program Director for a nonprofit community organization in one of Montreal's most socially diverse neighbourhoods. Over the years, he has been setting up permaculture gardens in schoolyards and on street corners, reproducing his own plants and fruit trees and disseminating knowledge about fruit and vegetable cultivation through multiple workshops at different venues across Montreal. Joëlle met Ben in 2013 at a workshop he was giving at the City Farm School, an urban agriculture training programme operating from within marginal and interstitial spaces at Concordia University. At the time, she was a market-gardener apprentice there.[1]

The meeting place for the workshop was in the NDG neighbourhood (Notre-Dame-de-Grâce borough), at the far end of Concordia University's Loyola campus, where City Farm School's in-ground production sites are located (see Figure 4.1). About a dozen market-gardener and schoolyard-gardener apprentices met right behind a tall residence building, on a piece of lawn next to a large medicinal herb garden and several variously sized collective garden plots.

It was pouring rain on that workshop day, and the temperature was ideal for transplanting the perennial plants and fruit trees that Ben had brought, partly from his own nursery production and partly from a nursery located on the Montreal Island. As the apprentices rubbed the roots of plants and fruit trees, shook up soil agglutinations, and dipped the matter into a bucket

Youth Urban Worlds: Aesthetic Political Action in Montreal, First Edition.
Julie-Anne Boudreau and Joëlle Rondeau.
© 2021 John Wiley & Sons Ltd. Published 2021 by John Wiley & Sons Ltd.

FIGURE 4.1 Vegetable garden beds covered with mesh, located in front of a medicinal garden plot and some fruit trees (top right) planted on the day of a food forest design workshop. Behind the garden is a residential street, while City Farm School's market stand is located in the building on the far left. *Source:* photo by Joëlle Rondeau, July 2014.

of water inoculated with mycelium and other fungi in order to kickstart a symbiotic communication network between the roots and the microorganisms living underground, they learned the principles of 'food forest' design and cultivation. Among other plants and tools, they teamed up with black and purple raspberries, grape vines, trellises, pear trees, pink champagne currents, alfalfa, oat, clover, and lupens, all of which they planted densely together in order to harness their synergistic potentials. On a flat area of grass lawn laid out in the iconic American campus style, a multispecies edible collective was arranged. By design, the metabolic actions of nitrogen-fixing plants (alfalfa, clover) benefit other species, while the long tap root of other plants (lupen among them) transports heavier minerals up into soil layers closer to the roots of fruit trees. Over time, the shade of the trees' canopies will offer cool microclimates to the plants below, while the trees themselves will provide natural habitats for birds and offer students and neighbours a little something tasty to eat, free of charge. Does urbanity affect the ways in which youth think about agriculture and grow food today? In this ethnography, we enter the urban political world of beginning and aspiring urban farmers.

The Market-Gardener Apprenticeship Program involves an eight-month apprenticeship at the City Farm School, taking place over a whole growing season, from seedling production at the Concordia Greenhouse in March to the closing of production plots and markets at Loyola campus in October. It is not part of the university's curriculum. In fact, City Farm School was constituted as a nonprofit organization two years after its founding in 2011, in order that it could continue operating on institutional lands while offering experience-based education in urban agriculture and selling crops at farmers' markets. The training programme was 'designed to create urban farmers who are interested in taking their veggies to market, while also working collectively to design and manage a typical scale community garden plot' (City Farm School 2014b). To this day, it is unique in the Province of Quebec and in Montreal in providing hands-on training, guest lectures, and teach-ins on small-scale organic food production and distribution, as well as food sovereignty and food politics.

The programme, however, shares similarities with urban farming training programmes that have emerged in North American postindustrial cities in response to growing social and professional demands for farming and horticultural training in urban environments, including Detroit's DTown Farm, Milwaukee's Growing Power, Chicago's City Farm, and Boston's Food Project. These emergent urban agriculture education infrastructure systems and knowledge networks are gaining increasing attention in popular and academic literature (Bryant 2012; Ewert 2012; Hanson and Marty 2012). Developed over recent years by actors outside of the formal institutional agriculture education infrastructure (e.g. community organizations, social enterprises, student collectives), they provide training on modes of food production and distribution specifically adapted to urban environments. Their production sites differ from conventional farms in that they are often interstitial, small-scale, and networked (Bryant 2012; Hanson and Marty 2012), making use of situational opportunities to produce food for urban communities and provide farming training.

In a similar fashion, City Farm School was created at Concordia University in 2011 by students, aspiring professional urban farmers, and community members. Its emergence on the downtown campus of a university that does not carry agriculture education or training programmes is quite significant. City Farm School was crafted by students and community members involved in the Concordia Greenhouse Project, a 'collectively run, consensus-based, nonprofit organization' whose mandate is to organize various activities on sustainable modes of food production and food issues in the rooftop greenhouse located on the 13th floor of the Henry H. Hall Building of Concordia's downtown campus. It was only after years of student activism and administrative work led in part by Sustainable Concordia that, in the academic year 2007–08, the greenhouse was progressively transformed into a community space geared towards urban sustainability and popular education. It had been abandoned by the biology department in the mid-1970s and the university had planned to dismantle it in 2002. However, university campus sustainability assessments reclaimed by the student community recommended that it be used instead as a space dedicated to ecological horticulture and community development in order to foster urban sustainability. Discussions between the university administration, a sustainability coordinator, students, and Sustainable Concordia led to its renovation and transformation.

This had a powerful attraction effect on Ellen, one of the greenhouse's first coordinators. When Joëlle met her to learn more about the development of the Concordia Greenhouse Project, she was a professional urban farmer working in Toronto and had been actively involved in growing vegetables on the open-air rooftop of a university building there, teaching production techniques to students, and selling crops to the university's food services and at a farmers' market on campus.

Ellen was living in British Columbia when she heard from a friend in Montreal that the People's Potato, the student collective at Concordia University mentioned by Étienne in the previous chapter, was clandestinely growing seedlings in the abandoned greenhouse. The history of this student collective illustrates how shifting modes of political action set the impetus for the beginning of these activities, in 1999, 'at a time of growth in socially and environmentally conscious politics at Concordia University, with the emergence of a strong anti-capitalist wing in the anti-globalization movement' (People's Potato 2014). As is stated on the collective's website (www.peoplespotato.com), 'Not satisfied with merely discussing antipoverty and food politics within the student body, the Potato's original founders attempted to address these issues in a tangible way'; that is, by serving by-donation vegan lunches. The attempt was thus to 'provide an alternative to the corporate run cafeterias on campus'. The greenhouse was used to grow some of the greens served in those meals. The People's Potato's endeavour, subversive of the monopolistic capitalist channels of food production and distribution on campus, seduced Ellen significantly: '*I thought that's the coolest thing I've ever heard . . . and I was already on the track of wanting to do urban agriculture as a career, so I thought this is perfect, I have two years left of my undergrad, I'll go do it at Concordia and that way I can volunteer at the greenhouse.*' Her words evoke a striking conception of proximate space and continuity, almost as if there were a subway between British Columbia and Montreal.[2] She lives in a world of networked urban places.

Ellen loves to be outdoors and active. She speaks energetically and with great passion. From the tone of her voice and the pace of her speech, you can tell that she is a go-getter, with a warm, generous, and unpretentious character. Most of the people Joëlle meets through City Farm School share these enticing personality traits; their presence carries a certain kind of intriguing flow of light and lightness that touches you and stays with you, marking your memories and inspiring you.

Ellen moved to Montreal in the 2000s and continued her undergraduate studies at Concordia University. By the end of her programme, she was hired to work as education coordinator at the greenhouse. '*I was lucky enough to get the job, to do that because I'd shown interest. So it was a strange thing for me because I was not a professional yet. I was just interested in learning*', she explains. In partnering with community members (the Montreal Permaculture Guild[3] among others), she began to organize educational activities in urban agriculture. This created a training space for beginning or aspiring urban farmers, providing hands-on learning opportunities in a field that had little to no professional recognition as such, in a city where formal training in urban agriculture did not exist. As Ellen says, '*I sort of felt like my role there was to create my own destiny, kind of. . . I wanted a space to learn and practice . . . I had to create that for myself and I knew that there were other people that wanted to learn so I put up call-outs and we gathered a movement of people. And . . . so basically this was happening where we were doing lots of workshops and we were realizing like, we couldn't really keep up . . . So City Farm School was a way of being like ok, we want to do this even better but we also want it to be . . . if it's gonna be really organized and . . . be like . . . meeting a need because there were so many people coming into our workshops, there was obviously a huge demand for people to both learn how to grow food, but also practice it. Because that was the thing about the greenhouse, that you could do both there. Like it wasn't just a place where you go to a workshop, it was a place where you could also plant and make mistakes and . . . enjoy it. Enjoy the process.*' Like the strikers we met in the previous chapter, Ellen wanted to open a different political space, doing more than claiming.

By 'bringing the farm apprenticeship to the city', City Farm School's Market-Gardener Apprenticeship Program is 'designed to prepare participants to become leaders in the emerging urban agriculture movement' (City Farm School 2014a). Thus, its mission consists not just in developing expertise in urban agriculture, but also in promoting 'a cultural shift towards more resilient communities able to meet the challenges posed by climate change by focusing on local food autonomy' (City Farm School 2014a). As one of its coordinators once told Joëlle, talking about the criteria used to recruit participants, '*we're an urban agriculture school, we're city farmers, we want people who are interested in city farming, you know what I mean? Who are wanting to make a difference in the city.*'

Over the years, educational opportunities at the greenhouse have thus been structured into a community-based city farming school aimed at filling the gaps of formal agriculture educational infrastructure in order to provide experience-based training in small-scale organic food production and distribution adapted to the urban environment. The politicized narrative inextricable from the School's mission, recruitment criteria, and history gives meaning to urban agriculture practices and training as a political form.

So, *'it's not just growing food'*, as Ben says. It's not just having fun by gardening together on the streets or in yards, either. These various political gestures – asserting the presence of edible plants in the urban environment, creating pop-up farmers' markets on campus, serving free vegan lunches to the university community – produce aesthetic political relations by taking advantage of situational opportunities. While City Farm School flies under the radar of formally recognized agriculture education institutions, it aims to create actors who can legitimately be present in the situations that they participate in creating with numerous non-human actors, thereby sustaining political action through their differentiated agentic capacities.

As a political form, urban agriculture also speaks to an attraction to differences that thrives in city life. It is the kind of attraction that, in the concrete city, draws people towards vibrant materials and life forces coming from a farmers' market on a university's downtown campus. In its initial year, City Farm School apprentices sold produce cultivated in planters on Mackay Street at a farmers' market set up by students. Ann loved it. She is an energetic urban farmer who completed the apprenticeship in those initial years and has since been actively involved in the coordination of the programme's activities. She remembers, laughing: *'[People] were like "oh, where does this come from, the greenhouse?" And I'm like "No, right there! Like, look! That's the tomato plant that you're eating off of." And people were like "Oh my gosh, oh my gosh!" They'd freak out, they were really excited!'*

The differentiated agentic activities producing such urban agricultural environments and situations engage our senses intensely; they have semiotic and material powers that make us interact viscerally with the land. For Ann, *'in terms of it being, like, a garden, it's like really productive and selling at markets and stuff . . . like, I find it important to be doing that – to be selling at markets even though there wasn't a lot of produce coming out of it. Uhm . . . just to sort of like put that idea in people's minds, you know, that, like, you can do that even on this tiny space and in those weird raised boxes and stuff like that.'*

The edible plants that surprise us on the street corner – like a raspberry plant in front of a coffee shop, for instance (see Figure 4.2) – these are *'the kinds of things that bring awareness in one's environment. It's something alive, that everyone knows. You know, the first thing that we did was to eat the berries*

FIGURE 4.2 Edible plants cultivated on a street corner in Villeray by a group of citizens under the name 'Mange Trottoir' ('Eat Sidewalk'). *Source:* photo by Joëlle Rondeau, July 2017.

on the plant,[4] says Juliette. After completing the Market-Gardener Apprenticeship, she enrolled in a landscape architecture programme with an interest in developing edible landscapes and one day owning her own farm.

Critical literature on urban agriculture and urban food movements has drawn attention to the kind of insurgent and lifestyle politics embedded in alternative urban food growing practices (Block et al. 2012; Lyons 2014; Galt, Grey, and Hurley 2014; Lewis 2015). That urban agriculture is a political act is not a new idea. How urban cultures more specifically affect this kind of political action – expressive of a transformation of the political process – has been less explored. Yet, '*wanting to make a difference in the city*' is precisely what motivated Joëlle to undertake the Market-Gardener Apprenticeship Program in 2013. After having participated in an urban farm project in Toronto upon the completion of her bachelor's degree, she came to Montreal to learn the skills and knowledge needed to develop an intergenerational collective rooftop garden in the city. It was while participating in City Farm School's apprenticeship programme that she felt compelled to further explore the professional and sociopolitical projects informing apprentices' desire to acquire urban agricultural knowledge. They appeared to 'bare potentials able to improve and enlarge our sensitivity, our comprehension and perhaps even our way of being', to quote Welsch (2002) (see Introduction). In other words, Joëlle found herself in several pregnant moments during this apprenticeship, participating in a myriad of everyday political gestures, unable to describe exactly what she felt touching her in action, moving her inside and out, changing the modalities of her engagement with the urban environment, with the land.

Following experiential insights gained through her own experience, Joëlle returned to the field a year later as a Master's student and aspiring researcher. With a new cohort of apprentices and of individuals who had completed the programme, she wanted to make sense of the urban political world that beginning and aspiring urban farmers cultivate with numerous earthly beings and lively matters.

Embodied Experiences of the Spatialities and Circulation of Food Commodities in the City

As an entry point into this urban political world, let us consider how Ann describes the significance and meaning of cultivating food: '*I feel like growing food and like, having the ability to do that is one of the most empowering things that you can do with your life. You know? To feed yourself and to feed your community and to be . . . like people talk about coming off the grid or whatever but, for me, I think it starts with food you know? To like, not be dependent on the worldwide farming system which is messed up and hurts a lot of people.*' Living in a city (especially in the Global North) means that sustaining your body's energy and health is an act that relies on resources often located in faraway places, which pass through long production and distribution chains connected by logistic algorithms operating predominantly on capitalist and industrial rationalities up to outlets where they are sold in exchange for money.

In Montreal more specifically, several factors have increased dependence on imported food. Long winters, agricultural trade policies that have drastically reduced the numbers of family farms, the eating habits of the settler communities that have claimed ownership of the land and disrupted Indigenous food systems, urban sprawl historically linked to industrialization and regimes of private property, and the concentration of power in the food distribution chain are only some of the elements that have increased Montrealers' dependency on long, globalized, corporate food chains. As is the case elsewhere, 'the metropolis dwells in a food plate, but not necessarily the one it feeds off due to the metropolis's cosmopolitan character and the dominant global character of the food system' (Brand and Bonnefoy 2011, p. 2; our translation).

Yet, eating is an immediate embodied experience. Food is *'something that you ingest, which gets into your body, which . . . it is very much linked to one's own health, to the individual'*,[5] according to Raphaëlle. Whether through shock documentaries, classroom discussions, international apprenticeship, or travel experiences, youths are more aware today of food politics and the consequences of their consumption practices. A multiplicity of media exposes them to the problems brought about by climate change, the industrialized food system, and agricultural trade policies. It defines some of the contours of this urban youth world, a shared space of commonality characterizing what they can sense and perceive. See Ellen's words, for instance: *'I was taking a lot of Latin American history classes and I became sort of politicized through those classes with the political and social struggles of like landless peasants in Latin America and how in these agrarian communities, people are becoming impoverished by the industrial food system basically, right? I became critical of industrial food systems and recognized that we are part of it because we are consumers.'* In this urban youth world, the production process of fetishized commodities is demystified. It shapes translocal sociopolitical consciousness. Thus, the interdependencies constitutive of globalized industrial food systems and their effectiveness are felt as visceral links connecting bodies and ecosystems. Ideology becomes edible. . .

Knowing the detrimental effects of their consumption acts and habits, the apprentices that Joëlle meets, just like Joëlle herself, have complex and conflicting relationships to consumer goods produced and made available for purchase through globalized, industrial chains. When Sophia was setting up her urban sprout farm after the completion of her market-gardener apprenticeship, getting as much second-hand equipment as possible was very important to her. She did not want to buy mass-produced products because, as she explains it, *'when you're buying a product like this, you're also participating in the labour hours of all these individuals and they are . . . they are slaves to you. And it's just like a very heavy uhm . . . network that you are supporting in doing so. And you are implicit in that work. Like, whether you like it or not, you're trusting whatever company it is to produce a good product but you aren't necessarily questioning how they are producing it. And . . . so . . . in buying their product, you are participating. And for me, that's a very disturbing notion because I don't want to . . . render . . . I don't want to take someone's freedom away and that's what I'm doing. So, I think, for me, that's part of the reason getting second-hand things is very important. Because it's reducing waste.'*

A paradoxical tension emerges here in the disconnections felt between producers, distributors, transformers, and consumers in absolute time and space, where they are spatially and temporally connected in networks with detrimental effects *infused in* the commodities that circulate within them.

As Sophia highlights: *'So if you're buying mass-produced food. Like, you are becoming . . . you're eating the injustice, you're eating the fossil fuels, you're eating . . . You're literally eating other humans in a way. I mean, that sounds awful but . . . people are giving their livelihoods to . . . getting less than minimum wage, living in fear of being sent back home, you know. That's just a really horrible disguised slavery, it's really awful.'*

A common thread in the conversations Joëlle has with beginning and aspiring urban farmers is this networked conception of space linking the local with the global through foodways, bodies, and materials. The accessibility of producing your own food, in this context, prompts a kind of 'resistance articulée' (F. Anderson, 26 March 2016, cited in Lamarque 2016, p. 86) in the punk, anarcho, do-it-yourself spirit that partly characterizes Montreal's urban feel. We find it in Ann's words, quoted previously: *'people talk about getting off the grid'*. She continues: *'To be able to look after yourself in a way that doesn't hurt anybody. You know, and that makes you feel good. And is a good thing, you know. For me, that's a big part of it, that's why I wanted to do it. I was just like "oh my god! I can't participate in this. How am I gonna do it? Ok I'm just gonna learn how to do it myself. That's fine. I can be independent. I don't have to . . . participate in this, like, shitty system, you know".'* From a political form, urban agriculture becomes an embodied political gesture. Nonlinearity, mobility, and affectivity have a significant effect on political action here. The gesture is as much about viscerally dewiring from hegemonic networks with detrimental sociopolitical and socioecological effects as it is about rewiring to alternative networks, spatializing, embodying, and ingesting food circulating through more-than-human alternative systems with positive effects.

Urban farmers' political gestures present a productive critique of the temporality associated with urban ways of food provisioning in a world that appears somewhat besieged by capitalist rationalities and product homogeneity. Consider Damien's perspective: *'food, I have to work in order to pay for it. Well, this idea, you can make it crumble a little by saying "maybe not necessarily" you know? Maybe you have to work something like 10 hours per week to make enough money to afford food. Well, then what about putting 10 in like trying to forage in the dumpsters of grocery stores food that is still safe and in good shape?'*[6] Damien's political act, as expressed here, is grounded in urban life's cyclical temporalities and everyday practices. It expresses an attempt at making time for alternative food provisioning tactics that subvert the metalogics of the dominant agroindustrial and capitalist food system. Damien grew up in Montreal's central neighbourhoods and knows these densely populated environments intimately. After high school, he started to get actively engaged in student activism and environmental activism. Now in his mid-twenties, his thinking on the city is informed by an ecological and anticapitalist mindset, as he has come to consider that '*the potential of the city is to . . . have created a sort of conduit that slips out of this [capitalist] economy and that – if we are well organized – we can take back and like . . . progressively get out . . .*'[7] This taking back is a deeply embodied, experiential political act, as he is '*trying to affect the economy around me by creating different linkages or . . . an insertion . . . to insert myself in the economy in a different fashion. So, you know, making loops. To render these loops efficient . . . I want us to save on nature for instance. Or to save on humans who are presently oppressed in their work environments.*'[8]

Growing or foraging food – and in these endeavours, weaving alternative food webs – is conceived as another way of circumventing the alienation that these youths feel in 9–5 work cycles and urban ways of food provisioning. This alienation is felt in relation to numerous non-human actors connected by the temporalities and equivalences of the '*lifestyle that the city dictates*', as Cynthia puts it. Some of the equivalences required for the reproduction of everydayness in the urban world of these educated, White youths trained for professional jobs in the service and knowledge economy are made explicit by Suzanne: '*People go from 9 to 5 in front of their computers. What's it for, actually? It's to get the salary that will pay for the house that you leave alone to itself while you go to work, you know? And for your two weekend days which are very precious. You spend one in tidying up and the other in resting. Hey! That's not a meaningful life!*'[9] Suzanne's words attest to a sense of alienation induced by this specific delimitation of space and time of the urban political economy. It translates into a lack of meaningful purpose with numbing and disorientating effects: '*People don't necessarily have a reason for living. I get why depression is rampant!*'[10] As Raphaëlle sees it, and lives it herself: '*I feel that if people had to work the land to survive, you know – not necessarily to get back to the times when you know . . . my grandparents really suffered, it was very hard, surviving and all that . . . but to the point where you have to work a bit to feed yourself. I think that a sentiment of accomplishment would be so much more present.*'[11]

As a kind of counter-actualization of this sense of dispossession and lack of meaning, these youths express the strong desire to transform their urban world, adjusting its temporal cycles and making space for modes of food provisioning that are de-alienated from the hegemonic circuits of the capitalist market economy spatializing food flows mostly through corporate outlets in the city. Take Simone's description of her ideal city: '*I see the city like . . . like an edible city. My ideal city would be one in which we can travel as easily by skateboard, by bike or any other means of transportation . . . I like the playful dimension of being able to feed ourselves just like we want. Where you can go look in dumpsters, find safe and healthy things, cook them, can them, do lactofermentation, whatever. Where you can go harvest fruits in the park . . . Have a garden on your balcony. It's true that we are faced with the reality of the workplace. I fully acknowledge that when you work from 9 to 5, you become tired, you may not have the energy for this, but I like the potentiality of making the claim that feeding oneself should not only be "you go to your grocery store, you make your groceries and you cook". No. You know? Or like you buy pre-cooked meals, or you eat out. No, food should also be available for you free of charge.'*[12] Simone's conception of an 'edible city' expresses a playful liberty of food choices, spatialized in the urban environment outside of a commodified value chain and actualized in situational creative acts. Like for the 'risk-takers' we will meet in Chapter 5, this 'potentiality' is what drives her. It defines the contours of a hopeful horizon. It is a political act that constitutes an active and imaginary appropriation of the urban space, echoing similar forms of political action in the repertoire analysed in Chapter 3.

The productive landscape of these Montreal youths is not confined to a bounded space, agricultural plot or otherwise. Likewise, the heterogeneity of temporal patterns in the urban environment is constitutive of their practices. More particularly, the cyclical (sequential) temporal patterns of plants are taken advantage of by the beginning and aspiring farmers Joëlle meets. For instance, Ann tells her that on her walks around the city she *'seedsave[s] like always.'* Why so? Because she loves it so much, she says. She explains: *'I start carrying a little plastic bag around with me, usually for that it's usually like flowers, like marigolds. You've got to dead-head them to make them come back . . . a lot of flowers . . . daisies, that kind of thing. I just grab seeds. All the time. Or like I see a pepper plant that's kind of like . . . you know, it's like dehydrated or something. I'll just grab a couple and keep them and plant them . . . [laughs]. Yeah.'* In these situations, with all their vitality, Ann and the seeds constitute themselves as political actors, legitimate in their endeavours and effectivity taking place over different timescales and through very different capacities and styles of action: those of a human and those of a seed. Ann tells Joëlle that she usually replants the seeds at City Farm School's own plant nursery project. Over the years, this project has become well known for providing thousands of seedlings at very low cost to urban agriculture community organizations in and around Montreal. *'They will go back out to all these different organizations'*, Ann continues, *'but it's like stuff that I randomly grabbed on a walk down the street.'* The distributed agency of seeds saved from planters thus transforms urban spaces, making them productive and edible. They act through dispersion rather than confinement.

It is easy to be awed and even humbled by seeds. *'There's something incredible in the idea of planting a seed,'* says Raphaëlle, *'and then see something pop out almost by itself.'* Reflecting back on the experience of growing seedlings for community organizations and their collective market-garden plots as part of the market-gardener apprenticeship they both undertook in 2013, Joëlle and Raphaëlle are still mesmerized by it all:

RAPHAËLLE *You know the lettuce seeds, how small they are, and you're like, 'I am gonna put this in the soil and . . .' Honestly, even now, I'm like, 'It's never gonna grow!' You know, there's only a bit of soil and I've put a bunch of seeds in there, I covered them.*

JOËLLE   *. . . watered them*

RAPHAËLLE *And you've got lettuce. It's a bit surreal as it is . . . There is something so intrinsic to life. And that is so easy . . . I think that it should be obvious, that it should be known, I think that people must experience this in their life.*

With the traditional conceptual lenses of political sciences, it would be difficult to understand something as mundane as planting an organic, heirloom seed as an object of political action. Yet, in a world of cities, these seeds' agentic capacities, as they are entangled in multispecies 'knots of embodied time' (Rose 2012, p. 128), can become a vector of critical political education and political effectivity. Consider Ann's perspective: '*Seeds to me is just so interesting – the first currency [humans] ever had. You know what I mean? Holy shit! This is the beginning of commerce . . . is seeds. So . . . to be attached to a history that long is like, I get goosebumps. I'm like, "oh my god, how do I, like, [a] little tiny human get to participate in that", it's so exciting!*'

Through these words and the excitement they carry, we grasp the extent to which Ann understands and perceives herself as participating in the long political and economic history of the coevolution of plants and humans. She feels related to the evolutive assemblages that have shaped this history, to the knowledges that have emerged through it and been passed on to generations. This understanding of time locates her existence, her body's vitality and agentic capacities in a temporal framework that resonates with the concept of enduring time, that is 'a time of continuity between past *and future*' (Rose 2012, p. 128; our emphasis). Deborah Bird Rose's analysis of such 'knots of embodied time' can help us better understand the temporal heterogeneity that is characteristic of urban farmers' aesthetic mode of political action with organic (self-reproducible) plants. To do this, following Rose, we have to make distinctions between three patterns of time: generational time (which 'involves flows from one generation to the next'), synchrony, and sequential time. 'Synchrony intersects with sequential time, and involves flows among individuals, often members of different species, as they seek to sustain their individual lives', Rose (2012, p. 128) explains.

In the case of seed foraging and growing, Ann expresses a situational opportunity where 'generational time intersects with synchronous encounter' (Rose 2012, p. 129). This intersection can be understood in fact as 'a site of embodied interface' (Rose 2012, pp. 129–130), and is as such deeply affective. This is where Ann gets goosebumps. The potentiality of generating a new existence – and new modes of coexistence – at this embodied interface where sequential temporal patterns intersect with the knowledge and traditions passed down from generation to generation is intensely felt as both aesthetic *power* and ethical responsibility – or, as Donna Haraway (2016) would put it, 'response-ability'. Ann makes this clear to us as she further reflects on the historical entanglement of humans and seeds, and the contemporary twist of patented seeds that are imbricated in the globalized capitalist economy: '*I see seedsaving as a technology, a type of shared knowledge and to try and put a patent on something that old . . . It's just mindblowing to me how anybody can ever allow that to happen because it's just like so detrimental to the way that we learn and the way that we live.*' For Ann, understanding this rupture of generational time through private property and capitalist teleology, at the intersection of synchronous encounter and sequential time in the entanglement between edible plants and humans, constitutes transversal knowledge: '*I feel like through seeds is a great way to understand the sort of contemporary aspects of capitalism that are really trying to like take ownership over ideas and concepts. So . . . if you understand that, then it opens up ways to understand all these other things which . . . potentially could lead to very systemic change.*'

We thus see that beginning and aspiring urban farmers' ways of relating to food and agriculture express a networked conception of space, as well as sequential, generational, and synchronous temporalities that give meaning to urban agriculture as an object of political action. They provide an urban logic of action that contrasts with the political process in a world of nation-states, because they are grounded in the immediacy of one's environment and everyday life. They lay bare multilinear, unforeseen, mysterious potentials that appeal on both representational and affective registers. Sophia synthesizes this well: '*I think urban agriculture does that. It's a change in mentality and realizing that we don't need this monoculture field. That food, something that everyone needs, which is a constant, can be done in a myriad of different ways, some very destructive uhm . . . for the environment and for other people, like migrant labour workers, for uhm . . . the world at large by dumping all these pesticides, etc., etc. Or it can be done in a sustainable way for the environment, for other people.*' This highlights very clearly a notion of variation that sees food and agriculture as objects of political action which materially take shape in and exist as effects of a varying nexus of more-than-human networked sociospatial relations involving other bodies, entities, and spaces.

This has ontological implications. As Gilles Deleuze writes in *The Fold* (1988, pp. 25–26), when variation is taken as the object, 'it is the notion of function that tends to stick out, but also the notion of object that changes and becomes functional . . . The object can no longer be defined by an essential form, but rather tends towards a pure functionality.' Deleuze calls this new object 'objectile'. He writes, '[w]ith this new status, the object does not relate to a spatial mold or, put otherwise, to a form–matter relation, but rather to a temporal modulation which involves a continuous variation of matter as well as the continuous development of form' (Deleuze 1988, p. 26). We find this in Ann's and Sophia's words, which evoke the temporal modulation and continual variation of both form and matter in the object-nexus of food, seeds, and agriculture. This nexus affects the subject for whom ingesting this 'objectile' is a temporal, bodily necessity. It puts them in a position from which they can grasp aesthetically – and take part in metabolically – this form of political action, producing difference in and through bodies (their own and those of others). The subject becomes 'subjectile', as Deleuze puts it.

'I think that's what's so powerful about it', says Sophia, 'it's that it's the great equalizer, like, who doesn't need food? Everyone needs food. And so then taking that obvious uhm . . . constant. You are able to find some point of contact, some point of . . . uhm uniting with someone else. A point of similarity and are then able to . . . present your argument in a way that is relatable . . . Whereas if you talk about something like . . . a pipeline. It might be not so relatable to some people because . . . yes they get gas, but they will not be impacted by an oil spill in Saskatchewan. It will really not impact them. Uhm . . . it will get in their watertable but it's just not directly applicable. But if you talk about the health, your health based on what you eat, if you talk about uhm . . . like it's just . . . everyone can relate because everyone needs food. It's what I think is so intriguing.'

In this context, learning the 'myriad ways' in which it is possible to produce food for yourself and for a community, with varying health and environmental outcomes on bodies (both human and non-human), becomes another way of transforming political relations through aesthetic modulations. This kind of political action is motivated not so much by strategic rationality towards a political goal as by pleasure, spontaneity, creativity, and the strong affective energies that circulate between and through bodies and are capable of energizing both growth and action.

The Urban Logic of Action of Urban Agriculture Practices

When these youths are asked whether they consider themselves militant people, only a few say they do. Usually, it is those who have been involved in guerilla gardening or environmental activism. Others instead express discontent and distrust at the political actions of social and ecological movements seeking clear and strategic outcomes. Ben says, '*I've never really been involved in any political movement. I don't think that's really effective. It often takes a long time to achieve things and they aren't necessarily big. Especially nowadays. You know, like, back when organics weren't the thing, somewhat for the people that were doing it, to come together and form an association and like, get, you know, the . . . laws in terms of regulation laws, in terms of what is organic, what is not organic and that kind of stuff, I think that was a really big and important step. But like now, I think, what you grow, how you grow it, when you're growing it, and with whom, all that I think is really a lot more important. Doing a project and doing it in your way that is really . . . pushes the boundaries and gets awareness and gets people involved. That changes things more than protesting or . . . in my opinion.'* He speaks here to a diffuse form of political action, evoking a clear conception of distributed political agency. This echoes Sophia's emphasis on food as a choice. Ben's logic of political action rests on the differentiated material effectivity of the choices we make, embedded as they are in a field of ecosystemic and socio-political relations. What factors in this political act are the differentiated agentic capacities of various species, techniques, tools, and people co-mingling in assemblages with differing emergent effectivity. How the action unfolds, who participates in this process, and the effects produced are all the more important in this political form. This resonates with Sophia's comment on the 'myriad ways' in which food can be produced and made available to others.

Ben's words also capture the strong affective relations that are sought out through these political gestures. The promise is that these gestures will enlarge sensibilities and move people. This expresses a profoundly affective aesthetic; changing the landscape of what people can sense or perceive and making them desire to get attuned to the movement of the action and 'get involved'. This form of political action is expressive of the transformation of the political process in a world of cities as compared to a world of nation-states.

More specifically, distrust in the nation-state motivates action here and now as part of heterogeneous agential collectives. It informs an urban logic of action. For instance, Madina, who also completed City Farm School's Market-Gardener Apprenticeship Program, states it explicitly in referring to responsibilities for ensuring equitable access to food and non-genetically modified seeds: *'The government has to step in but they're the ones that are protecting the wrong people, right? That's why I think like of these sort of . . . grassroots, service-style, like home gardening, you know . . . just doing it on your own is probably like, the way to go. The only way we can challenge, like, changing our food systems is if we . . . literally do it ourselves. But we can't do everything neither, you know like . . . it'd be interesting if you could get a network of farmers, like local like, if you get a body of people in a small area that can like specialize in certain things. You know like really small and just trade amongst yourselves. I wonder if that'd be like . . . You know like . . . People doing that together.'*

Youths who have been involved in traditional political movements, mostly anticapitalist and environmental social movements, express disengagement. In the case of the youths we spoke with, it often resulted from negative affects (blame and shame, among others) they felt as part of these movements, which reverberated with the goal of changing behaviours and enticing changes in environmental legislation. In contrast, they talked about strong empowering affects circulating through groups of people, plants, seeds, tools, and microorganisms that energized political action. For instance, when Raphaëlle became aware of the environmental problems related to climate change, she was moved politically: '*Once you're aware of all this, you can't ignore it.*'[13] She became involved in a group of climate change activists, distributing flyers on the streets. Once there, however:

> *I saw just how much people don't care. And this kind of activism shut me off, it sort of made me get that people, they don't . . . you know, just leave them alone, they don't want this. And then I realized that you can't coerce them. You can't change the world. Stop having the earth weight on your shoulders. And now, it's like a feedback loop that has made me realize that all in all, the only individuals who you can have influence on are those in your nearby environment. And I see it. So I have lost interest in activism, you know. It's too bad, I believe in it, I think it is important. But I don't have the personality to do it. It affects me too much . . . to see that like, a protest . . . all the effort that goes into it, nothing changes afterwards. It's not for me. I prefer to work . . . uhm . . . you know, with a community surrounding me . . . make a minimal change, yet influence maybe one person that knows me and this, this will be enough.*[14]

The possibility of quickly perceiving the emergent effectivity of one's action by asserting the presence of plants or being able to feed a community energizes action. So does the unpredictability of one's actions set in a field of relations constituting open-ended assemblages, configurations of human and non-human actors. The agentic capacities of new species, new pests, and unforeseen opportunities cause great excitement, which motivates beginning and aspiring urban farmers in their endeavours and learning.

These acts assert the presence of food organically grown in the city to reclaim space and change the relations that produce it, while at the same time asserting the presence of new kinds of farmers who can legitimately be present in the situations that they produce, thereby constituting political actors. This political form requires one to learn how to recognize and know with whom to mingle to produce aesthetic political action as an emergent effect of interdependent human and non-human agentic capacities. Learning the implicit grammar of this more-than-human urban agriculture scene plays on affective registers more than rational ones. In other words, one has to trust and follow one's own intuitions; one must get a sense of and a feel for things rather than leaning on knowledge acquired formally through rational and disembodied modes of knowing. Organic market gardeners are, after all, working with the living, in real-time and open environments. To know when, where, and how to intervene to optimize plants' vital agentic capabilities in a field of vibrant ecosystemic interdependences (without relying on synthetic pesticide and fertilizer ratios) is to learn to sense *variations* – in textures, tastes, smells, sounds, vibes, rhythms, and feelings – and intermodulate relationships where possible in an attempt to optimize synergies and repulse pests.

Acquiring experiential knowledge through hands-on practice is at the basis of the pedagogical relation taking place without institutional authority at City Farm School. As such, aesthetics is the predominant mode of knowing and learning; intuition and powerful affective attachments are considered driving forces. As Ann explains, '*that was sort of the approach to education. Just like . . . give the people the opportunity to fall in love with their gardens and get attached and really want to, but . . . you know what I mean? Once people fall in love with their garden, it's self-propelled; their knowledge and their, like, learning. And all you've done is like provide a space and the tools and some . . . and like access to some specific knowledge.*' In setting up the programme and its pedagogical opportunities, aesthetics was – and still is – considered a foundational element. Carol, another coordinator, mentions: '*I realize that giving more workshops and disseminating like quote–unquote knowledge or whatever . . . is something that needs to be very organized and you have to be ready. At the same time, it really comes from uhm . . . a feeling of wanting to share and create an environment that is like conducive to somebody experiencing something inspirational. Like those are the two things. "Get organized" is what you want, and to . . . share [knowledge] with people and hope that they are expecting this. And then also to share it in a way that is like fun and like inviting, you know.*' These words attest to the importance of creating an inviting and enabling aesthetic that allows individuals to be moved by affects which energize action and inspire. They also illustrate very well how affect moves between agents, creating such an enabling environment, passing through bodies and materials without finding its source in a unique individual, but instead being fuelled by bodies, reverberating through their expectations, moving on. This inspiring, enabling environment is probably what Joëlle felt touching her without being able to articulate it when she completed the apprenticeship in 2013; what was so captivating, enticing, and pleasurable. It felt and tasted wonderful too.

Learning how to act politically with a plant, a hose, a mycorrhiza is not a given for those youths who do not come from agricultural families and have little or no horticultural knowledge and training when they start their apprenticeship (as is the case for most of them). Apprentices come to perceive, recognize, and identify non-human actors with whom they can cultivate the city and create alternative food networks to the globalized industrial food system through hands-on learning experiences that involve sensory and empathic engagements in performing agricultural practices either alone or collectively, with little or no supervision.

During the lessons and work sessions, the use of anthropomorphic language sets out a pedagogical relation between human and other-than-human actors. This is an educative trick that makes it easier for apprentices to put themselves in a plant's or insect's 'shoes' and thus learn experientially how to better respond to other-than-human actors' own styles of action and capabilities. It forces them to draw from an empathic imagination in order to sensorially tune in to other-than-human specific sensory dispositions and inclinations and so get a better understanding of a shared urban political world from these actors' perspectives and umwelt. *'Just, like, try to understand it that way,'* Ann says, *'In like . . . think what's their goal. And you're an annual plant. Your goal is to reproduce, to pass on your genes. So, ok, so I'm like I'm gonna steel your flowers early on because you're gonna try to die on me and I don't want you to die. I know that's your goal – I'm really sorry.'* Mischievously, she adds: *'You know, you do have to apologize too, like, "I'm really sorry, but like, not yet . . . I'm gonna need more of you before . . ."* but then you save some seeds so you give it back. Right?'*

Whether in *'making strategic moves'* by harvesting kale leaves that are *'blocking the sun or impeding the air flow'* in order to keep the plant alive for continuous harvests all through the season, in evaluating whether grapes are ready for harvest according to their taste, or in learning how to co-act with a shovel's effectivity and clay soil *'that moves like that'*, these urban agricultural practices involve sensory education – learning experiential and haptic knowledge in movement, in action.

If both human and non-human actors are compelled, attracted, and attuned to the movement of action unfolding in multispecies entanglements, what are some of the modalities of power at play?

Seduction and Attraction in the Garden

Here we zoom in on seduction and attraction as twin modalities of power at play in aesthetic political relation, focusing more specifically on the charismatic capacities of non-human actors. 'Non-human charisma', a concept developed by Jamie Lorimer (2007), refers to the capacity of non-human actors to draw us into their world and, as such, draw affective responses from us. It is an emitting modality of power; it seduces and calls for a response. Through this power relation, urban farmers learn to be affected by non-human actors, get attuned to their various styles of action, and find themselves in a mysterious world.

Plants draw us into their worlds. '*They have temperaments*', as Ann says. If you attend to a plant's needs, you must pay attention to the '*things that they like*'. When she says this, Ann insists that she isn't making it up, that it '*comes from the way that people talk about it. People are like . . . and farmers, they'd be like, "oh yeah, like tomatoes like a struggle" or like . . . you know, they'll say things like "pepper like wind" and "eggplants like heat". You don't say they need it, you don't say that, like, it's necessary. You say like they like these things.*' We 'relate' differently to different plants. Ann doesn't find it hard to relate to plants: '*they're living creatures, they're awesome. They're so awesome.*' Fascination, attraction, and magnetism are the modalities of power at play here.

Lorimer (2007) distinguishes various types of non-human charisma which are useful for understanding some of the seductive capacities of fauna and flora. These modalities of power trigger powerful affective attachments that can be either positive or negative. Joëlle and Loren laughed a great deal during an interview when Loren admitted that she had not been able to kill a Japanese beetle (see Figure 4.3) throughout her apprenticeship, despite the fact that this invasive species was creating havoc in the garden. By contrast, she '*[didn't] have a problem killing aphids*'. She said that she found the Japanese beetle '*quite beautiful . . . they're gorgeous creatures . . . whereas an aphid, it's a little dot, you know? And so you don't see much of it, it's more like little dots*'. As an aspiring urban farmer, she felt better about herself with this realization, saying jokingly that as an aphid killer, she wasn't '*a total wimp after all*'.

The physical characteristics of some non-human others can trigger what Lorimer calls 'cuddly charisma' by drawing caring attention to them. Those

FIGURE 4.3 Japanese beetle (*Popilla japonica*). *Source:* photo by Joëlle Rondeau, August 2014.

in possession of physical characteristics similar to those of humans can seduce us more powerfully, as in the case of the Japanese beetles comparatively to the aphids. The basis of this charisma is what Lorimer calls 'ecological charisma'. Charismatic non-human beings' ecological affordances must be concurrent with the space–time ecological rhythms and ecological affordances of humans, who are warm-blooded mammals, 'mostly bipedal, between 1.4 and 1.9 metres tall, land dwelling, diurnal, and ocular centric' (Lorimer 2007, p. 916). Hence, when Loren says that she has no problem killing aphids, which appear to her as *'little dots'*, they are endowed with less ecological charisma than Japanese beetles, which have larger bodies, legs, and two visible eyes. Furthermore, the aesthetic appearance of the Japanese beetles – with their body's bronze and green metallic-looking outer shells – triggers awe and fascination. In this case, we can also conclude with Lorimer (2007, p. 920) that 'organisms such as insects, that are radically different to anthropocentric norms perform a *feral charisma*'.

Species can trigger strong emotional responses from humans at different stages of their lifecycles, their capacities and aesthetic appearances attracting others. As Ann mentions to Joëlle, *'Every year, this is one of the weirdest challenges, is that I try to cut down the number of tomatoes mostly. Because you end up with, like, 25 varieties of tomatoes that you are growing and it's very hard to manage that. It gets kinda out of control. But it's hard because I love so many of them, they're just so pretty. Like, they're so pretty as seedlings. So then some of them, like, I'm attached to some at the seedling level, where I'm like "Oh my god, you're so gorgeous and you smell so good", you know they're like purple or they have loby things or they're like really delicate. Like the Roman Candle is like this bizarre-looking fucking creature. It looks like a willow tree as a tomato . . . uhm . . . and it's really hard to keep it alive, but it's like . . . I'm in love with it a little bit. And then when you grow it out, it's shit. Like, it doesn't do very well in this climate. Like, it's not really the right plant to be growing here but I can't stop myself from growing it because I love it, you know [laughing]. Like, that kind of thing happens. Maybe more than it should.'* As this example makes explicit, these seductive modalities of action influence human gestures and attention, which can in turn influence the composition of species in the garden.

The effects of charismatic power relations between humans and non-humans are not fixed; they can change over time. Species endowed with feral charisma may trigger fear and repulsion, but, as Raphaëlle tells Joëlle, this perception can change with a better understanding of their role in one's environment: *'When I was little, I had a really bad phobia of earwigs. And a couple of months ago, I was harvesting lettuce with a knife. And I was seeing it . . . there were earwigs walking and I was trying not to catch one of them, but you know, I was conscious that they were there and I was happy with that, I told myself "well, ok, they are not on me, they're doing their own thing" . . . and just realizing that I had made it to the point where I was capable of accepting them. They are in their environment and I had no fear.'*[15] In this open-ended, dynamic encounter, Raphaëlle and the earwigs constitute themselves as political actors with a shared sense of purpose (however different their agentic capacities may be) in the co-production of the market garden, a shared environment. Connolly (2011) would call this a 'pregnant moment' in which, as proto-agents, the earwigs are disrupting Raphaëlle's sense of perception as she senses their unexpected vibrations. Raphaëlle perceives their presence, their vibration, and is proud of her new capacity to share a space–time with them without panicking. For Connolly, 'complex agency' or political action requires the involvement of two or more agents, but also a capacity to deepen sensitivity for others, a capacity for self-consciousness, the ability to master the environment to some degree, and the ability to work tactically on the self in response to external pressures and one's own reflective responses. The earwigs clearly do not satisfy all these conditions. However, they carry 'creative agency' in the sense that they disturb Raphaëlle's sense of perception. In doing so, Raphaëlle gains self-confidence with regard to her own agency and subjectivity. The earwigs' political effect is thus highly dependent on Raphaëlle's sense of perception and her interpretation of this perception; in other words, on Raphaëlle's experiential knowledge. Proto-agentic capacities only have indirect political effects, yet these effects are essential for spurring creative and then complex agency.

However, in the case of undesired species, attraction can be manipulated so as to control their movement and reproductive urges. As such, domination is a modality of power well used in ecological farming systems that do not rely on pesticides or synthetic fertilizers. For instance, a species attractive to pests will be planted next to cultivated plants to create a diversion for them. Humans thus play with species' seductive and attractive powers to the benefit of their own interests. Aesthetics acts here as a mode of human–non-human communication. An example is a trap used at City Farm School to capture Japanese beetles, which artificially reproduces the beetles' own pheromones, tricking them into thinking that it is a mate and trapping them when they approach. Humans have thus reproduced the beetles' agentic capacity – the emission of pheromones – to exert control over the attractive effect that it triggers on them. This is a power relation that also plays on a somatic register. The Japanese beetles recognize the pheromone artificially and strategically reproduced by humans because it is significant in their world or umwelt. Through this somatic interaction, humans trick and manipulate the beetles in order to preserve the leaves of cultivated plants for their own purposes.

Conclusion

The farming and training sites at City Farm School make visible socioecological and sociopolitical interdependencies between human and non-human others that can, through their varied styles of action and capacities, produce more fertile, biodiverse, and edible urban spaces. The presence of more than 100 plant varieties with different roles, capacities, and uses in an ecological market garden attracts insects, microorganisms, birds, and small animals that are rarely seen in Montreal.

What urban farmers have told and shown us is that urban ways of life are bringing new political forms to the fore. The motor of this process is not so much antagonism and contention as impulsion and aesthetics. Indeed, as we have seen in this chapter, these youths act rather spontaneously, jumping on opportunities intuitively with a nonconsequentialist outlook. The more-than-human interdependencies constitutive of everyday life in the urban environment bring about situational opportunities that inform beginning and aspiring urban farmers' practices, as Loren explains: *'there's all kinds of . . . interesting potentials that you don't even see coming. You know what I mean? Like . . . uhm and allies that you make and . . . unknown things that are gonna come up.'* Engaging in this open-ended, dynamic, and surprising swarm of activity is fun and thrilling. It can potentially enable possibilities and calls for responses.

In this process, pregnant moments lead to a transformation of the socially constructed sensory dispositions that delimit the conditions of detectability of non-human sources of agency in producing urban spaces where noncommodified foods can circulate and be organically grown. Aesthetic modes of learning contribute to bringing about an aesthetic political consciousness, deconstructing the naturalness of the socioecological and sociopolitical urban relations producing city dwellers' living environments. Theories of aesthetics have provided a useful lens through which to understand how human beings perceive non-human presence. Yet, what we see in the urban world of young urban farmers in Montreal is that sensing proto-agents also propels political action. Indeed, urban farmers' particular aesthetic dispositions shape their political subjectivity, their relation to space, time, and rationality, and consequently their broader engagement with the city. By changing their judgement of taste and their encounter with the urban sensory world, they transform their recognition of non-human beings into positive performances of sustainable food practices.

Notes

1. This apprenticeship experience, initially undertaken out of personal and professional interest and curiosity, prompted Joëlle to further explore – this time through academic research at Institut national de la recherche scientifique – the significance of urban agriculture training programmes in the development of a new generation of farmers and alternative urban food systems. She found herself in several pregnant moments during her apprenticeship. The following year, as a Master's

student, she returned to City Farm School to conduct fieldwork with the new cohort of market-gardener apprentices. This fieldwork consisted of participant observation over the course of the seasonal cycle using a GoPro camera mounted on her chest in order to capture interactions with plants and interviews with urban farmers (Rondeau 2017).

2. British Columbia and Quebec are separated by close to 5000 km.

3. The Montreal Permaculture Guild was offering free community workshops. Partnering with the group allowed for a great diversity of workshops to be held at the greenhouse with very little operational cost.

4. 'Le genre de chose qui éveille dans l'environnement des gens. C'est quelque chose de vivant, qui se mange que tout le monde connait. Tsé, la première chose qu'on a fait, c'est manger les framboises qui étaient dessus.'

5. 'Quelque chose que tu ingères, qui rentre dans ton corps, qui… c'est beaucoup lié à la santé de soi-même, à l'individu en tant que tel.'

6. 'La nourriture, j'ai besoin de travailler parce que je dois me payer de la bouffe. Ben cette question-là tu peux déjà un peu la faire trembler, pis comme dire ben. . . pas nécessairement tsé, peut-être que tu dois travailler comme 10 h par semaine pour ta bouffe, ben comme, what about 10 à essayer de trouver dans les ordures des épiceries, des aliments qui sont encore sains et en bon état. Donc là tu viens de mettre comme 10 h . . .'

7. 'Le potentiel de la ville, c'est de comme . . . d'avoir créé un un genre de canal qui s'échappe de cette économie-là [capitaliste] que, si on est bien organisé, on peut le récupérer pis faire comme . . . se sortir progressivement . . .'

8. 'j'essaie d'affecter l'économie autour de moi comme en créant des liens différents ou des . . . une insertion . . . comme m'insérer dans l'économie d'une façon différente. Donc, tsé, de faire des boucles justement. De rendre efficientes ces boucles-là . . . je veux qu'on économise la nature par exemple. Ou qu'on économise les humains qui, en ce moment, sont victimes d'oppression dans leur milieu de travail.'

9. 'Les gens vont de 9 à 5 devant leurs ordinateurs. C'est pourquoi en fait? C'est pour obtenir le salaire qui va payer la maison que tu laisses seule pendant que tu vas travailler . . . Tsé pour tes 2 jours de fin de semaine qui sont très précieux. T'en passes une à faire le ménage pis l'autre à te reposer. Eille! C'est pas une vie ça!'

10. 'Ils ont pas nécessairement une raison de vivre là, tsé. Moi je comprends qu'il y ait de la dépression!'

11. 'J'ai l'impression, si les gens devaient travailler la terre pour survivre là tsé pas nécessairement pour retourner au point où tsé, peut-être, mes grands-parents ont vraiment tsé souffert, tsé ç'a été vraiment dur,

la survie, tout ça . . . où il faut que tu travailles un peu pour te nour-
rir et tout ça. Je pense que . . . il y aurait tellement plus un sentiment
d'accomplissement.'

12.   'Moi je vois la ville comme . . . comme une ville comestible. Moi ma
ville idéale serait une ville où on peut se déplacer aussi facilement
dans n'importe quel type de transport, que ce soit en skateboard,
que ce soit en vélo . . . j'aime l'aspect ludique de pouvoir s'alimenter
comme on veut. Tu peux aller fouiller dans les poubelles, trouver des
choses saines, les cuisiner, les canner, faire de la lactofermentation,
peu importe. Tu peux aller cueillir les fruits dans le parc . . . Avoir un
jardin sur ton balcon . . . c'est vrai qu'il faut se confronter aussi à la
réalité du milieu du travail là. Je suis tout à fait consciente que quand
tu travailles de 9 à 5, tu es fatigué, tu n'as peut-être pas l'énergie,
mais j'aime la potentialité de dire "l'alimentation, ça ne devrait pas
être juste tu vas à ton épicerie, tu fais ton épicerie et puis tu cuisines".
Non tsé. Ou t'achètes des plats cuisinés ou tu manges au resto. Non,
tu devrais être capable de t'alimenter gratuitement aussi.'

13.   'Une fois que tu es au courant de tout ça, tu ne peux pas l'ignorer.'

14.   'J'ai vu à quel point les gens s'en foutaient. Et ça, ce genre d'activisme
là m'a vraiment éteint, ça a comme fait: eille les gens, là, y'ont
pas . . . fous-leur la paix, ils n'ont pas envie. Et là je me suis rendue
compte que . . . tu ne peux pas forcer les gens. Tu ne peux pas changer
le monde. Arrête d'avoir la Terre sur tes épaules là. Et là c'est comme
un retour pour me rendre compte que finalement, les seules personnes
sur qui t'as de l'influence, c'est ton environnement autour. Et je le
vois. Donc j'ai comme . . . perdu un intérêt pour l'activisme, tsé. C'est
malheureux, je crois à ça, je crois que c'est important, mais je n'ai pas
la personnalité pour le faire. Ça m'affecte trop . . . de voir que, une
manifestation . . . tout l'effort qui va là-dedans, ya rien qui change
après ça. C'est pas pour moi. Moi je préfère travailler . . . euh . . . tsé
en communauté autour de moi . . . faire une . . . faire un changement
minime, mais autour de moi peut-être, peut-être influencer une personne qui me connait et ça, ça va être assez.'

15.   'Quand j'étais jeune, j'avais comme une phobie des perce-oreilles là,
vraiment là. Et v'là mettons un mois ou deux, j'étais en train de récolter
pour le marché. Et puis tsé, je récoltais de la laitue avec le couteau. Pis je
voyais . . . y'avait des perce-oreilles qui se promenaient et puis j'essayais
de ne pas les prendre, mais bon, tsé, j'étais consciente qu'ils étaient là
et puis j'étais contente avec ça, je me suis dit, bon là, tsé, ils ne sont pas
sur moi, ils font leur affaire . . . puis . . . juste de voir à quel point, j'étais
comme rendue au point où . . . j'étais capable de les accepter. Ils sont
dans leur environnement, j'avais pas peur.'

FIGURE 5.0 'Skateboarding in the Metro'. Source: illustration by Lukas Beeckman.

Chapter 5

The Urban Political World of 'Risk-Takers': Provocative Choreographic Power

Hubert likes to wear sweatshirts with a hood and loose jeans. He abhors a three-day beard and has deep dark eyes that speak for themselves and illuminate or obscure his pale complexion depending on how he feels. He speaks softly. When we meet him, he expresses uncertainty about the 'relevance' of his experience for our research. Yet, his story and his social analysis are among the most forceful we have heard. At 26 years old, Hubert tends to change ideas and leave projects unfinished, be it a documentary he is working on, a musical tour of small alternative joints in the suburbs, or his undergraduate degree. When we meet him, he is dumpster diving.[1]

There is one thing that Hubert has never lost his passion for: skateboarding. When Julie-Anne meets him in front of the Québec National Library on a cool and grey afternoon, they agree to walk around the city so that he can tell her the story of his involvement in the 2012 student strikes. As they walk on Saint-Denis towards Boulevard René-Lévesque, he recalls:

HUBERT   *I would often go to demonstrations on my board.*
JULIE-ANNE   *Ahh, that's cool.*
HUBERT   *We could skate in places we normally can't [laughter].*
JULIE-ANNE   *Well, you're not the first one to say this. Even people who were not on skateboards, they told me how they liked, you know, they had the impression that they were, you know, on the street, you know literally.*
HUBERT   *Well, for me, it's a bit hard to skate because of that. You know, I prefer practising on the street. Because it's there that ... exactly, it's there that you're, you're for yourself completely. You occupy your body, you let your heart, your body, occupy space. You don't restrain yourself, except for your security.*

Youth Urban Worlds: Aesthetic Political Action in Montreal, First Edition.
Julie-Anne Boudreau and Joëlle Rondeau.

JULIE-ANNE   *Yes, yes. For sure. But, for example, on the sidewalk would you restrain yourself more? How would you compare that?*
HUBERT   *On my skateboard?*
JULIE-ANNE   *Yes, because of obstacles?*
HUBERT   *For me, the sidewalk and the street are the same. I occupy all the space, up there as well [pointing to the stairs of a university building], and the stair ramp as well if I can. So it's a generalized occupation. But in all of these cases, I'm not supposed to be there. So, so it can disturb people.*[2]

For Hubert, occupying the street means being completely with oneself: *'You occupy your body, you let your heart, your body, occupy space'*. It is a form of *'generalized occupation'* with no restrictions around physical objects such as sidewalks and stairs. Hubert synthesizes in this short conversation the meaning of occupation. Occupation as he describes it is not a strategic ideological repertoire of political action such as when Occupy Montreal camped in Square Victoria for about five weeks in the fall of 2011. Rather, it is a form of distributed agency between his body, his skateboard, the sidewalk, and the casual walker. Occupation, in other words, is a dance with the street, the stairs, the mother pushing a stroller, the surveillance camera. Occupation is a choreography.

'But in all of these cases, I'm not supposed to be there. So, so it can disturb people.' Hubert ends by expressing his awareness that his bodily presence, his speed, his dance with the street may disturb others. He speaks to a certain degree of legal, physical, and social risk. Hubert, like the other dumpster divers, Greenpeace building climbers, explorers of abandoned industrial buildings, practitioners of extreme sports, and graffiti writers we will encounter in this chapter, is strongly critical of the risk-management framework that dominates contemporary Montreal. Unafraid of fear, Hubert and the others sense fear as a political act. Fear is for them a form of social relation and political gesture.

If police officers see Hubert as a provocative, risk-taking, and dangerous youth using the street in inappropriate ways, he would not describe himself as such. He does not see himself as a voluntary risk-taker. To the contrary, when he occupies the street, he sees not danger but spiritual opportunities. How does such political action unfold? What modalities of power are mobilized? What types of political subjectivity are constructed? This chapter explores the idea of distributed agency through the concept of urban choreographies. It discusses Hubert's and others' embracing of fear in relation to what Rancière would call the 'police', the hegemonic regulative framework of risk-management and the fear of fear. Dancing with the city and embracing fear produces provocative subjectivities which mobilize seduction as a form of political action. Spatial transgression disturbs the 'distribution of the sensible' by visibilizing other ways of moving and being with the city.

The Risk-Management Context

Since the end of the Cold War, traditional safety concerns of the nation-state (protecting its territory, civil protection, public order) have gradually been enlarged to cover the concerns of the general population in its everyday experience, including fields of action such as health and well-being. This is what is called 'human security' by international institutions. Following 11 September 2001, Canada decided to base its anti-terrorism work on a Canadian Security and Intelligence Community, understood as a flexible system of cooperation between different organizations in charge of public safety: police services, civil protection, fire safety, correctional services, and national security. Similarly, in Québec, the Centre National de Veille de la Sécurité Publique was created in 2002, later becoming the Centre des Opérations Gouvernementales in 2006, with a monitoring mandate (surveillance and alert) in addition to the anticipation and coordination of actions.

These institutional changes follow a more generalized transformation of the welfare state's role in public protection. The Canadian, Québec, and Montreal framework for ensuring protection now follows an actuarial logic (Boudreau 2013), involving identifying 'at-risk' groups or territories in which to socially intervene in order to prevent future problematic behaviour. In the 2000s, the 'dangerous' target was the figure of the gang member; today, it is predominantly the figure of the radicalized youth. Skateboarders and 'voluntary risk-takers' constitute a distinct category, whereby they are not necessarily racialized but they are considered somewhat 'irrational' and provocative because of their unnecessarily risky behaviours.

Authorities mobilize actuarial techniques of probabilistic calculation in order to detect risks and act preventively. This is based on the premise that risk is an objective – and thus calculable – element of social life (Borraz 2008). In the field of police action, this has come to be known as the 'new penology' (Feely and Simon 1992). It refers to an understanding of the criminal as a bundle of risk factors. The criminal act is no longer seen as an act of transgression, but rather as a statistical probability for a vulnerable group. It is thus a normal aspect of the social system that cannot be eradicated, but which we ought to *manage* through prevention. In order to do so, various techniques have been implemented: crime prevention through urban design; social and spatial interventions in 'at-risk' territories; community policing;

the use of at-risk individuals to control others (youth patrols, urban stewards); racial profiling; and zero-tolerance zones (regulating delinquency in a space, not regulating the delinquent). Some of these techniques and their effects on racialized youth were explored in depth in Chapter 2. The youth we meet here have different backgrounds and positionalities.

The most important aspect of these transformations of security politics over the last two decades is shown by the changing roles and forms of 'protection'. With the elimination of many of the welfare state's regulating tools (monetary policies, protection through social redistribution, etc.) and the state's increasingly visible inability to protect citizens from crime, terrorism, natural catastrophes, and health hazards, the neoliberal state has had to find new ways to legitimize its presence. Its authoritative (penal) functions remain fairly intact, and have even been strengthened through a series of measures criminalizing poverty. However, its social functions have evolved from an emphasis on social redistribution to one on individualized responsibilization (workfare, insistence on individual performance, etc.). The state no longer promises happiness for all, but rather an efficient management of risks. In this system, 'good citizens' are required to work on themselves, to become socially 'useful', to avoid unnecessary risk…

Urban Dancers and Diviners: Choreographic Power as Political Action

In 1961, Jane Jacobs published an analysis of urban insecurity that still resonates today. In her essay 'Eyes on the Street', she argues that informal surveillance mechanisms through a lively neighbourhood sociability are more effective than repression and modernist architecture (Jacobs 1961). What do eyes on the street see? Jacobs pointed to the fact that local inhabitants can easily detect a rupture in the 'sidewalk ballet' that characterizes the daily routine of local streets, and thus act if or even before danger appears.

In 1971, Erwin Goffman published an extensive study of dramaturgy in public spaces, asking how people keep face when they encounter strangers. He speaks of civil inattention, the process whereby strangers demonstrate they are aware of others sharing the same space, without transgressing their personal boundaries, without bumping into them, without imposing on them (Goffman 1971).

More or less a decade later, Lefebvre and Régulier (1985) proposed a methodology of 'rhythmanalysis'. Through the figures of the medical doctor who harmonizes the body's organs, or the poet (like Nico or Patrick; see Chapter 2) who has the power to affect our senses with the harmony of words, Lefebvre and Régulier call for an analysis of urban rhythms in order to understand how harmonization, attuning, and tempo produce urban space. The city is produced through natural and cosmic cycles as well as through human labour. Human labour requires social organization, and this modifies natural cycles. Industrialization and urbanization tend to produce linearity and repetition. But cyclic rhythms always fight back. This tension between cycles and linearity is not something Lefebvre and Régulier wish to study abstractly. Instead, they argue that studying rhythms requires feeling them through our bodies and attuning them to urban space. Rhythmanalysis, they conclude, is a way to think with the body, as illustrated by the urban farmers we met in Chapter 4.

Sidewalk ballets, civil inattention in public spaces, and urban rhythmanalysis all speak of choreography. Choreography is succinctly defined by dance and performative studies professor SanSan Kwan (2013) as 'the conscious designing of bodily movement through space and time'. When Hubert speeds on Saint-Denis Street, avoiding crashing into the mother pushing a stroller, avoiding the gaze of the surveillance camera, joyfully skating down the stairs, he is performing a choreography, adjusting his bodily movements through space and time. Movement (agency) is distributed – harmonized – between his body, his skateboard, the cameras, the mother, and the street.

But choreography is more than a kinaesthetic relation between body, time, and space. It can be constraining, as when the body is choreographed – consciously designed – as Kwan (2013) explains. Lefebvre and Régulier (1985) focus on how linear rhythms produced by industrialization and urbanization appeal to choreography as constraining, as producing repetitive movements. But choreography can also be enabling, when habits of the body generate performance. Hubert's choreography is enabling; his skateboarding skills and the habits of his skating body enable him to avoid obstacles and to feel bliss. Together, the *choreographed* – which is more visible from the top-down perspective of someone who sees Hubert skating through crowded Saint-Denis – and the *choreographic* – which is visible from the standpoint of Hubert's bodily subjectivity – form what Campbell (2013) calls *choreographic power*.

Choreographic power emerges from tensions between the choreographed and the choreographic. Improvised bodily practices such as Hubert's skateboarding on Saint-Denis produce ruptures in the normative use of the street. At the same time, this very choreographic challenge affirms and sustains the norms. The sudden appearance of Hubert's dancing speed, this choreographic transgression of the street's habitual rhythm, make the choreographed norm visible. When speed erupts, we realize that the usual pace of pushing a stroller on the sidewalk (choreographed use) is what it is. It is at a walking pace that we know how to avoid obstacles and be civilly inattentive. Hubert transgresses this coded rhythm, in the sense that he disturbs the sensorium of the street by changing its rhythm. This transgression is neither progressive nor regressive; it simply modifies, for a few seconds, the habitual pace. Such disturbance is what makes spatial transgression a political gesture, but its political effect will come only when these myriads of spatial transgressions are interpreted by their perpetrators as political acts.

In short, choreographic power can serve as a heuristic device for rendering political gestures knowable and thinkable beyond words. As we walk on Saint-Denis Street and Hubert describes his passion for skateboarding, he zooms in on politics as a precognitive encounter between bodies, material artefacts, and spaces. Such encounters involve finesse, attuning, and magnetism. Indeed, as Hubert concludes, *'it's a really intense affirmation because there is no unity, ehh, there's no skateboarding organizing committee. You know, it's a spread-out culture.'*[3] The *'affirmation'* Hubert describes here is the presence of 500 to 600 skaters on the street during Gold Skate Day, which used to take place annually in June. The impromptu presence of so many skating bodies on that specific day caused police officers to close the streets: *'there's many skaters on the streeeet!'*

Hubert describes these annual events as political acts. To him, Gold Skate Day is political because it performs unity in a dispersed and diffuse skating world: *'sometimes we came down, there were skaters from 9 to 50, 55 years old.'*[4] Political acts are creative moments that break from the routine and, through their unfolding, legitimate the actor. Gold Skate Day, now gone, used to assemble a diverse crowd of skaters during the Tamtam events at the bottom of Mount Royal (see Chapter 1), who would take the street together. Participating in this collective occupation built on everyday political gestures choreographed by skaters in their normal transgression of Montreal street paces. Political gestures are acts of transgression involving the body in everyday routine. Hubert regrets the disappearance of Gold Skate Day (the political act breaking the routine), but still performs political gestures: *'when we would skate, we would all leave together. A route was distributed the night before, on the skater blogs. Most people didn't know about this I think. But yeah, in the end this was over. So we would go let's say to spots like Peace Park, a place where skaters have gone since it was constructed I think in the 1980s or the beginning of the 1990s. So, there we don't have the right to skate because there are tickets issued for a municipal bylaw concerning urban furniture.'*[5] Hubert's participation in Gold Skate Day shows that occupation of the street as an embodied, singular gesture when skating and occupation as a political act can go together.

The notion of choreographic power enables us to think with our bodies. Even if we do not skate ourselves, feeling speed in our bodies, the eruption of skaters disrupting our walking, cycling, or motorized rhythms reveals the power of municipal codes, as well as the power of transgressive speed. But to understand this political relation between control and transgression, we need to be sensitive to the materiality of the city, to what is between human bodies on the street. Being able to perform in the city, as skater or simply as walker, we need to decode it, to be able to perform within certain registers. Decoding largely operates through sensing; that is, 'reading, reproducing and domesticating the urban soundscapes, the visual overflow, the styles, the smells, and a physical landscape that can be read through everyday mythologies of past actions, heroes, martyrs, events, danger' (Hansen and Verkaaik 2009, p. 12). Certain people, like Hubert and other urban dancers we will meet shortly, have more performative charisma than others. They are, as Hansen and Verkaaik (2009, p. 17) so beautifully suggest, 'diviners of urban space, people needed for their knowledge and agility', for their 'dangerous abilities'. Skating, dumpster diving, building exploration, and graffiti writing are practices that require the ability to read the landscape and sense its potentialities beyond its prescribed use. Urban diviners are people who have these aesthetic abilities and, through their practices, can transgress the choreographed street. The traces they leave – a piece of graffiti, an accelerated heartbeat as we realize a skater has zoomed right by us, the smell of an opened trash container being scavenged, a banner hung on the top of a bridge by a Greenpeace activist – carry their own charisma. In the previous chapter, we discussed with Lorimer (2007) the charismatic agency of non-human beings. Choreographic power emerges from the charismatic agency of urban diviners and the traces they leave in the city; by appealing to our senses, these traces are a constant reminder of what a place could be beyond its normalized use. Urban diviners make these other potentialities visible: an industrial building could be an art gallery; a street could be an acrobatic stage; a back alley full of trash containers could be a food pantry.

Through his rhythmic transgression, Hubert constantly decodes the city, making it readable and meaningful to others, to the mother surprised by his eruption as much as to the police officer whose job is to control (choreograph) rhythms. One day, Hubert was exiting a subway station. As he reached the door, he put his feet on his skateboard and opened it. He heard two police officers running behind him. *'So just the surprise of seeing them run, to see they were nervous because they thought they would have to pursue me because I saw them and they thought I would run off. So they were, they were in an action movie mode.'*[6] Their unusual 'action movie' pace surprised him. *'I was in reaction mode, rapid reaction in the face of potentially dangerous people. So I was like really, I wasn't able to follow, to be sufficiently lucid to have a constructive conversation.'*[7] The officers asked him to show his identity papers. *'And then I tell them: "well, what's happening?", it's not clear to me, I'm just like, you know, I know they're mad at me because I'm on my board, but the way they were running when I opened the door, I thought they were going to catch someone with a gun behind me [laughter].*[8] Hubert took some time to read the situation, still surprised by the drama of their race towards him. This is what can be called double aesthetic appearance: Hubert on his board inside the station constituted a body out of place for the officers; in turn, the officers' running as if chasing someone with a gun surprised Hubert. He didn't identify himself promptly as they demanded, so he received two tickets: one for skating inside the station, the other for obstruction of the officers' work. Hubert's face is mad with indignation as he tells the story:

HUBERT   *When it comes and gets you like this just in your ... 'two metres*
              that I put my foot on the board when there's nobody around'
              [laughter], and that I'm right next to my home, and that I'm try-
              ing to mind my business, I don't disturb anyone.
JULIE-ANNE   *Yeah, yeah.*
HUBERT   *I don't break anything.*
JULIE-ANNE   *Yeah, yeah, it's like powerlessness in the face of a big, well of power*
              that falls on you [laughter].
HUBERT   *A big machine, when it starts you can't do anything. Once they*
              had decided they would give me a ticket.[9]

When '*the machine starts*', Hubert says, '*you can no longer do anything*'. Even if he was not disturbing or breaking anything, even if he was home (close to his house), even if he was displaying civil inattention by '*minding my own business*', Hubert suffered the officers' choreography. Yet, we still consider Hubert an urban diviner because, as he says, '*it's a way to say also, to re-establish skateboarding as something that was born against all odds on the street, something wild, urban, not domesticated, that you can't put in a park with fences and that will stay there*'.[10]

Skating, like practising other urban sports such as parkour, 'is an ascetic and aesthetic form of self-negation geared toward the removal of suffering in the city. By focusing on the aesthetics of gymnastic movements, the spiritual experience of physical rigour, and communion with one's (urban) environment, they [traceurs, skaters] pursue something about bodily experience that ventures beyond rational knowledge' (Atkinson 2009, p. 192). In his ethnographic study of parkour in Toronto, Atkinson (2009, p. 170) describes this practice of 'dangerously' dancing with urban space and artefacts as an 'aesthetic-spiritual reality of the self through poiesis'. Poiesis, he pursues, 'can provide moments of catharsis and liberation for people, or moments of ecstasies, wherein the conscious and calculating mind is "let go" and the body and mind move as one' (Atkinson 2009, p. 178). Urban diviners produce embodied knowledge that helps decodify the city. They do not seek power, they simply let themselves dance, producing aesthetic appearances as their speed or movements surprise and reveal normal paces and codes.

Voluntary Risk-Takers? Fear and Youth Politics[11]

Urban diviners have the 'dangerous ability' to produce knowledge about potentialities of urban space that cannot easily be appropriated and controlled. They have choreographic power, the power to arrange movement in time and space at a pace different from the choreographed norm. Perhaps for this reason, these youths are often called 'voluntary risk-takers'. The literature on risk-taking and youthfulness tends to seek psychological explanations for behaviour that puts one's physical and social integrity in danger. Le Breton (2004), for instance, explains adolescent risk-taking behaviour in terms of the search for identity, a lack of self-confidence, and the narcissistic restoration characteristic of adolescents. Lupton and Tulloch (2002) hold that voluntary risk-taking occurs at a particular moment in one's life trajectory and suggest that the willingness to take risks is built through experience, interaction with others, and learning from different individuals. Participants in extreme sports, for example, search for an emotional intensity that will allow them to escape the alienation of daily life and to live in the present moment.

Lyng (1990) similarly explains 'high-risk' behaviour as a constructed identity in a particular sociohistorical period, highlighting the social dimensions of individual risk behaviour. The term 'edgework' describes an activity associated with a threat to one's physical or mental well-being, as practised by individuals with a particular technical expertise, who experience a series of subjective sensations (feelings of self-realization and omnipotence) while doing so. Fear is part of the experience of edgework, and overcoming it opens the door to rewarding sensations. Edgework will thus counterbalance the alienation felt by the individual, by allowing them to experience a very intense sense of 'self' and completely freeing them from societal pressures. Lyng (1990) concludes that edgework is a form of 'experimental anarchy' through which individuals push the boundaries of social conventions in order to explore the fringes of reality and fulfil their quest for authenticity (see also Ferrell 1993).

While Hubert and the other urban diviners and dancers we will meet in this chapter acknowledge that the activities they take part in do present a certain degree of risk, for the most part they consider them to be safe because, through practice, they have learned to control the hazards and gradually push their own limits. Self-control and self-work are central to mastering such techniques. As Michel, a highline professional, explains, there is risk involved in everything we do, '*from coming into this world to crossing the street on a red light*'. Michel is 25 years old. He moved to Montreal from a small California town about four years ago to learn French and get to know the place his mother comes from. He decided to stay because he found in Montreal a community of people who shared his '*vision of life*'. He likes Montreal, but finds it too quick, too noisy, too rapid. He is thinking of moving to the Eastern Townships (a region of Quebec located about 170 km south of Montreal) so that he can hear the crickets chirp at night. Michel practises slackline for a living, even though he earns very little from it (about $4000 last year). He works as a street entertainer in the Quartier des Spectacles during summertime, hanging himself from a line. He teaches the sport, he organizes expeditions, he gives shows. He sees himself as evolving between the circus world and the world of extreme sports.

About six years ago, Michel saw a video of someone walking on a wire about 3000 m up, without protection. It impressed him because he was afraid of altitude and felt very stupid. The same day, he bought himself a slackline and trained alone for about seven months, until he could find balance (see Figure 5.1). '*I got addicted to slackline. Once I held my balance the first time, I loved it.*' Michel presents himself as someone who cares for his body:

FIGURE 5.1 Slackliner in Parc Jarry. April 2014. *Source:* photo by Maude Séguin-Manègre.

he doesn't drink, smoke, or use drugs; he eats well and practises yoga. '*For the first seven months, I never knew anybody to do slackline with,*' he recalls as we have lunch at the Commensal, a vegetarian restaurant formerly located inside the Maison du développement durable on Ste. Catherine Street, '*then I showed some friends and nobody really wanted to do it with me until I started getting kicked out of the parks.*' He could not figure out why he was not allowed to practise his sport when others could do as they wished. So he went to his small town's Parks and Recreation Department. '*They said it was too dangerous. I did tons of research and I found that thousands of people get admitted to emergency rooms each year after playing on jungle gyms and soccer, and I never found anything on slackline injuries…*' But the city replied with an ordinance stating that no ropes or wires should be attached to trees. '*So I made an amendment and presented to the City Board, and this is when people started taking interest. And my buddies joined in with me and I think everybody loves an opportunity to fight against authority, so naturally my buddies jumped in with me and they started slacklining through that.*' The amendment was passed, and after six months it entered the statutes. This small California town was the first place in the world to incorporate slackline in its city code.

Michel has had numerous injuries, breaking twelve bones in total. He has had two knee surgeries. But those injuries were the result of skateboarding. He skated for seven years before he started slacklining. He has had one serious injury from slacklining, and that was a separated shoulder. He finds his practice of slackline much healthier (physically and mentally) than skateboarding. Yet, like Hubert and others, he insists that 'danger' provides him with a feeling of living life to the fullest: '*You gotta experience life. I mean sure, I'm turning upside down on top of cement. I wouldn't necessarily choose to install my line over cement. But I think the presence of danger brings you a certain awareness and I find bliss in this awareness. Sometimes I walk hundreds of feet off the ground unattached to my line and never do I feel so alive. I think when you feel that threat of death or danger it puts you completely in the moment where you really need to be ultimately focused on what you are doing. I find bliss in ultimate focus.*'

The idea of 'risk' represents a linear relationship to the future. Western conceptions of time have predominantly been linear because of fear of the inevitability of death. Linear time is seen as rational only because death 'is the law that presses against the seeming relativities of time in particular situations' (Greenhouse 1996, p. 4). In other words, fear of death is a historically situated feeling, one that is contested by urban diviners and other 'risk-takers' such as Michel. Hobbes built his political theory on the premise that fear of death has to be 'created', that citizens ought to be convinced of the benefits of fearing death. During his revolutionary times, fear of death was not prominent.

Glory and honour were considered politically 'virtuous' emotions. However, Hobbes argued, rationality rests on fearful individuals. Fearing death meant a new relation to time, characterized by rational and reasonable precautions and the anticipation of negative consequences. The anticipation of negative consequences is what is called 'risk'. It imposes, as Lefebvre and Régulier (1985) suggest, repetition and linearity. Fear of death, Hobbes demonstrated, opens space for the constitution of rational individuals who are no longer as sensitive to the opinion of others as when they are governed by glory and honour. Unlike fear, honour and glory require that others recognize an individual's actions as glorious or honourable. Fear of death, in opposition, only requires a rational calculation of consequences and prudence.

Rhythmanalysis shows that urban life comprises more than one rhythm: linearity (directional time) for sure, but also cycles (circular time), tempos (pace), and moments (situational time). Risk-taking such as slacklining or skateboarding involves searching for limits. While none of the youths with whom we speak are afraid of dying from their practice, they challenge the rational and reasonable norm of prudence that derives from Hobbes's philosophy about the fear of death. In contrast with rationalized norms of precaution and fear of fear, urban diviners embrace fear: it makes them feel alive. For many youths, going beyond personal limits is felt as empowering. As Michel explains, fear is a motivational factor in pushing oneself to the limits and surpassing one's abilities:

MICHEL   *Fear is a healthy sensation. Without fear we would be in grave danger. So my personal philosophy on fear is: accept it, embrace it, appreciate it, but don't let it hold you back from doing what you know you're able to do …*

JULIE-ANNE   *So you have confidence in yourself?*

MICHEL   *Ultimate. It made me grow into loving what really makes me scared.*

Venturing out of one's comfort zone to take risks enables deeper knowledge of oneself and, ultimately, the ability to reach a higher level of consciousness (Lupton and Tulloch 2002). '*The beauty of being scared is that you're pushing yourself past your capacity. In your practice you're growing as a human, so when you go past your fear you're growing, and growing is what I believe is the reason for our existence. To live, to love, to enjoy, and to grow.*' Michel explains that he can manage and control risks through practice and calculated gestures: '*The level of danger with slackline is really following the level of your practice or your stupidity. When you start slackline, it's not that dangerous unless you're really stupid. The more you get into your practice, the more dangerous it becomes because you are trying new things.*' Similarly, when we ask Julien, who has practised

BMX, to define risk, he tells us that it means trying something that you have never done before. However, he goes on to say that when you reach a certain level of professional practice, the chances of getting hurt are greatly diminished: '*if you are capable of doing certain tricks, then you will just add a variant to it, which makes it new. You know that you are already comfortable doing that, so just adding something will be dangerous, but you know that you have better chances of getting it. And when you reach a certain level you are able to have more control when you fall.*'[12]

When it comes to climbing buildings for Greenpeace, Antoine stresses that '*it's only risky if you lose control of your actions and if you don't think through what you are about to do.*' He goes on to say that it is necessary to remain calm and think clearly in order to avoid losing control – loss of control can be caused by trying to climb too quickly or by panicking. Countless hours of training and an in-depth knowledge of the techniques and equipment used by Greenpeace are required, in order to increases your self-confidence.

Some voluntary risk-takers, like Antoine, Michel, and Julien, see themselves first and foremost as professionals who, in order to excel in what they do, need to push themselves beyond their personal limits and overcome their fears. They use the feeling of fear to their advantage as a driving force to improve themselves. Risk-taking is thus seen by these youths as a means for fulfilment, empowerment, and self-realization based on emotional control and technical skills. Self-realization defines a relationship to the norm that is underpinned by favourable measurement against an ideal. It is a logic that seeks individual betterment through performance. Lyng (1990, p. 871) explains that 'edgework involves not only activity-specific skills but also a general ability to maintain control of a situation that verges on total chaos, a situation most people would regard as entirely uncontrollable ... Most edgeworkers regard this skill as essentially cognitive in nature, and refer to it as a special form of "mental toughness".' This is indeed what is described by Michel, Julien, and Antoine. They emphasize the cognitivism of their acquired skills.

However, they also describe another important facet of risk-taking, one that comes closer to poiesis as a method for revealing 'different' human truths, closer to the spiritual and aesthetic work of urban diviners. For them, cognitive and aesthetic work are intimately related. Lyng attends to this continuum by specifying that 'instead of seeing risk taking compelled by an internal need to satisfy urges or attain rewards [the logic of self-realization], the edgework model views risk takers being drawn into these activities by the seductive power of the experience' (Lyng and Matthews 2007, p. 78). Speaking in terms of edgework instead of risk-taking highlights the choreographic power of these activities, in the sense that it highlights the distributive agency between the body, the slackline, the spectator, and the urban landscape. Cédric puts it marvellously: '*The moment your awareness kicks in, whatever you're exposed to at that moment, that's what you're going to adhere to. If you're not aware of the things influencing you, then they can't shape you.*'

Cédric is 40 years old. He grew up in the neighbourhood of Verdun and still lives there in the same house (originally built for war veterans) that belonged first to his grandparents, then to his parents, and now to him. He started skateboarding when he was around 13 years old and later became a graffiti artist. He was influenced by movies like *Beach Street* and started spreading tags with his name. As he tells us during a meeting on Ste. Catherine Street, he was considered a troublemaker throughout his youth in the 1980s: '*There were bike paths but we were constantly told to get off them because we weren't on bikes so we were getting ticketed all the time. That ostracization led to us listening to punk music. Punk was different from other mainstream music and punk culture is about "fuck the authority" so you adopt that mentality, which leads to conflict with youth and authority.*' But he sees himself as a success story because most people thought that he would never amount to anything. He founded a graffiti festival more than 15 years ago. He also does advocacy work with disadvantaged youth in Verdun and the South-West district.

Literally, working the 'edge' means negotiating the frontier between life and death, order and chaos. While risk-taking is more clearly a temporal idea (the anticipation of future negative consequences), edgework has a more spatial connotation. Cédric explains that bridges, abandoned buildings, and highways are attractive to graffiti artists (see Figure 5.2) because '*nobody bothers you there. The surfaces lend well to it as well. Police don't hang out there. Authorities don't. The funny thing is that condo owners may also use these spaces to walk their dogs and so they are trespassing too. You're both doing something illegal but for two different reasons and different perceptions. Sometimes those dog walkers will call the cops on you. They feel that their presence is more legitimate. I think the cop should give them both a ticket because they are both trespassing.*' For him, the 'edge' is about spatial intuition, the ability to read and feel space. What is important is not 'risk' but feeling the environment.

CÉDRIC   *I have done extreme sports all my life, I have done graffiti for a long time, I practise risk in business on a daily basis, on projects that I take on. If anybody was to reflect on the true risk that's involved, there really is no risk involved. It's not a driving force, not personally anyway. What's important for me is not about pushing my limits and putting myself in harm's way ... There is no risk. The notion of risk is not a driving force. It's a reality.*

JULIE-ANNE   *So do you put into place any strategies to manage that risk?*

FIGURE 5.2 Graffiti art, underpass, Rosemont, May 2007. *Source:* photo by J.A. Boudreau.

CÉDRIC   *Well yes, but they are natural, it's second nature now. There are things that come into play so quickly into your mind you know how to avoid a negative outcome. I don't think risk is a driving force and I don't even believe someone who says that it drives them.*

Hubert expresses a similar idea when we ask him if he felt 'at-risk' while participating in illegal night demonstrations during the 2012 student strikes:

HUBERT   *Well, I was feeling threatened, but more conceptually than physically [laughter]. I felt they could exert laws against me.*

JULIE-ANNE *Arrest you or something?*

HUBERT   *Like searching me, you know, anything … and that was a worry I have almost all the time because … because I skate on the street a lot.*

JULIE-ANNE *Yes, so you can always be …*

HUBERT   *So I'm always on the lookout for police officers, and if there is one, I always try to disarm my emotions first. In order to be really, I try to, to, if we're at the point of having a dialogue that would lead to my arrest or a ticket, well I try to look innocent, and [laughter] and not be too emotionally involved or else not … well. To look submissive. If this is what it takes, it's disgusting but …*[13]

Hubert expresses his ability to feel the space: '*I am always on the look-out.*' He occupies space that is attractive to him, just like Cédric chooses certain highway underpasses to paint. Both know they are trespassing, and both know what to do if they get caught: '*avoid being emotionally involved*', in Hubert's words, or draw upon '*second nature*' knowledge about '*how to avoid a negative outcome*', in Cédric's. This is choreographic power generated from an intimate relationship between the body, the artefact, and the street. It is more than cognitively acquired skills used for self-control and to master certain techniques. There is a strong affective component that has to do with spatial perception and intuition. In dumpster-diver Justine's words, it is all about the '*capacity to marvel at what comes to you.*' This creates unexpected forms of shared urban knowledge; it helps decodify the city. It reveals 'different' human truths (poiesis), the potentialities of urban space. This is the work of urban diviners; it is more than simply individually acquired skills.

It is political work in the sense that it challenges social norms about rational precautions – especially for women. Olstead's (2011, p. 91) research on female edgeworkers shows that 'the women's confrontations with precautionary messages illuminate the context of their edgework as a gendered economy of risk that resists recognizing them as "takers", but only its recipients.' It is also a political act because it often puts edgeworkers in direct confrontation with authorities – sometimes with productive results, as when Michel secured a new city ordinance for slacklining, sometimes not. For instance, Cédric was arrested and sued for a quarter of a million dollars for having tagged railway property. He decided to face the police when they arrived and challenged the law: '*That is more about being an advocate or being an activist when it comes to something. The only thing we were guilty of was trespassing. The thing about graffiti is that you have to be caught in the act. If you're not caught in the act, everything is hearsay. There is no proof that it was me who did it. When you know those things, there is no risk.*' Why did he decide to paint railway property in the first place? '*There was a little bit of political awareness*', he admits. He recalls how '*skateboarding taught me to take risks, to fall down and get back up again, how to confront authority. We fought to have ramps built. We had to petition to do things … But we weren't marginalized youth. We were still going home to dinner at 6p.m. that was cooked for us, going to high school. We were middle-class kids in a middle-class neighbourhood so we had nothing to be mad about. But the system disenfranchised us. It taught us how to fight for something.*' This is how he learned to be an activist.

But these youths are not political only through direct confrontations with the law. Cédric expresses a much subtler vision of politics, something close to precognitive and affective political gesture: '*It's [graffiti] not about legality or illegality. It's about ego and ignorance, individual, identity. … It's not against the system. This isn't about politics changing the world, it's about writing your name on a wall. It's not about freedom of speech. It may be for some graffiti writers depending on where you live and if you have no rights. It has to be case per case. Each context is completely different.'* He pursues again how he affectively and intuitively reads urban space: *'it's about awareness. If you're tagging on someone's building, at the end of the day, it's easy to clean off, not a big deal. But what if the owner is an 85-year-old woman who just lost her husband and she is alone and nobody is there to help her. Imagine if someone did that to your grandmother? So why not see this woman as your grandmother. You can go make it right, clean it or fix it at least, so that you can make a contribution.'* MAN, a 27-year-old graffiti artist who asks to be identified by his artist name, corroborates this: *'We have street rules: no churches, no schools, and no houses. We don't respect people who don't respect these rules.'*[14]

Cédric expresses a sense of the political similar to what Teresa Caldeira (2012) found in her study of graffiti, *pixações* (the style of tagging characteristic of São Paulo), and bikers. She introduces her paper as follows:

> Expressed as both artistic production and urban performance, they not only give the subaltern new visibility in the city but also express new forms of political agency. However, these interventions are contradictory: they affirm rights to the city while fracturing the public; expose discrimination but refuse integration. They test the limits of the democratization process by simultaneously expanding the openness of the democratic public sphere while challenging it with transgressive actions ranging from the mildly illicit to the criminal. (Caldeira 2012, p. 385)

In São Paulo, Caldeira studied marginalized youth and their modes of expression through 'imprinting and moving', but the youth with whom we speak in Montreal generally do not come from a subaltern background. Yet, as in São Paulo and many other cities around the world, 'they choose aggression and transgression as their mode of articulation while simultaneously speaking the language of rights and liberties and affirming a deep pleasure in freely moving around the city' (Caldeira 2012, p. 386). As a political gesture, youth expressivity reveals subversive truths and potentialities in urban space. In this sense, expression has political effects on the city largely through the charisma these forms of expression carry and their ability to speak aesthetically. Sometimes, these diffuse political gestures are articulated as ideological statements, as when a building climber hangs a banner for Greenpeace; sometimes, they lead to institutionalization, as when Michel secured an amendment to the city code; but most of the time they have more diffuse political effects through aesthetic communication that foster awareness of the normalizing consequences of choreographed power.

Collective Edgework: Distributed Agency Through Provocation and Seduction

'Awareness' refers in Cédric's analysis to affective attuning to the space around you and the feelings of others. Cédric disputes confrontational interpretations of his edgework. He speaks instead of affective attuning, of empathy. Michel, on the other hand, emphasizes embodied provocation: *'Have fun. Push yourself. Live. Breathe. Just let go of that ideal that the normal everyday society pushes on you of get a job and do what you are told. Buy a house and buy a car and do what society tells you to do. You just want to do what you want to do, be free, be alive and live in the moment. That philosophy is encouraged through the practice of slackline because it is really a practice of the present moment. If you are not focusing on right now, you are going to fall. If you are thinking of walking the line completely you are thinking too far into the future. I think that is the shared ideal of living in the present moment. We all like that.'*

Provocation is an aesthetic modality of power. It entails revealing what does not work with social norms by affectively appealing to the senses to instil desire or disgust. Provocation causes trouble, in Butler's (1990) sense of a scandalous and sudden intrusion which produces unanticipated agency. We already spoke of the figure of the urban diviner. In the Greek tradition of the cynic, the practice of parrhesia plays a similar role: expressing subversive truth that will have important effects on the entire polis. This subjectivity is constituted through continuous work on the self, experimenting to become someone else, something more. Such a description fits very well with Hubert and with Michel. They do not seek to be scandalous like the 'badass' would (Katz 1988), but they do seek to provoke and to disturb daily urban rhythms. Their intentioned actions as urban dancers/movers conflict with choreographed rhythms. When and where politics will emerge out of these provocations is unanticipated and goes beyond individual efforts.

This will perhaps become clearer with the story of Nathalie. She was born in Pointe-aux-Trembles in a self-employed arts-and-craft family. She describes her sister as more conventional, while she is more 'trash'. We ask her what it means to be conventional. She responds it is *'To have integrated the capitalist consumption model, schedules (to have weekends), popular TV, popular music, fashion clothing. Follow the masses.'*[15] Nathalie rejects consumerism, just like her parents did. They represent the only authority she doesn't challenge. Nathalie studies art because the last thing she wants is to 'make the economy roll'. Nathalie is a dumpster diver (see Figure 5.3).

FIGURE 5.3 Dumpster diving, September 2014. *Source:* photo by Maude Séguin-Manègre.

The dumpster diver is in many ways a provocateur, a troublemaker, because they tend to instil disgust: '*Most of all in [the neighbourhood of] Hochelaga, with neighbours. It's colourful, Hochelaga. There is the "shrew" with her cigarette who starts to insult you.*'[16] Dumpster divers eat 'garbage soup'. Justine, a former restaurant worker and now a dumpster diver, confirms this negative social reaction: '*Well, it's logical. It's how we were raised. We learned that if you drop something on the counter, it's no longer good, so in the trash … And working in restaurants, it gives you even more the desire to save food and to adopt such extreme behaviour. The rule is to throw out food, so you need to hide if you want to take food. It pushes to a form of delinquency. It's a sure fascination for food that is really personal.*'[17] For Justine, finding something beautiful in the trash is an accomplishment: '*I give myself little challenges like that. I was happy to find new stuff. Now I want bagels. The thrill brings me much. I like culinary improvisation. When access to commercial bins was forbidden, I decided to be invisible. I was never really afraid. It's just food. There are people who tell me that at two in the morning a girl should not be alone in a back alley, that it's stupid. But I say, nobody is interested in going into a back alley at that time.*'[18]

Justine, like Nathalie, describes the beautiful and provocative aesthetics of dumpster diving. She speaks of her '*fascination for food*', its creativity and texture, of food as a conduit for improvisation. Nathalie is more explicit on the spatiality of this aesthetic: '*So you need to find the alleys where there are market containers, and to go when it closes at 6 or 9 p.m. You have to go regularly, picking your spot. You have to bring many bags to separate portions in advance, a knife to take out bad pieces. We scavenge, but not too close to the bottom because there is more juice. You do it less during the summer. From March to June mostly; during the summer when it's too hot it's not good, and during the winter it freezes. It demands organization.'*[19] Then, as Justine explains, *'there is a ritual. You take everything out, you wash everything. It's important to do that. We can get organized in dumpster-diving groups. When you speak about it, you're careful about what you say, because often people are repulsed at the idea of the dumpster. The interesting spots are more in the Mile-End.'*[20] Justine adds details to this description of distributed agency: *'And when you go to people's houses, you can see from their apartment if they are doing it. There are clues like higgledy-piggledy stuff, glass jars.'*[21]

The best spots, the back alley, the many bags to separate found items, the jars: these are material artefacts that relate Justine and Nathalie to the city, to mainstream and alterity. Instead of understanding political subjectivity as self-contained sovereign individual actors, dumpster divers constantly cross gaps, join other agents. Nathalie has recently stopped dumpster diving because she moved out of her apartment, where she could share the work with her roommates and neighbours. *'It's easier in a group. And it's really convivial. It's a gang trip, exploratory.'*[22] When she was living in this *'bohemian commune'*, as she describes her place in Hochelaga, she was not at school so she had time to coordinate activities and send people to dumpsters. She did the cooking. *'It can't be just free for all, it needs organization, it's a fragile structure.'* She ended up leaving because *'it was less fun, I was being vulturized and too many people were doing nothing.'*[23]

Nathalie's description of dumpster diving emphasizes the pleasure of provocation. But the pleasure she describes is not as individual as that of Hubert, or Michel, or Julien. She speaks of collective pleasure, of a collective negotiation of the edge. In her feminist exploration of sadomasochist edgework, Newmahr (2011, p. 692) argues that contrary to Lyng's masculinist conception of edgework as competitive, skilful control and conquest of fear, there are many 'situations in which the risk taking is interdependent, in which edgeworkers need one another in order to navigate the edge, or collaborative – that is, in which edgeworkers construct and constitute the boundaries for one another.' Collaborative edgeworking works by converting fear into something that is sensually appealing. It works, in other words, through seduction, through suggestion and enticement. As a modality of power involving emitting (seduction) and receiving (attraction) agents, seduction is fundamentally relational and collaborative.

Nathalie describes collaborative dumpster edgeworking in the Hochelaga loft, but she also speaks of collaborative edgework between place-hackers and police officers. She is an urban explorer, someone who enters abandoned urban places such as empty industrial buildings (see Figure 5.4). She likes spending time in places where she does not necessarily have the right to be. She finds it beautiful: '*It's like playing cat-and-mouse with police officers or security guards. It gives a thrill, but I find that really beautiful to go to these places. To access this beauty, you need to break authority. Even if you risk getting caught.*'[24] '*Playing cat-and-mouse with police officers*' is a seductive-attractive modality of power relation: '*All your senses are sharpened because you know you are guilty because you have no right to be there. You can feel guilty if you get caught. It gives a thrill, it's not just in order to defy authority. It's just a step to reach your goal of exploration.*' Police officers also experience a '*feeling of thrill at catching someone in the act.*'[25] It is a collaborative form of edgework between the trespasser and the officer that produces a strong affective charge, described by Nathalie as a '*thrill*'. MAN speaks instead of a liberated energy: '*Before doing it, you are anxious; while you are doing it, you are thrilled; and after, you can breathe, let go a certain form of energy.*'

MAN grew up in the central neighbourhood near McGill University, commonly known as the 'McGill ghetto', where students congregate. He lived on and off the street. He describes himself as '*rebellious*', '*angry*'. He is

FIGURE 5.4 Building to be destroyed on Van Horne, adorned with the tag *peur* ('fear'), September 2014. *Source:* photo by J.A. Boudreau.

a powerful example of the provocative urban diviner: '*Sometimes I got kicked out because there were situations where obviously things got a little violent, you know. It's very normal because they didn't know how to react to someone who was like me, very rebellious. I didn't know how to react because I'm just being myself. I don't know any better, really. Now we are in very good term me and my parents and they understood that there are certain things that just don't work. You can't put a lion in a cage and not expect it to not go nuts. It's the same thing with me. They tried different things to calm me down and I just went crazier. Now we all just realized that people just need to be.*'

For Nathalie, beauty can only be accessed by '*breaking authority*' and communicating with others who are sensitive to it. 'Sensitive' is a key word here: Nathalie explains how shared affective memories, or what Katz (1988) calls 'aesthetic finesse', require being able to recognize and elaborate on the sensual potentialities of a situation. For example, when Greenpeace activists Antoine and Marc describe their encounters with police officers, they speak of various intuitions with regards to who will help them and who will cause more problems. Marc explains that first-line police officers and security guards are always more nervous, while it is easier to deal with sergeants and lieutenants: '*Well, patrollers lose control. They don't understand what is happening and they don't know how to negotiate or interact with activists. They react brutally. I suppose this provides them with a sense of authority.*'[26]

Such aesthetic finesse reveals Marc's affective memory of past encounters with state authorities and shapes his relationship to them. Aesthetic finesse is the main 'dangerous ability' of urban diviners. In their relation to the state or other authorities (such as MAN's parents), they do not simply claim rights or resist power and domination, they also negotiate a space of action by building on their aesthetic finesse and affective memory. Through acts of self-display, movement, and expression, urban diviners modify their relations with authority, one situation at a time.

Yet, for Nathalie, Marc, MAN, and Antoine, fear envelops them and radiates from them. In fearful situations (climbing buildings or diving in dumpsters), the idea of free-standing, autonomous individuals remains in the background. When, in a specific moment and place, something happens (e.g. escaping from police officers when painting a graffiti), actors engage in the situation by giving it a shared meaning (i.e. the fear/thrill of escaping). They thus designate this moment as important (they will remember it, describe how it unfolded, what route they took to escape, how they felt). This makes the situation recognizable, and individuals as much as objects participate in a form of collective situated action. MAN vividly describes an encounter with police officers: '*One time, I was finishing the lines of my piece. It was winter and the guy spotted me. He pursued me. He was kind of fat but he was still running fast. It lasted some 15–20 minutes' running. It was total panic. I didn't know where I was, I ran in people's gardens. A lady was cooking. I am vomiting while running and climbing because of the adrenaline. Extremely intense situation. After a while, I think I'm ok and I see the guy on the phone with the police again, and it's another 20 minutes' running. I don't want to get caught, I don't want trouble. And it's my name also. Sometimes they don't care, sometimes they do. People don't respect our culture because they don't know how it's difficult. We know it. Buddy fell from a roof while doing this, or buddy broke his leg, or his little brother was hit by a train ... Graffiti, we love it because it's dangerous. We love it because it's tough. We love the challenge. This run was the best, the last one was with the police. I gave everything, the Olympic sprint. I traversed the park, I ran, it was the end. And a bus stopped at that moment right on the corner. 15–20 minutes, I was breathing. People were looking at me like "what the fuck happened to him?"*[27] (see Figure 5.5). MAN's description is completely embodied. He provides details on his muscles, his stomach, his lungs, the outside temperature, the woman cooking, the man on the phone. He describes strong relational empathy with buddies who fell, who died. He describes how when he stopped at the bus stop, he looked really out of place. He describes how the situation was provocative because it was about attraction to thrill and revulsion felt by onlookers at the sight of his sweating, out-of-breath, vomit-covered body.

FIGURE 5.5 Van Horne and avenue du Parc, September 2014. *Source:* photo by J.A. Boudreau.

Aesthetic political relations operate through seduction and attraction/repulsion, involving the strange feeling of being sucked into the situation, as within a magnetic field. But how can we understand such 'mobile, tactical, evanescent and morally ambivalent dynamics of power that seem to have no predictable ontology of [their] own' (Hansen and Verkaaik 2009, p. 21)?

Conclusion

Beginning with Hubert's description of street occupation as choreographic power, this chapter has explored how distributed agency works by attuning movements in time and space. As a heuristic device for knowing and seeing political gestures, choreographic power highlights how transgressive urban rhythms can reveal the norm. When they erupt, skateboards, tags, and dumpster odours produce unexpected knowledge about urban spatiotemporalities. They reveal potentialities, what these spaces could be. The literature on voluntary risk-taking tends to emphasize youthful psychological tendencies towards daring and narcissistic affirmation. While will and interest are definitively part of these forms of youthful expression, our encounters with 'risk-takers' in Montreal reveal different aspects of this urban world.

Focusing on the 'edge' more than simply 'risk', the young Montrealers we have spoken to in this chapter are very sensitive to the materiality of their action: the street, the line, the skateboard, the trash can. By transgressing urban rhythms through this distributed agency materialized in choreographic power, they reveal other forms of knowledge. They work as urban diviners. For them, there is no risk, but instead 'spiritual' opportunity for empowerment, self-realization, and decodification. This works through their trusting their senses and not only their rational and cognitive capacities. It works through their being able to read space, to feel it. It works through aesthetic finesse.

The edge is often not negotiated individually, although men tend to emphasize their individual self-discipline, training, and conquest of fear more than do women. The edge is often negotiated collectively: between them and artefacts, between them and the police, between them and the casual walker, between them and the digital diffusion of their videos. Working the edge is both a political gesture and a political act. It is most obviously a political act when it is supported by an ideological discourse against consumerism, when a city ordinance is secured, or when there is a direct confrontation with the police. It is also a political act when it openly challenges the rational precautious norms of the risk-management system in which we live, such as when 600 skaters assemble on the street for Gold Skate Day. But most of the time, it functions through less visible political gestures, through choreographic power. It builds on provocative and embodied practices that work through affective modalities: seduction/attraction. Edgeworkers construct provocative subjectivities that instil attraction or repulsion, such as exploring industrial sites or cooking a paella from discarded food.

Notes

1. We have not been in touch with him lately, so it is unclear if he is still scavenging for food in commercial trash containers in Montreal's back alleys.
2. 'Moi je faisais souvent les manifestations en skate.' / 'Ahh ça c'est cool.' / 'Là on pouvait faire du skate dans des endroits où on peut pas d'habitude [rires].' / 'Ben t'es pas le premier qui me dit ça. Même les gens qui faisaient pas de skate, y me disaient comment ils aimaient ça. Tsé ils me disaient qu'ils avaient vraiment l'impression, tsé d'être dans la rue, tsé littéralement là.' / 'Ben moi, c'est un peu pour ça aussi que je fais du skate. Tsé je préfère pratiquer dans la rue. Parce que c'est là que … c'est justement, c'est là que t'es, t'es pour toi-même complètement. T'occupes ton corps, tu laisses ton cœur, ton corps occuper l'espace. Tu te restreins pas, ben sauf pour ta sécurité là.' / 'Oui oui, c'est sûr. Mais par exemple, sur le trottoir tu te restreindrais plus? Comment, comment tu comparerais ça?' / 'En skateboard?' / 'Oui. À cause des obstacles?' / 'Pour moi le trottoir pis la rue c'est la même chose. J'occupe l'espace. Tout en-haut là aussi [en pointant vers les escaliers d'un bâtiment de l'université], pis la rampe d'escalier aussi je peux. Fait que c'est une occupation généralisée. Mais dans tous les cas je suis pas supposé être là. Fait que, fait que ça se peut que ça dérange les gens.'
3. 'c'est assez intense comme affirmation, parce qu'il n'a pas d'unité euh, y a pas de comité de skateboard. Tsé c'est une culture un peu éparpillée.'
4. 'Des fois on a descendu, il y en avait des jeunes de 9 ans à des jeunes de 50 ans, 55 ans.'
5. 'quand on déambulait en skate … c'est qu'on partait tous ensemble. On avait une trajectoire qui était remise comme la veille, ben au sein des skaters sur les blogs-là. La plupart du monde était pas au courant je pense. Mais c'est ça, vers la fin y en avait pu de ça. Pis là on allait admettons à des spots comme par exemple à la Place de la paix, à un endroit où les skaters y vont toujours depuis qu'elle a été construite je

pense, les années 80, fin 80 ou début 90. Fait que là, on a pas le droit de skater à cause qui a beaucoup de contraventions au nom d'un règlement municipal qui s'applique à l'utilisation du mobilier urbain à des fins pour lesquelles il n'est pas conçu.'

6. 'Pis juste la surprise des voir courir, de voir qu'ils étaient sur les nerfs, parce que eux ils s'attendaient à devoir me poursuivre parce que moi je les aurais vu pis je serais reparti en courant. Fait qu'eux ils étaient, ils étaient, en en mode film d'action.'

7. 'Sur le coup, j'étais en mode réaction-là, réaction rapide face à du monde potentiellement dangereux. Fait que j'étais comme vraiment, j'étais pas capable de suivre, d'avoir l'état de lucidité nécessaire pour avoir une conversation constructive.'

8. 'Pis là je leur dis, "ben qu'est-ce qui se passe, qu'est-ce qui est en train de se passer?", Moi je trouve ça pas clair, je suis juste comme. Tsé je sais qu'ils m'en veulent parce que je suis sur mon skate, mais la manière qui courraient quand j'ai ouvert la porte, je pensais quasiment qu'ils s'en allaient attraper quelqu'un qui avait un gun en arrière de moi là (rires).'

9. 'Que quand que ça vient te chercher comme ça jusque dans ton … "deux mètres que je mets le pied sur une planche quand il y a personne autour là" [rires], pis que je suis à côté de chez-moi, pis que, je suis en train de faire mes petites affaires, je dérange personne.' / 'Oui oui.' / 'Je brise rien.' / 'Oui oui. C'est un peu une impuissance face à comme toute une, ben tout un pouvoir qu'ils te tombe dessus [rires].' / 'Toute une machine, quand elle commence tu peux plus rien faire. Une fois qu'eux ils avaient décidé qu'ils nous donnaient un ticket.'

10. 'c'est une manière en bout de ligne aussi de comme rétablir le skate comme étant quelque chose qui est né envers et contre tous dans les rues, quelque chose de sauvage, d'urbain, qui est pas domestiqué, que tu peux pas mettre dans un parc avec une clôture pis qui va rester là.'

11. Parts of this section were previously published in Boudreau, Liguori, and Séguin-Manègre (2015). The PIERAN project consisted of a short set of 11 interviews with 'voluntary risk-takers', exploring fear in the construction of political subjectivities.

12. 'Ben si t'es capable de faire tel ou tel trucs, ben tu vas juste rajouter une variante dedans. Ça va en faire un nouveau. Tu sais que t'es déjà à l'aise de faire ça, donc juste de rajouter quelque chose oui ça va être dangereux, mais tu le sais que t'as plus de chance que tu l'ailles. Pis à un certain niveau, t'es capable de maîtriser tes chutes.'

13. 'Ben je me sentais menacé, mais plus conceptuellement que phy-
siquement [rires]. Je sentais qu'ils pouvaient émettre des lois contre
moi.' / 'T'arrêter où je sais pas quoi? Oui.' / 'Comme me fouiller, tsé
n'importe quoi … pis ça c'est déjà une crainte que j'ai presque tout
le temps. Parce que … parce que je fais du skate dans les rues pas
mal.' / 'Oui fait que tu peux toujours te faire euh …' / 'Fait que je
suis toujours à l'affût de si il y a un policier, pis si y en a un j'essaie de
désamorcer mes émotions toujours. Pour essayer d'être vraiment, tsé
j'essaie de, de, si on est rendu avoir un dialogue qui pourrait finir à ce
que moi je me fasse arrêter où que j'ai une contravention, ben j'essaie
de faire l'innocent, pis de [rires] pis de pas être émotionnellement
impliqué ou sinon de pas … voyons, de paraître soumis. Si il faut, pis
c'est dégueulasse là mais …'

14. 'On a des règles de la rue : pas d'églises, pas d'école et pas de maison.
On ne respecte pas le monde qui ne respecte pas ces règles-là.'

15. 'Avoir intégré le modèle capitaliste de consommation, d'horaire (avoir
ses fins de semaine), télé populaire, musique populaire, vêtements à la
mode. Suivre la masse.'

16. 'Surtout dans Hochelaga avec les voisins. C'est coloré Hochelaga. Y'a
la «mégère» cigarette au bec qui commence à t'insulter.'

17. 'Ben c'est logique. C'est comme ça qu'on a été élevés. On a appris
que si t'échappes quelque chose sur le comptoir c'est pu bon alors
dans la poubelle … Pis travailler en restauration ça te donne beaucoup plus envie de sauver la nourriture pis d'adopter des comporte-
ments extrêmes là-dedans. La règle c'est de jeter la nourriture, alors
il faut se cacher pour prendre la nourriture. Ça pousse à une certaine
délinquance, c'est une certaine fascination pour la nourriture qui est
personnelle.'

18. 'Je me donne des petits défis comme ça. J'étais contente de trouver
des trucs nouveaux. Là je veux des bagels. Le thrill ça m'apporte
beaucoup. J'aime l'improvisation culinaire. Quand on a interdit
l'accès aux poubelles d'un commerce, je me suis mis en tête de pas
me faire voir. Je n'ai jamais vraiment eu peur. C'est seulement de la
nourriture. Y'a des gens qui me disent qu'à 2 h du matin une fille
toute seule dans une ruelle c'est stupide. Mais selon moi ça intéresse
personne d'aller dans une ruelle à cette heure-là.'

19. 'Alors il faut trouver les ruelles et les containers des marchés, et y
aller aux heures de fermetures 18 h ou 21 h. Faut y aller régulière-
ment, trier sur le volet. Faut apporter plein de sacs pour portionner à
l'avance, un couteau pour enlever les morceaux pu bons. On fouille

pas trop dans le fond parce que y'a du jus. T'en fais moins l'été. De mars à juin surtout, l'été quand c'est trop chaud c'est pas bon et l'hiver ça gèle. Ça demande de l'organisation.'

20. 'il y a un rituel. Tu sors tout et tu laves tout, c'est très important de faire ça. On peut s'organiser des groupes de dumpster diving. Quand tu en parle tu fais attention à ce que tu dis, parce que souvent les gens sont révulsés à l'idée du dumpster. Les spots intéressants sont plus dans le Mile-End.'

21. 'Pis quand tu vas chez des gens tu vois avec leur appartement si ils en font. Y'a des indices comme des trucs en vrac, des pots Mason.'

22. 'En gang ça se fait mieux. Et c'est très convivial, c'est un trip de gang, explorateur.'

23. 'Ça peut pas être juste free for all, il faut une certaine organisation, c'est une structure fragile … c'était moins le fun, je me faisais vautouriser et trop de gens faisaient rien.'

24. 'C'est jouer au chat et à la souris avec les agents de police ou de sécurité. Ça donne un thrill, mais je trouve ça vraiment beau d'aller dans ces endroits-là. Pour accéder à cette beauté-là, il faut briser l'autorité. Même si tu risques de te faire pogner.'

25. 'Tous tes sens sont aiguisés parce que tu sais que t'es coupable parce que t'as pas le droit d'être là. Tu peux te sentir coupable si tu te fait pogner. Ça donne un thrill, c'est pas juste dans le but de défier l'autorité. C'est juste une étape pour arriver à tes fins d'exploration … sentiment the thrill de pogner quelqu'un sur le fait.'

26. 'Ben les patrouilleurs ils perdent un peu le contrôle. Ils savent pas ce qui se passe, pis ils savent pas comment négocier ou interagir avec les activistes. Ils réagissent très raide. J'imagine que ça leur donne un sens de l'autorité.'

27. 'Une fois j'étais sur les dernières lignes de mon piece. C'était l'hiver et le gars il m'a spotté, il m'a poursuivi, il était assez gros mais il courrait quand même vite. Ça a duré 15–20 minutes de course. C'était la panique totale. Je ne savais pas où j'étais, je courais dans les jardins du monde, une dame qui était en train de cuisiner. Moi, à cause de l'adrénaline, je suis en train de vomir en courant et en grimpant. Situation extrêmement intense. Après un moment je pense que je suis correct et je revois le gars au téléphone avec la police et c'est un autre 20 minutes de course. Je veux pas me faire attraper, je veux pas le trouble. Et c'est mon nom aussi. Des fois ils s'en foutent, des fois ils s'en foutent pas. Les gens n'ont pas de respect envers notre

culture parce qu'ils ne savent pas comment c'est difficile. Nous on le sait. Buddy il est tombé du toit en faisant ça, où buddy il s'est cassé la jambe ou son petit frère il s'est fait frappé par le train ... Le graffiti on aime ça beaucoup parce que c'est dangereux. On aime ça parce que c'est difficile. On aime le challenge. Cette course-là c'était la meilleure, la dernière c'était la police. Là j'ai tout donné, le sprint olympique. J'ai traversé le parc, j'ai couru et c'était la fin. Et il y a un bus qui a arrêté juste au coin. 15–20 minutes je soufflais, les gens me regardaient "what the fuck happened to him?'"

Conclusion

What does it mean to live in a highly unequal urban world where the role, the place, and the forms of the state (and its powers) are eminently variable, elastic? How does that affect social and political change? Can we continue working with the same definition of what constitutes the political? Do words such as 'progress', 'progressive', 'equality', 'freedom', and 'revolution' resonate on the Left the same way they did only a few decades ago? Perhaps others would feel less quaint, such as 'spirituality', 'radicalness', 'disruption', 'DIY', 'experiential', 'experimentation', 'connection', or 'openness'? Old words do not disappear; they persist in political imaginaries. But others appear and become more salient. The question then becomes: What do these new words reveal about the underlying logic of political action in the contemporary period?

We are told that the world has undergone important structural changes in the last four decades, leading to global urbanization and a changing role for the national state (see for instance Brenner and Schmitt 2014). We wanted to observe these structural changes from the point of view not of *the* universalist urban world, but of multiple youth worlds expressing diverse experiences of urbanity from Montreal (see for instance the feminist, critical race, and queer critique by Oswin 2016). Montreal, a node in a world of cities, may not hold much weight in the global urban moment, but it has a specific aesthetic feel – charged with potentialities – that we have sought to describe in this book. A theory of aesthetic relations became meaningful in accounting for and making sense of transformations in the political process whereby structural effects of power and political change are experienced and embodied, not always rationally contested and negotiated – sometimes fled, planted, eaten, mastered, or beat-boxed on the street, in living rooms, in parks, in community centres. Urban cultures are challenging the very meaning and contours of the political process.

Living in a world of cities calls for epistemological and methodological interventions that do not discredit or invalidate the co-mingling of plural ways of coming-to-know in and through urban worlds. As the youths encountered in this book put it, their worlds are always-already in the making, through a multiplicity of agentive forces irreducible to the figures, the knowledges, or

Youth Urban Worlds: Aesthetic Political Action in Montreal, First Edition.
Julie-Anne Boudreau and Joëlle Rondeau.
© 2021 John Wiley & Sons Ltd. Published 2021 by John Wiley & Sons Ltd.

the ruling instruments of city planners, academics, urban movement leaders, the police, corporate managers, or developers. They call for the development of heterotopic thought and practices.

We have sought to learn from the perspectives of racialized youths, urban farmers, 'voluntary risk-takers' such as dumpster divers, building climbers, and students taking to the streets during the 2012 'Maple Spring'. The urban youth worlds that they create and sustain sensorially, aesthetically, sometimes only in fleeting moments, make up not only frameworks for reading the world, but a physical and existential sense of location where they can constitute themselves as actors to affect sociospatial and political change.

We situated the analysis in our experiences of political action and the effects of the accumulation of these political forms in these diverse youth urban worlds. Rather than a dichotomous and hierarchical conception whereby structure determines agency, this approach to urban politics seeks to emphasize continuity in global connections affecting urban life, seen from various scales and perspectives (see Figure 1).

Entering, or sometimes being pulled into these worlds, we sought for the arbitrary and the unpredictable in urban cultures by following various modalities of power and their manifestations, rather than focusing on structural patterns of economic, political, environmental, and social urbanization seen 'from above'. The urbanization of capital, to paraphrase Harvey (1985), affects the urban experience and produces specific spaces of hope (Harvey 2000), what Lefebvre (1970) describes as the urban revolution. These historically situated structural and geopolitical conditions produce material and embodied

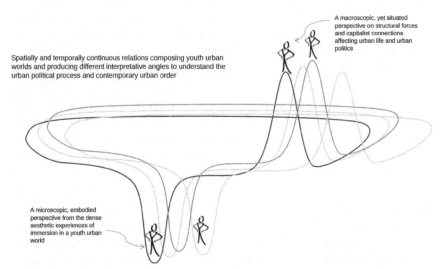

FIGURE 1 Conceptualizing urban politics. *Source:* adapted from Boudreau (2017, p. 56).

effects. Our focus in this book has been to explore these effects, because we believe starting from the micro is a means to produce different interpretative angles through which to understand the contemporary urban order.

This is why, to come back to Tivon's words (Chapter 2), we used cameras manipulated by youths, seeing with them the scanning surveillance cameras pointed back towards them as they took their shots. To use Fred's description of the student strike (Chapter 3), we described liminal moments of urbanity, like when the sound of pots and pans echoed by the glass and steel buildings energized the crowd's self-directed movements and its significance, rather than focus the analysis on institutionally calculable political changes. We marvelled, with Raphaëlle and Ann (Chapter 4), at the encapsulation of generational temporalities and inventive life in seeds collected and redistributed from street planters, rather than focus on urban resilience through urban agriculture practices. And, following Hubert's choreographic skateboarding (Chapter 5), we decoded the city through his rhythms to reveal unexpected 'urban truths' rather than studying actuarial risk-management techniques.

Understanding how political action unfolds while tracing the effects of power requires ethnography. It requires studying not only institutions and specific political actors, but specific spatialized worlds. Gaining access to these worlds takes time and the development of trustful, ethical relationships with 'epistemic partners' (Holmes and Marcus 2008).

As conceived in this book, an urban world is constructed through interactions with the spaces and objects of the city as much as with other people, non-human entities, and artefacts. As the preceding chapters show, youth urban worlds come to constitute platforms for political action where youthfulness (*more than* a set of biological and psychological factors) is a social position and a distributed mode of political action decentred from the state. This is why we feel closer to the conceptualizations of youthfulness developed from the standpoint of cities in the Global South. In Mexico City, Douala, and Teheran, intellectuals from the Global South speak of youthfulness as a relational social location characterized by a generous notion of friendship; they speak of youthfulness as dispersion, discordant moments, or travelling and circulation.

A world is characterized by specific sensory experience, by a shared space of commonality. The intensity of the aesthetic, sensorial relations that are sustained and created in these youth urban worlds sometimes stands in sharp contrast with other worlds appearing coeval within the same place. Hubert notices this explicitly as he reflects on his experience of the 2012 student strikes, saying: *'as some people are thinking they are going to die from the tear gas, others are buying Pop-Tarts. There is no universal cohesion where everything occurs at the same time. Nothing stops because something is happening.'*[1]

Forms of Aesthetic Politics Influenced by Youthfulness and Contemporary Conditions of Urbanity

The stories of this book speak to how living in a world in which urban cultures are hegemonic gives force to aesthetic political relations in ways that were not possible in a world of nation-states. Urban cultures tend to bring forth a discontinuous relationship to time wherein immediacy, multiple rhythms, and circularity are more prominent than a linear conception of progressive historical change. Urbanity further favours networked, or topological, conceptions of space. Significant places are connected by youths in their mental mapping to make up an affective collection of situations, and the street plays a major role. Youths narrate how they open and close spaces of political action; they do not take the national state space as a pregiven for action. They disdain a confined sense of space and time.

In the past decade, aesthetics has returned forcefully to political philosophy. In urban studies and political geography, it is probably the work of Jacques Rancière that is most fashionable (Grange and Gunder 2019; Tolia-Kelly 2019; Blakey 2020). We are inspired by his 'distribution of the sensible', the idea of a shared structure that regulates how we perceive the world through our senses. At one level, in the hegemonic urban world, we experience time and space differently to how we do so in the world of nation-states. But, of course, not everyone has access to this urban world, or else access is highly differentiated. Those walking under the banner of the 'right to the city' constantly remind us of this fact. Their interventions can be seen as exposing relations of exclusion and inclusion, the polemical order of the distribution of the sensible that affects who can participate in a political order held in common. Youths are at the forefront of this urban world.

What we have sought to demonstrate, however, is that if we ascribe the political only to moments of rupture that expose a polemical distribution of the sensible, we lose multiple contiguous dimensions and nuances playing out in urban aesthetic politics. The political moment is sometimes very difficult to identify because it is enmeshed in a myriad of small gestures and daily affective flows. The political is cumulative, simultaneous, messy, and unclear. It cannot be ideologically pure or identifiable through sharply defined moments of rupture.

This is why we draw attention to the importance of attending to the accumulation of political forms along a continuum of political gestures and political acts in order to analyse political relations beyond the obvious forms of organized protests or eminently visible provocative actors. Political gestures are aesthetic political forms that involve the body in aesthetic ways (marching in a demonstration, screaming at a police officer, going to a punk concert) and to which we ascribe political meaning, but which may not necessarily register attention or be performed with an intent to register attention (and thus create an aesthetic disturbance in a polemical order of the distribution of the sensible). *Political acts*, on the other hand, are creative moments that break from the routine. What is important to emphasize is that through their unfolding, they legitimate the actor, who can be present in the situation they participate in creating. Participating in such situations requires aesthetic finesse, the attuning of sensory dispositions and conditions of perceptibility to recognize and elaborate on sensual possibilities (Katz 1988, p. 9). The accumulation of political acts in our everyday lives (some of which may create political appearances that we can only admit to for some time) and their transformation into a politicized, recognizable narrative over time is what we call 'political action'. The political unfolds through many different aesthetic forms and temporalities in an urban world. These are not always readily available to anyone. They depend on one's positionality and the relational, sensual possibilities that situations afford or allow one to create, momentarily, with a range of political actors. Nonetheless, they have political effects.

Political science and Marxist critical studies have tended to describe the political as fundamentally dichotomous. They represent it as a struggle between opposite interests (in mainstream language), or between the dominant and the dominated (in Marxist terms). Relational philosophies, such as the work of Bruno Latour (2005), have challenged this dichotomous understanding and emphasized instead the way action unfolds through various types of relations that constitute subjects as they are acting. This is what we mean by 'performative'. Montreal youth show that embodied ways of coming together produce urban space. Appearance and visibility in public space are an essential political form in the current urbanized structural context, as Butler (2015) demonstrates in her analysis of the global wave of protests and occupations occurring in 2011.

However, many relational approaches have largely evacuated the primary element of the political: power. If everything is relational and performative, this gives the impression that there are no frictions, tensions, abuses, exploitations. . . The stories from Montreal narrated here are full of unequal power relations, abuse, exploitation, injustice. But instead of taking these as a dichotomous relation between the powerful and the victim, we have chosen to trace power through its materialized and embodied effects in specific moments, aesthetic experiences, and places. In other words, instead of ascribing a certain amount of power to different sets of actors (as in, capitalists and elites have more power than marginalized youths) or locating power in specific institutions (the state, the school, the market), we have been attentive to how different modalities of power produce effects that are visible through ethnography. We do not conceive of power as what makes you act or what initiates an action (empowerment, resistance). We conceive of it instead as visible traces: as the effect of action. Power is something we feel as the effect of certain gestures or acts. It is not a mere resource to be strategically deployed. Nor is it simply a motor, the energy that propels action. Power is conceived here as modalities of action, such as manipulation, domination, authority, and coercion. The effect of each modality is specific.

We wished more specifically to draw analytical attention to two modalities of power that youths in Montreal speak of: seduction and provocation. Unlike much of what political analysis usually focuses on in both mainstream and critical perspectives (coercion, manipulation, domination, authority), seduction is not commonly studied. Both seduction and provocation become very visible when we feel an aesthetic appearance. This is when action-oriented perception is suspended. It is when we feel something happening, when we admit it is touching us, having an effect on us. But it is also when we cannot put words on what is happening, cannot strategically decide. It is when we feel surprised, attracted, or repulsed by what is appearing to us. It is when common political concepts such as interests, identity, resistance, and strategy are not operative.

Seduction and provocation are powerful ways of acting politically. Political scientists have marginally explored these two modalities of power with regards to the seductive work of political campaigns, or provocative public personalities (Neuman et al. 2007). These studies tend to focus on seduction and provocation as strategies for action. This is how we began our exploration of seduction in Chapter 2. We briefly mentioned there how it is instrumentally used to face police officers. Seduction provides empowerment to racialized youths for whom provocation is unavailable. Provocation, just like transgression, is a privilege that not everyone has access to. Élisabeth angrily reminds us of this fact. Racialized youths have an acute understanding of structural forces that affect how they are perceived and, in turn, influence their political subjectivities. For instance, Stéphane explains that 'the system' produces a group dynamic producing police abuse of power. Tom highlights that with time, a neighbourhood's reputation produces inertia; the name Little Burgundy, he explains, 'holds weight' and produces fear. In response, seduction is one tactic these youths develop. Most of those with whom we have spent time in the MapCollab project have a detailed analysis of the gentrification process affecting their neighbourhood. They suffer from racialization processes that force them into predefined categories, and they develop embodied tactical responses that empower them. But, despite the racialized regime of perceptibility curtailing their movements, they assert aesthetic agency in ways that move us to engage with Blackness inscribed and re-circuited in the urban fabrics of their neighbourhoods and beyond. They produce knowledge through an epistemology of Blackness.

Beyond tactics and strategies, seduction and provocation tend to work affectively and precognitively. In Chapter 3, protesters identified the crowd, the red square, and Anarchopanda as the dominant figures of the student strikes. These non-human and anonymous figures work through seduction. They are not intentionally seductive, but they are undoubtedly affectively attractive, and sometimes provocative. Anarchopanda, for instance, is loved for his care and risk-taking. Similarly, we saw how ideological convictions are as affective and situated (because they generate interpersonal conflicts) as they are rational and argumentative. Here, the affective directly feeds into the cognitive through seduction. Strikers had an elaborate discourse against neoliberalism and capitalism. But this was not the main reason why they got involved in the strike. Rather, they emphasized improvisation and the process through which they gradually got 'sucked in' to the strike. Structurally, their actions were meant to resist neoliberalization. But if we analyse them beyond this binary ontology, strikers were more sensitive to the immediate effects of experiential victories. Their action was guided by the logic of the street more than a logic of response to institutional moves. They did not speak of progress, or even of revolution (or only very little). Instead, their mode of orientation towards the future was intimately tied to their present experience of opening new spaces of political action.

In Chapter 4, we saw that non-human earthly beings' seductive capacities and attractive effects vary along different types of non-human charisma, which we have characterized, following Lorimer (2007), as cuddly charisma, feral charisma, and ecological charisma. Attraction and manipulation draw human and non-human creatures into one another's worlds in a reciprocal embrace. These modalities of power affect urban farmers' distribution of care and attention, which influences in turn what is cultivated, whose interest it serves, and the distribution of the sensible in this political ecology spatializing food and agricultural resources in its emergent more-than-human outcomes. Most urban farmers began their agricultural work because of their awareness of the damaging effects of global political economic food production structures. Yet, entering their urban world with an ethnographic sensitivity unveils that their analysis of this global structure is primarily circulatory: they speak of global food flows in a very embodied and materialized manner. Sophia, for instance, insists that *you're eating the injustice*. More than a dichotomous ontology, urban farmers describe how they 'dewire' and 'rewire' in alternative networks, *'making loops'* as Damien says. As with the strikers, they emphasize tangible and experiential change through hands-on training and affective relations, making *'minimal change'* one person and one seed at a time.

We continued this argument in Chapter 5 with the concepts of edgework and choreographic power. As a tension between the choreographed (the norm) and the choreographic (acting at the street level by attuning movements in time and space), choreographic power makes the norm visible. By occupying the street as Hubert says, by disturbing the normal rhythm, the edgeworker reveals what we do not see anymore. In this sense, choreographic power is a heuristic device to make political gestures visible beyond words. It enables us to think with our bodies. When the speeding skateboarder appears, their abnormal speed makes us realize what the normal speed is. Edgeworkers are urban diviners. They express subversive truths through choreographic power. They enact power through provocation. Nathalie and Justine, as dumpster divers, instil disgust. They delight in the collective pleasure of provocation. Their scandalous intrusion, like that of speeding Hubert on his skateboard or MAN running away from the police, is what produces their agency. But unlike ideological confrontations, provocation is not dichotomous. It is inherently relational: the idea is not to confront the police officer, the strolling walker, the supermarket client. It is to affect: to instil strong feelings of disgust, fear, admiration. By causing trouble, the urban diviner does not confront the norm with rational argumentation, they reveal it through inconformity. Through provocation, urban diviners negotiate a space of action. They do not see a battle with political enemies, but a spiritual opportunity for empowerment, self-realization, and decoding (producing new knowledge about the city). As Cedric puts it: *'it's not against the system . . . it's about awareness'*. It's about being aware of the world in which we live, sensing it, revealing, decoding it.

The performance of youth visibility in public space is often seen as transgressive. Transgression means pushing the limits of social acceptability. As such, transgression carries certain risks. Our explorations of aesthetic political forms in the preceding chapters show that such risks can be mediated through cognition, collective presence, or actuarial logics, to varying degrees depending on one's positionality. Masculine edgeworkers have, for instance, talked about learning to overcome fear by calculating risks rationally. In the case of women edgeworkers, urban farmers, and students bracing arms as they face the police, we have seen that a sense of collective support is crucial to mitigating risks in affirming their aesthetic agency to co-create situations which legitimize them as political actors. Racialized youths disproportionately face actuarial logics set in place to mediate risks, as these logics create and reproduce race as a marker of social differentiation.

Transgression challenges the way things are ordered, sensed, perceived, and recognized. For this reason, it has important political effects. More than a simple breach of a rule, transgression is affectively charged, operating through aesthetic relations. It provokes indignation or fascination. We personally immersed ourselves in the youth urban worlds described here with fascination for their transgressions. For the youth who transgress, daring to break taboos produces exaltation, fear, sometimes culpability. But in all cases, it affirms political subjectivities: the power to act and to have an effect in the world. It recreates worlds, rearranges the distribution of the sensible, the symbolic order, the regulation regimes in place. It is an affirmation of aesthetic agency. In Chapter 1, we argued that the contemporary period of urban hegemony favours aesthetic forms of political action and that youths are at the forefront of this. The intensive character of these transgressions, their multiplication around the world, and their increasing visibility and connectivity speak to an urgent need to adjust our definitions of the political.

Montreal in a World of Cities

What is criticism if not a reflexive operation about a 'reality'? Any reflection also requires a (temporary) withdrawal from the relentless rhythm of everyday life. It requires a certain 'distance'; even to extract oneself, momentarily, from the viscosity of the 'real' and the material. But this cognitive (reflexive) oper-ation is more convincing when it is also based on a sensitivity to this 'reality'; that is, the ability of one's body to feel, perceive, and listen to the world around it. Criticism is therefore not only an abstraction from reality, but also a sensitive gesture that contributes to producing it. Criticism can be an immersive experi-ence. It lives in the kitchen of a suburban bungalow, in a café in the Mile End, in the common room of a community organization. New spaces are opened for such critique to emerge, where speech can be freed, inspiring other forms of language, redesigning the kitchen, café, or common room.

Montreal may no longer play the central role it did in the 1960s for the global Black movement, but it is the standpoint from which we wrote this book. Some political gestures and political acts performed in youth urban worlds explored here have been influenced by 'universes of opera-tions' – specific ways of doing, interacting, and being in the world crystallized over time, in Montreal, because of the constant movement and intermingling of Black people. This is why it was essential, in Chapter 1, to attend to the significance of Black movements and the Montreal Black community for the circulation of Third World decolonization ideas and liberation theories, fol-lowing their political effects and historical traces in Montreal streets, cafés, apartments, and beyond as they variously became meaningful (and reinter-preted) from the various urban standpoints of youth groups in the urban political moment of the 1960s and 1970s.

Montreal is a small node in the urban world today. In comparison with cities elsewhere and megalopolises of the Global South, where more than half the urban population is under 30 years old, young people in Montreal do not have the weight of numbers to temporally and spatially create extensive platforms for political action out of their youthfulness, but they act through dispersion, taking advantage of situational opportunities. They conjoin temporalities and spatialites to create and sustain youth urban worlds that affect sociospatial and political change aesthetically in the contemporary global urban moment.

The stories we have presented in this book cannot cover the multiplicity of youth worlds in Montreal. We did not speak of Indigenous urban youths and their dynamic cultural production, youths living on the street and their contribution to the local punk scene, 'radicalized' youths active in Extreme Right movements, transgender youths . . . the list goes on.

To conclude, we wish to turn again to Kabisha's words. This book is an ethnography. That means we have immersed ourselves in specific youth worlds, but we remained always outsiders. As much as we tried to give a voice to youths, we did not surrender our authority or erase the different positionalities which stabilize it, temporally and intersectionally. Although we treated youth words as more than representations, accounting for embodied and felt aesthetic political gestures, we can only empathically describe what these youth feel – we cannot pretend we feel the same. Kabisha is right:

> *They miss out. Those who write our stories for us, thinking they know our beginnings, middles, and ends.*
>
> *Thinking our stories are as simple as what they've heard in quick, depthless public discourses, discourses run by people who are more like them, people who are outsiders: extracting their chosen pieces from our stories. These outsiders, they are not us insiders. They cannot, they do not relate to us.*
>
> *They miss out on the strength that emerges out of rubble. They miss out on the stories of resurgence, and celebration. They miss out on humour that erupts from the lowest points of our bellies.*
>
> *They miss out on complexities and specificities.*

She wrote this piece for a collective writing project closing the Map-Collab experiences (Ateliers MapCollab 2018). Ethnography certainly has its limits. But with a sensibility to the aesthetics of political relations, we hope these youth stories about Montreal have opened the door to more *'stories of resurgence, and celebration'*.

Note

1. 'pendant qu'il y en a qui pensent qu'ils vont mourir sous les bombes lacrymogènes, ben il y en a d'autres qui sont en train d'acheter des Poptarts. Il y a pas de cohésion universelle où il se passe tout en même temps. Il y a rien qui arrête parce que d'autres choses se passent.'

References

Acampora, C.D. (2007). An introduction (with obvious affection for Gloria Anzaldúa). In: *Unmaking Race, Remaking Soul: Transformative Aesthetics and the Practice of Freedom* (ed. C.D. Acampora and A.L. Cotten), 1–17. Albany, NY: SUNY Press.

Acampora, C.D. and Cotten, A.L. ed. (2007). *Unmaking Race, Remaking Soul: Transformative Aesthetics and the Practice of Freedom.* Albany, NY: SUNY Press.

Alfred, G.R. (1995). *Heeding the Voices of Our Ancestors.* Don Mills, ON: Oxford University Press.

Allen, J. (2003). *Lost Geographies of Power.* Oxford: Routledge.

Alsalman, Y. (2011). *The Diatribes of a Dying Tribe.* Montreal, QC: Write or Wrong/ Paranoid Arab Boy Publishing.

Amin, A. (2004). Regions unbound: towards a new politics of place. *Geografiska Annaler: Series B, Human Geography* 86 (1): 33–44.

Amin, A. and Thrift, N. (2002). *Cities: Reimagining the Urban.* Cambridge: Wiley.

Andersen, C. (2014). *'Métis': Race, Recognition, and the Struggle of Indigenous Peoplehood.* Vancouver, BC: UBC Press.

Ateliers MapCollab. (2018). *Mon quartier, notre vie. Regards transatlantiques.* Montreal, QC: Del Busso Éditeur.

Atkinson, M. (2009). Parkour, anarcho-environmentalism, and poiesis. *Journal of Sport and Social Issues* 33 (2): 169–194.

Austin, D. (2013). *Fear of a Black Nation: Race, Sex, and Security in Sixties Montreal.* Toronto, ON: Between the Lines.

Barbeau, B. (2017). Le racisme systémique fera bien l'objet d'une consultation publique à Montréal. *Radio-Canada.ca*, 17 August. https://ici.radio-canada.ca/ nouvelle/1118672/racisme-discrimination-systemiques-consultation-publique-montreal (accessed 16 September 2020).

Bayat, A. (2010). *Life as Politics: How Ordinary People Change the Middle East.* Redwood City, CA: Stanford University Press.

Becker, H.S. (1973) [1997]. *Outsiders: Studies in the Sociology of Deviance.* New York: Free Press.

Becker, H. (1982). *Art Worlds.* Berkeley, CA: University of California Press.

Benjamin, F. (2012). *Le Saint-Michel des Haïtiens.* Montreal, QC: CIDIHCA.

Bennett, A. (1999). Subcultures or neo-tribes? Rethinking the relationship between youth, style and musical taste. *Sociology* 33 (3): 599–617.

Berleant, A. (1992). *The Aesthetics of Environment.* Philadelphia, PA: Temple University Press.

Youth Urban Worlds: Aesthetic Political Action in Montreal, First Edition.
Julie-Anne Boudreau and Joëlle Rondeau.
© 2021 John Wiley & Sons Ltd. Published 2021 by John Wiley & Sons Ltd.

Berleant, A. (2012). *Aesthetics Beyond the Arts: New and Recent Essays*. New York: Routledge.

Bernstein, A. and Mertz, E. (2011). Introduction. Bureaucracy: ethnography of the state in everyday life. *Political and Legal Anthropology Review* 34 (1): 6–10.

Bhabha, H. (1994). *The Location of Culture*. London: Routledge.

Bilge, S. (2012). Mapping Québécois sexual nationalism in times of 'Crisis of Reasonable Accommodations'. *Journal of Intercultural Studies* 33 (3): 303–318.

Blakey, J. (2020). The politics of scale through Rancière. *Progress in Human Geography*. doi: 10.1177/0309132520944487.

Blanc, N. (2013). Aesthetic engagement in the city (trans. M. Rosen). *Contemporary Aesthetics* 11: ffhalshs-00982738.

Block, D.R., Chávez, N., Allen, E., and Ramirez, D. (2012). Food sovereignty, urban food access, and food activism: contemplating the connections through examples from Chicago. *Agriculture and Human Values* 29 (2): 203–215.

Boileau, G. (1991). *Le silence des messieurs: Oka, terre indienne*. Montreal, QC: Éditions du Méridien.

Born, G., Lewis, E., and Straw, W. ed. (2017). *Improvisation and Social Aesthetics*. Durham, NC: Duke University Press.

Borraz, O. (2008). *Les politiques du risque*. Paris: Presses de Sciences Po.

Boudreau, J.A. (2013). Jeunes et gangs de rue: l'informel comme lieu et forme d'action politique à Montréal. *ACME: Revue électronique internationale de géographie critique* 12 (3): 520–550.

Boudreau, J.A. (2017). *Global Urban Politics: Informalization of the State*. Cambridge: Polity Press.

Boudreau, J.A. (2018). Contextualizing institutional meaning through aesthetic relations: a pragmatist understanding of local action. In: *The Routledge Handbook of Planning and Institutions in Action* (ed. W. Salet), 245–256. New York: Routledge.

Boudreau, J.A. (2019). Informalization of the state: reflections from an urban world of translations. *International Journal of Urban and Regional Research* 43 (3): 597–604.

Boudreau, J.A. and Labrie, M. (2016). Time, space, and rationality: rethinking political action through the example of Montreal's Student Spring. *Human Geography* 9 (1): 16–29.

Boudreau, J.A., Liguori, M., and Séguin-Manègre, M. (2015). Fear and youth citizenship practices: insights from Montreal. *Citizenship Studies* 19 (3–4): 335–352.

Bourdieu, P. (1979). *La distinction: critique sociale du jugement*. Paris: Éditions de Minuit.

Bourdieu, P. (1993). *La misère du monde*. Paris: Éditions du Seuil.

Boutin, M. (2009). Le nationalisme révolutionnaire. *L'aut'journal*, April 3. http://lautjournal.info/20090403/le-nationalisme-r%C3%A9volutionnaire (accessed 16 September 2020).

Braidotti, R. (2015). Punk women and riot grrls. *Performance Philosophy* 1 (1): 239–254.

Brand, C. and Bonnefoy, S. (2011). L'alimentation des sociétés urbaines: une cure de jouvence pour l'agriculture des territoires métropolitains? *VertigO-La revue électronique en sciences de l'environnement* 11(2).

Brenner, N. and Schmid, C. (2014). The 'urban age' in question. *International Journal of Urban and Regional Research* 38 (3): 731–755.

Bryant, J. R. (2012). *Urban farming in Atlanta, Georgia: the seed of neoliberal contestation or hybridized compromise? Master's thesis*, Athens, GA: Georgia State University.

Burdett, R. and Sudjic, D. (eds.) (2010). *Living in the Endless City*. London: Phaidon.

Butler, J. (1990). *Gender Trouble: Feminism and the Subversion of Identity*. London: Routledge.

Butler, J. (2015). *Notes Toward a Performative Theory of Assembly*. Boston, MA: Harvard University Press.

Caldeira, T.P.R. (2012). Imprinting and moving around: new visibilities and configurations of public space in São Paulo. *Public Culture* 24 (2): 385–419.

Campbell, E. (2013). Transgression, affect and performance: choreographing a politics of urban space. *British Journal of Criminology* 53 (1): 18–40.

Canadian Press, The. (2018). Group opposed to controversial play SLĀV calls for commitment to discussion on race, diversity. *The Globe and Mail*, 11 July. https://www.theglobeandmail.com/arts/article-robert-lepages-controversial-play-slav-to-continue-run-across-quebec/ (accessed 16 September 2020).

Carlson, A. (2019). Environmental aesthetics. *The Stanford Encyclopedia of Philosophy*. https://plato.stanford.edu/archives/win2019/entries/environmental-aesthetics/ (accessed 16 September 2020).

Carel, I. (2006). Feu sur l'Amérique. Proposition pour la révolution nord-américaine, de Charles Gagnon: analyse et mise en perspective. *Bulletin d'histoire politique* 15: 149–161.

Castells, M. (1972). *La question urbaine*. Paris: F. Maspéro.

Castells, M. (1999a). *The Rise of the Network Society*. Volume 1 in the Information Age Series. Oxford: Wiley.

Castells, M. (1999b). *The Power of Identity*. Volume 2 in the Information Age Series. Oxford: Wiley.

Castells, M. (1999c). *End of Millennium*. Volume 3 in the Information Age Series. Oxford: Wiley.

Castonguay, S. and Dagenais, M. (2011). Introduction. In: *Metropolitan Natures: Environmental Histories of Montreal* (ed. S. Castonguay and M. Dagenais), 1–16. Pittsburgh, PA: University of Pittsburgh Press.

CBC. (2017a). 'That won't happen again': City of Montreal apologizes for ad criticized for lack of diversity. *CBC News*, 28 April. http://www.cbc.ca/news/canada/montreal/montreal-video-ad-diversity-1.4089759 (accessed 16 September 2020).

CBC. (2017b). Quebec's controversial consultations into systemic racism get new mandate, name. *CBC News*, 18 October. http://www.cbc.ca/news/canada/montreal/quebec-consultations-systemic-racism-overhaul-1.4360661 (accessed 16 September 2020).

Chambers, I. (2017). *Postcolonial Interruptions, Unauthorised Modernities.* London: Rowman & Littlefield.

Chiasson-Lebel, T. (2012). Introduction. Grèves et tensions dans les universités et les cégeps. *Nouveaux cahiers du socialisme* 8: 1–7.

City Farm School. (2014a). Our mission. http://www.cityfarmschool.com/our-mission/ (accessed 16 September 2020).

City Farm School. (2014b). Market gardener full internship. http://www.cityfarmschool.com/market-gardener-apprenticeship/ (accessed 16 September 2020).

Clarke, J. (1976). Style. In: *Resistance Through Rituals* (ed. S. Hall and T. Jefferson), 175–191. London: Routledge.

Clifford, J. and Marcus, G. ed. (1986). *Writing Culture.* Berkeley, CA: University of California Press.

Cohen, A.K. (1955). *Delinquent Boys: The Culture of the Gang.* New York: Free Press.

Coleman, P. (2018). *Equivocal City: French and English Novels of Postwar Montreal.* Montreal, QC: McGill-Queens University Press.

Collectif Débrayage. (2016). *Fuck Toute!* Montreal, QC: Sabotart.

Collins, P.H. (1998). *Fighting Words: Black Women and the Search for Justice.* Minneapolis, MN: University of Minnesota Press.

Connolly, W.E. (2011). *A World of Becoming.* Durham, NC: Duke University Press.

de la Cadena, M. (2010). Indigenous cosmopolitics in the Andes: conceptual reflections beyond 'politics'. *Cultural Anthropology* 25: 334–370.

Deleuze, G. (1988). *Le pli.* Paris: Les Éditions de Minuit.

Dickenson, V. (2011). The herons are still here. In: *Metropolitan Natures: Environmental Histories of Montreal* (ed. S. Castonguay and M. Dagenais), 37–50. Pittsburgh, PA: University of Pittsburgh Press.

Dikeç, M. (2015). *Space, Politics and Aesthetics.* Edinburgh: Edinburgh University Press.

Dillabough, J.-A. and Kennelly, J. (2010). *Lost Youth in the Global City: Class, Culture and the Urban Imaginary.* New York: Routledge.

Dorries, H., Henry, R., Hugill, D., et al. (2019). *Settler City Limits: Indigenous Resurgence and Colonial Violence in the Urban Prairie West.* Winnipeg, MB: University of Manitoba Press.

Douay, N. (2012). L'activisme urbain à Montréal: des luttes urbaines à la revendication d'une ville artistique, durable et collaborative. *L'Information géographique* 76: 83–96.

Dubet, F. (1987). *La galère: jeunes en survie: enquête.* Paris: Éditions du Seuil.

Duneier, M. (1999). *Sidewalk.* New York: Farrar, Straus and Giroux.

Dupuis-Déri, F. ed. (2013). *À qui la rue? Répression policière et mouvements sociaux.* Montreal, QC: Les Éditions Écosociété.

Eagleton, T. (1990). *The Ideology of the Aesthetic.* Oxford: Wiley-Blackwell.

Economides, A. and MacWirther, C. (2017). L'autoroute Ville-Marie: vision monumentale et division sociale. In: *Vivre Ensemble à Montréal: Épreuves et Convivialités* (ed. A. Germain, V. Amiraux, and J.-A. Boudreau), 155–162. Montreal, QC: Atelier 10.

Edmunds, J. and Turner, B.S. (2005). Global generations: social change in the twentieth century. *The British Journal of Sociology* 56 (4): 559–577.

Everett-Green, R. (2018). Robert Lepage and Quebec's angry summer, in two acts. *The Globe and Mail*, 7 August. http://www.theglobeandmail.com/canada/article-robert-lepage-and-quebecs-angry-summer-in-two-acts/ (accessed 16 September 2020).

Ewert, B.M. (2012). Understanding incubator farms: innovative programs in new farmer development. Master's thesis, Missoula, MT: University of Montana.

Farias, I. and Bender, T. (2010). *Urban Assemblages: How Actor–Network Theory Changes Urban Studies*. London: Routledge.

Feely, M.M. and Simon, J. (1992). The new penology: notes on the emerging strategy of corrections and its implications. *Criminology* 30 (4): 449–474.

Fennario, T. (2017). Montreal turns 375 but acknowledges that Tiohtià:ke is much older. *APTN News*, 17 May. https://aptnnews.ca/2017/05/17/montreal-turns-375-but-acknowledges-that-tiohtiake-is-much-older/ (accessed 16 September 2020).

Ferrell, J. (1993). Crimes of style: urban graffiti and the politics of criminality. Boston, MA: Northeastern University Press.

Finnegan. R. (1998). *Tales of the City: A Study of Narrative and Urban Life*. Cambridge: Cambridge University Press.

Fortin, A. (2013). La longue marche des carrés rouges. *Recherches sociographiques* 54 (3): 513–529.

Foucault, M. (1978) [2004]. *Sécurité, Territoire, Population: cours au Collège de France, 1977–1978*. Paris: Éditions Gallimard.

Galland, O. (2011). *Sociologie de la jeunesse*. Paris: Armand Colin.

Galt, R.E., Gray, L.C., and Hurley, P. (2014). Subversive and interstitial food spaces: transforming selves, societies, and society–environment relations through urban agriculture and foraging. *Local Environment* 19 (2): 133–146.

Gauthier, M. and Guillaume, J.F. (1999). *Définir la jeunesse?: D'un bout du monde à l'autre*. Sainte-Foy, QC: Éditions de l'IQRC.

Ghertner, D.A. (2015). *Rule By Aesthetics: World-Class City Making in Delhi*. New York: Oxford University Press.

Gilroy, P. (1993). *The Black Atlantic: Modernity and Double-Consciousness*. Cambridge, MA: Harvard University Press.

Goffman, E. (1971). *Relations in Public: Microstudies of the Public Order*. New York: Basic Books.

Grange, K. and Gunder, M. (2019) The urban domination of the planet: a Rancièrian critique. *Planning Theory* 18 (4): 389–409.

Greenhouse, C.J. (1996). *A Moment's Notice: Time Politics Across Cultures*. Ithaca, NY: Cornell University Press.

Hage, G. (2012). The everyday aesthetics of the Lebanese transnational family. ASA Firth Lecture 2012. https://www.theasa.org/downloads/publications/firth/firth12.pdf (accessed 16 September 2020).

Hall, S. ed. (2012). *Representation: Cultural Representations and Signifying Practices*. London: SAGE.

Hamel, P. (1991). *Action collective et démocratie locale: les mouvements urbains montré-alais*. Chicoutimi, QC: J.-M. Tremblay.

Hamilton, G. (2018). Indigenous consultants distance themselves from Robert Lepage play 'Kanata' over lack of native actors. *National Post*, 17 July. https://nationalpost.com/entertainment/theatre/indigenous-consultants-distance-themselves-from-robert-lepage-play-kanata-over-lack-of-native-actors (accessed 16 September 2020).

Hampton, R. (2012). Race, racism and the Quebec student movement. *New Socialist*, 8 July. http://newsocialist.org/race-racism-and-the-quebec-student-movement/ (accessed 16 September 2020).

Hansen, T.B. and Varkaaik, O. (2009). Introduction. Urban charisma: on everyday mythologies in the city. *Critique of Anthropology* 29 (1): 5–26.

Hanson, D. and Marty, E. (2012). *Breaking Through Concrete: Building an Urban Farm Revival*. Berkeley, CA: University of California Press.

Haraway, D.J. (2016). *Staying With the Trouble: Making Kin in the Chthulucene*. Durham, NC: Duke University Press.

Harel, S. (2014). Introduction: Le chant choral des villes. In: *Représenter l'urbain: Apports et Méthodes* (ed. S. Breux, J.-P. Collin, and C. Gingras), 9–37. Québec City, QC: Les Presses de l'Université Laval.

Harvey, D. (1973). *Social Justice and the City*. Baltimore, MD: Johns Hopkins University Press.

Harvey, D. (1985a). *Consciousness and the Urban Experience*. Baltimore, MD: Johns Hopkins University Press.

Harvey, D. (1985b). *The Urbanization of Capital*. Volume 2 in Studies in the History and Theory of Capitalist Urbanization. Oxford: Blackwell.

Harvey, D. (1989). *The Condition of Postmodernity: An Enquiry Into the Origins of Cultural Change*. Oxford: Blackwell.

Harvey, D. (2000). *Spaces of Hope*. Berkeley, CA: University of California Press.

Harvey, D. (2008). The right to the city. *New Left Review* 53: 23–40.

High, S. (2013). Embodied ways of listening: oral history, genocide and the audio tour. *Anthropologica* 55 (1): 73–85.

Highmore, B. (2010). *Ordinary Lives: Studies in the Everyday*. London: Routledge.

Holloway, J. (2002). *Change the World Without Taking Power: The Meaning of Revolution Today*. London: Pluto Press.

Holmes, D.R. and Marcus, G.E. (2008). Para-ethnography. In: *The SAGE Encyclopedia of Qualitative Research Methods* (ed. L. Given), 596–597. Thousand Oaks, CA: SAGE.

Hooks, B. (1995). *Killing Rage: Ending Racism*. New York: St Martin's Press.

Ioanes, A. (2017). Feeling and form. *Minnesota Review* 89 (1): 57–70.

Jacobs, J. (1961). *The Death and Life of Great American Cities*. New York: Random House.

Jazeel, T. and Mookherjee, N. (2015). Aesthetics, politics, conflict. *Journal of Material Culture* 20 (4): 353–359.

John, P. (2009). Why study urban politics? In: *Theories of Urban Politics* (ed. J.S. Davies and D.L. Imbroscio), 17–24. London: SAGE.

Johnson-Schlee, S. (2019). What would Ruth Glass do? London: aspects of change as a critique of urban epistemologies. *City* 23 (1): 97–106.

Junquera, J.J. (2003). *Las Pinturas Negras de Goya*. London: Scala.

Katsiaficas, G. (1987). *The Imagination of the New Left: A Global Analysis of 1968*. Cambridge, MA: South End Press.

Katz, J. (1988). *Seductions of Crime: Moral and Sensual Attractions in Doing Evil*. New York: Basic Books.

Kenny, N. (2011). Corporeal understandings of the industrializing environment. In: *Metropolitan Natures: Environmental Histories of Montreal* (ed. M. Dagenais and S. Castonguay), 51–67. Pittsburgh, PA: University of Pittsburgh Press.

Krause, S.R. (2011). Bodies in action: corporeal agency and democratic politics. *Political Theory* 39 (3): 299–324.

Kwan, S. (2013). *Kinesthetic City: Dance and Movement in Chinese Urban Spaces*. Oxford: Oxford University Press.

Labrie, M. (2015). Mouvement étudiant du printemps 2012 au Québec: exploration du répertoire d'action mobilisé. *Métropoles* 16: 5118.

Laferrière, D. (1985). *Comment faire l'amour avec un nègre sans se fatiguer*. Montreal, QC: VLB Éditeur.

Lamarque, J. (2016). *L'appropriation de la culture punk: étude ethnographique du punk montréalais en 2015*. Master's thesis, Montreal, QC: Université du Québec à Montréal.

Lambert-Pilotte, G., Drapeau, M.-H., and Kruzynski, A. (2007). La révolution est possible: portrait de groupes autogérés libertaires au Québec. *Possibles: 'Les jeunes réinventent le Québec'* 31: 138–159.

Latour, B. (2005). *Reassembling the Social: An Introduction to Actor–Network Theory*. New York: Oxford University Press.

Lax, T.J. (2014). In search of Black space. In: *When the Stars Begin to Fall: Imagination and the American South* (ed. T.J. Lax), 8–20. New York: The Studio Museum in Harlem.

Le Breton, D. (2004). The anthropology of adolescent risk-taking behaviours. *Body & Society* 10 (1): 1–15.

Lefebvre, H. (1970) [2003]. *The Urban Revolution*. Minneapolis, MN: University of Minnesota Press.

Lefebvre, H. and Régulier, C. (1985). Le projet rythmanalytique. *Communications* 41: 191–199.

Lévesque, L. (1999). Montréal, l'informe urbanité des terrains vagues. Pour une gestion créatrice du mobilier urbain. *Les Annales de la Recherche Urbaine* 85: 47–57.

Lewis, T. (2015). 'One city block at a time': researching and cultivating green transformations. *International Journal of Cultural Studies* 18 (3): 347–363.

Lorimer, J. (2007). Nonhuman charisma. *Environment and Planning D: Society and Space* 25 (5): 911–932.

Lupton, D. and Tulloch, J. (2002). Life would be pretty dull without risk: voluntary risk-taking and its pleasures. *Health, Risk & Society* 4 (2): 113–124.

Lyng, S. (1990). Edgework: a social psychological analysis of voluntary risk taking. *American Journal of Sociology* 85 (4): 851–886.

Lyng, S. and Matthews, R. (2007). Risk, edgework, and masculinities. In: *Gendered Risks* (ed. K. Hannah-Moffat and P. O'Malley), 75–98. Milton Park: Routledge-Cavendish.

Lyons, K. (2014). Urban food advocates' tactics to rebuild food systems: convergence and divergence in food security and food sovereignty discourses. *Dialogues in Human Geography* 4 (2): 212–217.

Magnusson, W. (2010). Seeing like a city: how to urbanize political science. In: *Critical Urban Studies: New Directions* (ed. J.S. Davies and D.L. Imbroscio), 41–53. Albany, NY: SUNY Press.

Manaï, Bochra (2015). La 'mise en scène' de l'ethnicité maghrébine à Montréal. PhD thesis, Montreal, QB: Université du Québec, Institut national de la recherche scientifique.

Manaï, B. and Touré Kapo, L. (2017). Assignation à participer: quels espaces pour les jeunes montréalais? In: *Vivre Ensemble à Montréal: Épreuves et Convivialités* (ed. A. Germain, V. Amiraux, and J.-A. Boudreau), 76–79. Montreal, QC: Atelier 10.

Mannheim, K. (1952). *Essays on the Sociology of Knowledge*. London: RKP.

Marcotte, G. (1997). *Écrire à Montréal*. Montreal, QC: Boréal.

Marcus, G. (1989) [2009]. *Lipstick Traces: A Secret History of the 20th Century*, 20th anniversary edition. Cambridge, MA: Harvard University Press.

Maunay, S. (2015). Coup de pied dans la fourmilière. *Journal Métro*, 23 December.

Maynard, R. (2017). *Policing Black Lives: State Violence in Canada from Slavery to the Present*. Halifax, NS: Fernwood Publishing.

Melucci, A. (1989). *Nomads of the Present: Social Movements and Individual Needs in Contemporary Society*. Philadelphia, PA: Temple University Press.

Merrifield, A. (2013). *The Politics of the Encounter: Urban Theory and Protest Under Planetary Urbanization*. Athens, GA: University of Georgia Press.

Mills, S. (2011). *Contester l'empire: Pensée postcoloniale et militantisme politique à Montréal, 1963–1972*. Montreal, QC: Éditions Hurtubise.

Mills, S. (2016). *A Place in the Sun: Haiti, Haitians, and the Remaking of Quebec*. Montreal, QC: McGill-Queen's University Press.

Munn, N.D. (1992). The cultural anthropology of time: a critical essay. *Annual Review of Anthropology* 21: 93–123.

Muñoz, J.E. (1999). *Disidentifications: Queers of Color and the Performance of Politics*. Minneapolis, MN: University of Minnesota Press.

Murphy, J.M. and Omar, S.M. (2013). Aesthetics of resistance in Western Sahara. *Peace Review* 25 (3): 349–358.

Nanay, B. (2016). *Aesthetics as Philosophy of Perception*. Oxford: Oxford University Press.

Nancy, J.-L. (1993). *Le sens du monde*. Paris: Éditions Galilée.

Nelson, C. (2016). *Slavery, Geography and Empire in Nineteenth Century Marine Landscapes of Montreal and Jamaica*. New York: Routledge.

Neuman, W.R., Marcus, G.E., Crigler, N., and Mackuen, M. (2007). *The Affect Effect: Dynamics of Emotion in Political Thinking and Behavior*. Chicago, IL: University of Chicago Press.

Nevins, J. (2018). Montreal jazz festival cancels show with white actors performing slave songs. *The Guardian*, 5 July. https://www.theguardian.com/music/2018/jul/05/slav-montreal-international-jazz-festival-cancelled-racist-songs (accessed 16 September 2020).

Newmahr, S. (2011). Chaos, order, and collaboration: toward a feminist conceptualization of edgework. *Journal of Contemporary Ethnography* 40 (6): 682–712.

Olstead, R. (2011). Gender, space, and fear: a study of women's edgework. *Emotion, Space and Society* 4: 86–94.

Oswin, N. (2016). Planetary urbanization: a view from outside. *Environment and Planning D: Society and Space* 36 (3), 540–546.

Ouimet, M. (2009). Louis-Joseph-Papineau, la planète francophone. *La Presse*, 4 May. http://www.lapresse.ca/actualites/education/200905/04/01-852906-louis-joseph-papineau-la-planete-francophone.php (accessed 16 September 2020).

Panagia, D. (2009). *The Political Life of Sensation*. Durham, NC: Duke University Press.

Papastergiadis, N. (2014). A breathing space for aesthetics and politics: an introduction to Jacques Rancière. *Theory, Culture & Society*, 31 (7–8): 5–26.

Pelletier, R. (1992). La révolution tranquille. In *Le Québec en jeu: Comprendre les grands défis*. (ed. G. Daigle and G. Rocher), 209–624. Montreal, QC: Les Presses de l'Université de Montréal.

People's Potato. (2014). Annual Report 2014.

Pilcher, J. (1994). Mannheim's sociology of generations: an undervalued legacy. *British Journal of Sociology* 45 (3): 481–495.

Radio-Canada. (2017). La consultation sur la discrimination systémique change de nom et de mandat. *Radio-Canada.ca*, 18 October. https://ici.radio-canada.ca/nouvelle/1062104/racisme-discrimination-systemique-mandat-change-forum-valorisation-diversite (accessed 16 September 2020).

Ralph, L. (2014). *Renegade Dreams: Living Through Injury in Gangland Chicago*. Chicago, IL: University of Chicago Press.

Rancière, J. (2000). *La partage du sensible: esthétique et politique*. Paris: La fabrique éditions.

Recollet, K. (2010). *Aural Traditions: Indigenous Youth and the Hip-Hop Movement in Canada*. PhD thesis, Peterborough, ON: Trent University.

Reid, M. (1972) *The Shouting Signpainters: A Literary and Political Account of Quebec Revolutionary Nationalism*. Toronto, ON: McClelland & Stewart.

Rondeau, J. (2017). Une autre relève agricole: Analyse des rôles des acteurs d'une formation en agriculture urbaine dans la production d'espaces et de pratiques agricoles alternatives au système alimentaire agro-industriel en milieu urbain. Master's thesis, Montreal, QC: Institut national de la recherche scientifique.

Rose, T. (1994). *Black Noise: Rap Music and Black Culture in Contemporary America*. Middletown, CT: Wesleyan University Press.

Rose, D.B. (2012). Multispecies knots of ethical time. *Environmental Philosophy* 9 (1): 127–140.

Ross, D. (2016). 'Vive la vélorution!': Le Monde à Bicyclette and the origins of cycling advocacy in Montreal. In: *Canadian Countercultures and the Environment* (ed. C. MacMillan Coates), 138–161. Calgary, AB: University of Calgary Press.

Saito, Y. (2017). *Aesthetics of the Familiar: Everyday Life and World-Making*. Oxford: Oxford University Press.

Saito, Y. (2019). Aesthetics of the everyday. *The Stanford Encyclopedia of Philosophy*. https://plato.stanford.edu/archives/win2019/entries/aesthetics-of-everyday/ (accessed 16 September 2020).

Sarkar, M. and Allen, D. (2007). Hybrid identities in Quebec hip-hop: language, territory, and ethnicity in the mix. *Journal of Language, Identity & Education* 6: 117–130.

Sarrasin, R., Kruzynski, A., Jeppesen, S., and Breton, É. (2012). Radicaliser l'action collective: portrait de l'option libertaire au Québec. *Lien Social et Politiques* 68: 141–166.

Savard, A. and Cyr, M.-A. (2014). La rue contre l'État: actions et mobilisations étudiantes en 2012. In: *Un Printemps rouge et noir, regards croisés sur la grève étudiante de 2012* (ed. M. Ancelovici and F. Dupuis-Déri), 59–86. Montreal, QC: Les Éditions Écosociété.

Shapiro, M.J. (2010). *The Time of the City: Politics, Philosophy and Genre*. London: Routledge.

Simmel, G. (1903) [1976]. *The Metropolis and Mental Life: The Sociology of Georg Simmel*. New York: Free Press.

Simon, S. (2006). *Translating Montreal*. Montreal, QC: McGill-Queens University Press.

Simone, A. (2005). Urban circulation and the everyday politics of African urban youth: the case of Douala, Cameroon. *International Journal of Urban and Regional Research* 29 (3): 516–532.

Simone, A. (2010). *City Life from Jakarta to Dakar*. London: Routledge.

Simone, A. (2016). 'It's just the city after all!' *International Journal of Urban and Regional Research* 40: 210–218.

Skelton, T. (2010). Taking young people as political actors seriously: opening the borders of political geography. *Political Geography* 42 (2): 145–151.

Sloterdijk, P. (2011). *Bubbles. Spheres Volume I: Microspherology*. Los Angeles, CA: MIT Press.

Stephens, J. (1998). *Anti-Disciplinary Protest: Sixties Radicalism and Postmodernism*. Cambridge: Cambridge University Press.

Stone, C. L. (1989). *Regime Politics: Governing Atlanta 1946–1988*. Lawrence, KS: University Press of Kansas.

Straw, W. (2002). Scenes and sensibilities. *Public* 22 (23): 245–257.

Straw, W. (2014). Scènes: ouvertes et restreintes. *Cahiers de recherche sociologique* 57: 17–32.

Surprenant M.E. and Bigaouette, M. ed. (2013). *Les femmes changent la lutte. Au cœur du printemps québécois*. Montreal, QC: Les éditions remue-ménage.

Tarrow, S. (1998). *Power in Movement: Collective Action, Social Movements and Politics*. Cambridge: Cambridge University Press.

Tayler, F. (2018). Mainmise, 1970: situating Québec within planetary geographies. *Mémoires du livre* 10 (1).

Thibaud, J.-P. (2010). La ville à l'épreuve des sens. In: *Ecologies urbaines: états des savoirs et perspectives* (ed. O. Coutard and J.-P. Lévy), 198–213. Paris: Economica-Anthropos.

Thomas, T.L. (1997). *A City With a Difference: The Rise and Fall of the Montreal Citizen's Movement*. Montreal, QC: Véhicule Press.

Thrasher, F.M. (1927). *The Gang: A Study of 1313 Gangs in Chicago*. Chicago, IL: University of Chicago Press.

Thumbadoo, R.V. (2017). *Ginawaydaganuc and the Circle of All Nations: The Remarkable Environmental Legacy of Elder William Commanda*. PhD thesis, Ottawa, ON: Carleton University.

Tolia-Kelly, D.P. (2019). Rancière and the re-distribution of the sensible: the artist Rosanna Raymond, dissensus and postcolonial sensibilities within the spaces of the museum. *Progress in Human Geography* 43 (1): 123–140.

Touraine, A. (1992). Beyond social movements? *Theory, Culture & Society* 9 (1): 125–145.

UNFPA. (2014). The power of 1.8 billion adolescent, youth and the transformation of the future. In*: State of World Population 2014*. https://www.unfpa.org/swop-2014 (accessed 16 September 2020).

Urteaga Castro Pozo, Maritza. (2012). De jóvenes contemporáneos: trendys, emprendedores y empresarios culturales. In: *Jóvenes, culturas urbanas y redes digitales* (ed. N.G. Canclini, F. Cruces, and M. Urteaga Castro Pozo). Madrid: Fundación Telefónica and Ariel.

Vallières, P. (1969). *Nègres blancs d'Amérique: Autobiographie précoce d'un terroriste québécois*. Montreal, QC: Parti pris.

Vernet, L. (2017). Le goût des autres: tamtams, Piknic Électronik et autres jeux de la sociabilité publique. In: *Vivre Ensemble à Montréal: Épreuves et Convivialités* (ed. A. Germain, V. Amiraux, and J.-A. Boudreau), 41–52. Montreal, QC: Atelier 10.

Vihalem, M. (2018). Everyday aesthetics and Jacques Rancière: reconfiguring the common field of aesthetics and politics. *Journal of Aesthetics & Culture* 10 (1): 1506209.

Ville de Montréal. (2011a). Consultation publique 'Policiers et citoyens, ensemble pour la communauté montréalaise'. Commission permanente de la sécurité publique. May.

Ville de Montréal. (2011b). Right of Initiative to public consultation. Portail officiel. http://ville.montreal.qc.ca/portal/page?_pageid=6717,60353574&_dad=portal&_schema=PORTAL (accessed 16 September 2020).

Ville de Montréal. (2017). Montréal, proud of its Indigenous roots: Montréal's new coat of arms and flag. http://ville.montreal.qc.ca/pls/portal/docs/page/prt_vdm_fr/media/documents/depliantdrapeau_8.5x11_ang-hr.pdf (accessed 16 September 2020).

Viot, P., Pattaroni, L., and Berthoud, J. (2010). Voir et analyser le gouvernement de la foule en liesse. Éléments pour l'étude des rassemblements festifs à l'aide de matériaux sonores et visuels. https://www.ethnographiques.org/2010/Viot-Pattaroni-Berthoud (accessed 16 September 2020).

Wacquant, L.J.D. (2004). *Body & Soul: Notebooks of an Apprentice Boxer*. Oxford: Oxford University Press.

Warne, C. (2014). Subcultural theory in France: a missed rendez-vous? In: *Subcultures, Popular Music and Social Change* (ed. The Subcultures Network), 49–64. Newcastle-upon-Tyne: Cambridge Scholars Publishing.

Warren, J.-P. (2008). *Une douce anarchie: les années 68 au Québec*. Montreal, QC: Les Éditions du Boréal.

Warren, J.-P. (2012). Fondation et production de la revue Mainmise (1970–1978). *Mémoires du livre* 4 (1).

Welsch, W. (2002). Rethinking identity in the age of globalization – a transcultural perspective. *Aesthetics & Art Science* 1: 85–94.

Whyte, W.F. (1943). *Street Corner Society: The Social Structure of an Italian Slum*. Chicago, IL: University of Chicago Press.

Wilkins, A.C. (2008). *Wannabes, Goths, and Christians: The Boundaries of Sex, Style, and Status*. Chicago, IL: University of Chicago Press.

Williams, J.P. (2007). Youth-subcultural studies: sociological traditions and core concepts. *Sociology Compass* 1 (2): 572–593.

Young, I.M. (1990). *Justice and the Politics of Difference*. Princeton, NJ: Princeton University Press.

Index

n here refers to the note in the text

Youth Urban Worlds: Aesthetic Political Action in Montreal, First Edition.
Julie-Anne Boudreau and Joëlle Rondeau.
© 2021 John Wiley & Sons Ltd. Published 2021 by John Wiley & Sons Ltd.